SANITY and SURVIVAL

in the

NUCLEAR AGE

Psychological Aspects of
War and Peace

SANITY and SURVIVAL
in the
NUCLEAR AGE

Psychological Aspects of War and Peace

Originally published as
SANITY and SURVIVAL

JEROME D. FRANK
Ph.D., M.D.

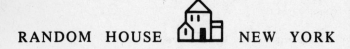

RANDOM HOUSE   NEW YORK

First Edition

987654321

Copyright © 1967, 1982 by Jerome D. Frank

Originally published as *Sanity and Survival: Psychological Aspects of War and Peace*

All rights reserved under International and Pan-American Copyright Conventions. No part of this book may be reproduced in any form or by any means, electronic or mechanical, including photocopying, without permission in writing from the publisher. All inquiries should be addressed to Random House, Inc., 201 East 50th Street, New York, N.Y. 10022. Published in the United States by Random House, Inc., and simultaneously in Canada by Random House of Canada Limited, Toronto.

Library of Congress Cataloging in Publication Data

Frank, Jerome David, 1909–
    Sanity and survival in the nuclear age.

    "Formerly entitled: Sanity and survival: psychological aspects of war and peace."
    Bibliography: p.
    Includes index.
    1.   International relations—Psychological aspects.
I.   Title.
JX1255.F7   1982   327'.01'9   82-9872
ISBN 0-394-33229-6   AACR2

Manufactured in the United States of America

Preface

by J. WILLIAM FULBRIGHT

SO FREQUENTLY is it pointed out that the human race has acquired the means of its own destruction that the shocking fact no longer shocks us. Everyone has heard it but no one takes it seriously; statesmen readily acknowledge the ability of the human race to destroy itself and then proceed to act as though it were not a fact at all. It is known but not believed, perhaps because it is impossible, or at least very difficult indeed, really to believe something that one has not seen or felt or touched or experienced.

Most of what we learn, certainly in the field of politics, we learn by trial and error, which is to say, by going about our affairs in a customary way until, by experience of error, we learn that the customary way is no longer workable and, accordingly, we revise it. It is a perfectly good way of learning as long as the error itself is not fatal or irreparably destructive. In matters of war and peace in the nuclear age, however, we cannot afford to learn by experience, because even a single error could be fatal to the human race. We have got to learn to prevent war without again experiencing it; we have got to change the traditional ways of statecraft without benefit of trial and error; and, in addition, we have got to be right not just in most but in *all* of our judgments pertaining to all-out nuclear war.

It is, to understate the matter, a notable challenge, calling most urgently for new ideas and new perspectives. It no longer suffices to seek the means of preventing war by studying the means by which it has traditionally been waged in the hope of adapting these to the conditions of the nuclear age. I share Dr. Frank's opinion that the new strategic studies, with their computerized calculations of the numbers of millions of people who might be lost or saved depending upon one pattern or another of nuclear attack and retaliation, are irrelevant to our basic needs. They are irrelevant because, as Dr. Frank points out, they are based on the false premise that the traditional system of war and peace can be salvaged. What is wanted is something new, something perhaps radically new, for the maintenance of peace in the nuclear age.

The power drive of men and nations traditionally has been checked by the power drive of other men and other nations. On every level of human activity, from the family to the nation, there operates a principle of countervailing force which, more often than not, makes for a rough equity by preventing any one person, group, or nation from gaining domination over all others. The Founding Fathers wrote this principle into the Constitution of the United States and it has worked well: vesting in each of the three branches of government certain means of restricting the power of the others, our Constitution has protected liberty by harnessing power against power, ambition against ambition. The genius of the system is that instead of relying on the virtue and voluntary restraint of office holders—qualities which, though not unknown, are highly unreliable—it utilizes human nature, not as one wishes it were but as it is, for protection against tyranny.

The system of countervailing force in international relations is known as the balance of power. It has, until recently, worked tolerably well; it has not prevented all wars but it has almost certainly prevented some wars, and since the rise of the nation-state system in the seventeenth and eighteenth centuries, it has prevented any one nation from gaining permanent domination over all others. It has done so, however, at accelerating cost:

a quarter of a century of general European war was required to defeat the aggression of revolutionary and Napoleonic France; in the twentieth century two world wars, taking tens of millions of lives and culminating in the dropping of atomic bombs on Hiroshima and Nagasaki, were required to defeat the aggressions of Germany and Japan.

The balance of power system can be said to have worked in the past in that bids for world domination were defeated, albeit at horrendous cost; but another war, fought with nuclear weapons, would involve incomparably greater cost. No "war game," no "scenario," however scientific and sophisticated, could possibly give us a picture of what the world would be like after a holocaust of unimaginable horror. Even if organized societies survived a nuclear war, what would the state of civilization be? What would become of nations and ideologies as we now know them? And, perhaps most important of all, what would the state of mind of the survivors be? What capacity would they have, in the wake of the greatest catastrophe in human history, to lay the foundations of a better world? Both world wars wrought profound changes in the world, changes neither foreseen nor desired by the leaders and peoples of the nations which fought those wars; all that we can say with confidence about the consequences of a nuclear war is that none of us can conceive what they would be.

For these reasons, the principle of countervailing force is no longer a workable basis for organizing the world. Although it has prevented the imposition of a global tyranny, it has not prevented global war, and the survival of our species requires a system that will prevent global war, not just by "crisis management," which may prevent a particular crisis from getting out of hand, but permanently and reliably. The new principle that is required is a principle of *community,* one which will end the no longer tolerable anarchy of unlimited national sovereignty. As Dr. Frank writes in his epilogue, "survival today depends on reducing, controlling, channelling, and redirecting the drive for power and the impulse to violence and fostering the countervailing drives toward fellowship and community."

The first, indispensable step toward the realization of a new concept of community in the world is the acquisition of a new dimension of self-understanding. We have got to understand, as we have never understood before, why it is, psychologically and biologically, that men and nations fight; why it is, regardless of time or place or circumstance, that they always find *something* to fight about; why it is that we are capable of love and loyalty to our own nation of ideology and of venomous hatred toward someone else's. We have got to understand whether and how such emotions satisfy certain needs of human nature and whether and how these needs could be satisfied in a world without war.

Only on the basis of an understanding of our behavior can we hope to control it in such a way as to ensure the survival of the human race. It is toward the development of this kind of understanding that Dr. Frank has written this book. He says that he is "convinced that love and trust are as powerful determinants of human behavior as hate and suspicion." Though perhaps less convinced, I am no less hopeful, and, in any case, I gladly defer to an expert in the field.

CONTENTS

SANITY and SURVIVAL in the NUCLEAR AGE

Psychological Aspects of
War and Peace

RARELY ARE we able to state that a book altered our lives. In my case I'm fortunate that the book *Sanity and Survival in the Nuclear Age* provided an outline for me of a course that had to be followed. I first read the book in 1967 while a medical student at the Johns Hopkins University School of Medicine. At the time I had been selected to go to the Soviet Union as a medical exchange student. The urging of the book—that we seek to develop patterns of cooperation to avoid a nuclear holocaust—clarified for me a path of action that could be taken to contribute to the prevention of nuclear war. This lead me to work for increased Soviet/American health cooperation and to prepare the details for the 1972 US/USSR Health Cooperation Agreement. In 1978 the ideas contained in this book, together with the experience of working with Soviet physicians, led me along with Dr. Bernard Lown to propose that Soviet and American physicians work together against the nuclear arms race. With the help of other American physicians, the foundation of the organization known as International Physicians for Prevention of Nuclear War was established. The development of this organization and the powerful movement of physicians around the world for prevention of nuclear war were fostered by the ideas and teachings of Dr. Jerome Frank, which are stated so forcefully in this book.

Dr. James E. Muller
Assistant Professor of Medicine, Harvard Medical School
Co-Founder, International Physicians
for Prevention of Nuclear War

Introduction

THE EVENTS that have transpired in the fifteen years since this book first appeared have not necessitated any significant changes in the text. The reader should have little difficulty in detecting any facts that have become outdated.

Certain general developments that have aggravated the nuclear peril, as well as a few that may offer some grounds for hope, deserve brief mention. On the negative side, technological improvements in nuclear delivery systems and warheads have continued to proceed at a breakneck pace. Negotiations, however, proceed much more slowly; by the time agreement is reached to ban a weapon, it is already obsolete. A good example is the antiballistic missile. As the variety and complexity of nuclear weapons increase, the prospect of gaining control of them through the negotiating process recedes.

The increasing accuracy of nuclear weapons has led to a shift in policy from preventing nuclear war through mutually assured destruction to waging nuclear war by destroying the enemy's missiles through first strike (the counterforce strategy) and by seeking to limit nuclear exchanges geographically. That is, nuclear weapons, instead of being built not to be used, are now ostensibly designed to be used. Their first-strike capabilities along with constantly shortening delivery times are eroding the stability of deterrence. Instability has been further increased by the continued proliferation of nuclear weapons within countries, the spread of civilian nuclear power plants, some of which can make weapons-grade plutonium, and the growing number of countries who are suspected of having nuclear weapons.

As the proliferation and increasing accuracy of nuclear weapons have made city shelter programs obsolete, civil defense planners have shifted their efforts to devising plans for evacuating people from the most threatened cities to presumably less threatened areas. These plans, involving the movement of masses of people under highly stressful conditions to areas that themselves are susceptible to nuclear attack, are *prima facie* unworkable, thus contributing to rising emotional tensions.

On the other hand, some developments have generated a spark of hope that the apparently catastrophic progression of events can yet be halted. Examples continue to multiply of the uselessness of nuclear weapons to solve the kind of international and internal conflicts that are racking the world. For example, it is difficult to conceive how the use of nuclear weapons in the Middle East could accomplish anything other than destroying all the combatants, nor could they contribute to the resolution of the conflicts in Afghanistan and San Salvador.

Furthermore, the fact that the world has rocked along for another fifteen years without a nuclear holocaust—contrary to the expectations of many of us—suggests that there may be factors making for stability that have escaped notice. One may be that, since any nuclear exchange, even if limited at the start, would have a very high probability of escalating to a civilization-destroying holocaust, no national leader would start a nuclear war as the result of a rational calculation. Unfortunately, accident or failure of judgment under extreme stress still remain as potential causes of nuclear catastrophe.

Perhaps the greatest ground for hope is the recent worldwide surge of political activities aimed at halting the nuclear arms race. At last people in many nations and with a variety of political views seem to recognize consciously the danger of nuclear weapons. When organizations as conservative as the American Catholic hierarchy and the American Medical Association are implicitly or explicitly campaigning against nuclear arms, it cannot be long before such activities influence national policies.

Since the fate of humanity lies in the hands of political and military leaders, perhaps the most important contribution psychologists should be able to make is to deepen our understanding of the psychological forces that keep leaders trapped in the nuclear arms race. A few thoughts that have occurred to me since writing this book may aid further understanding.

Leaders, by definition, perceive reality in terms of power relationships. They seek power for instrumental purposes—that is, to bend the world in the direction that they believe to be good—but also for its own sake. The accumulation of power becomes an end in itself. As Henry Kissinger put it, power is an aphrodisiac.

Power has two components: the ability to accumulate the means of power and the will to use them. The latter includes willingness not only to run greater risks and endure more hardships than one's enemies, but also to inflict as much damage on them as is required to prevail. Thus in international security establishments toughness is valued. Members who suggest conciliation or compromise with hostile nations soon lose credibility and influence.

In structured societies struggles for power are guided and constrained by rules that provide mechanisms for resolving conflicts without resort to violence. In the still anarchic international arena, however, the outcomes of power struggles are ultimately determined by which adversary can bring more destructive forces to bear and show the greater determination to use them. All of today's national leaders started their climb to power in a world of conventional weapons, so they are masters of the prenuclear international game, in which war was the final resort and the nation that possessed superior weaponry and will won. Thus war has been reinforced by success over millennia.

When humans are faced with an entirely new and unprecedented problem, such as the abrupt emergence of nuclear weapons, they try to make it appear like a familiar one and handle it by methods that have worked in the past. National leaders therefore still try to accumulate more and better nuclear weapons than their adversaries, even though they know intellectually that "Comprehensive military supremacy for either side is a military and economic impossibility."[1]

While prenuclear weapons from spears and clubs to bombs

and shells served as demonstrations both of real strength and of will power, nuclear weapons have abruptly and permanently broken the connection between weaponry and strength in one respect, but not in another. Perceived and actual reality still coincide in that the strategic nuclear weapons of one adversary gravely menace the other. They differ sharply, however, in that, beyond a level long since passed by the United States and the U.S.S.R., accumulating more powerful and sophisticated strategic weapons decreases the security of all nations, including the possessors. As these weapons cannot actually be used against another nuclear power without enormous damage to the user, their only remaining function is to demonstrate superior will.

Thinking and behavior are guided more by the perception of reality than by its actuality. As long as nuclear weapons are perceived as simply bigger conventional ones, the country that has the smaller or less technically advanced stockpile will see itself as weaker and will be perceived as weaker by its opponents and allies. It will therefore act as if it actually were weaker—that is, it will be more easily intimidated, will act less decisively in crises, and will be in danger of losing its allies and tempting its opponents to seize the initiative. Thus the pursuit of power and security through illusory nuclear superiority is in reality a race for prestige. The nuclear arms race is an especially dangerous form of psychological warfare. It is an effort to achieve psychological security at the expense of actual security.

Both personal qualities and organizational forces trap leaders in the pursuit of the will-o'-the-wisp of nuclear superiority. Personal qualities include an orientation to action, optimism, and the leaders' need to believe they can control events. By definition leaders are persons of action. A leader's effectiveness depends on the ability to deal with practical problems as they arise. Even if leaders had the leisure to indulge in the flights of fancy necessary to invent innovative solutions to unprecedented problems, they are seldom temperamentally fitted to do so. So they continue seeking to acquire larger nuclear arsenals than their adversaries because this is how they have always dealt with conventional weapons.

Leaders' confidence that anachronistic solutions to nuclear

problems can work is reinforced by their optimism. To be successful a leader must enter every conflict expecting to win. Moreover, the higher the position a leader has attained, the more victories over defeats he or she has experienced; so the confidence of national leaders that they can prevail has been heavily reinforced. The realization that nuclear wars are unwinnable can make but slow headway against this accumulated experience.

Finally, leaders must believe that they can control events, and seek at all costs to preserve this belief in the face of uncontrollable eventualities. To this end, military establishments churn out innumerable scenarios of limited or localized nuclear conflicts, all of which are manifestly unworkable. Since a single error would be disastrous in a nuclear battlefield, command and control would have to be perfect for these scenarios to work. Such perfection has rarely been achieved under battle conditions, even with conventional weapons, and it is inconceivable with nuclear ones. Not only have these weapons never been tested in actual combat so there are large uncertainties about how they would behave under such circumstances, but they are known to produce electromotive pulses that disrupt electronic communications. Although efforts are being made to shield command and control systems against these pulses, no one can be confident that these efforts have succeeded.

Organizational features of the leader's role are at least as important as personal qualities in keeping leaders in thrall to the nuclear arms competition. This conclusion is suggested by the outstanding military and civilian leaders who, although pursuing nuclear policies when in power, denounce nuclear weapons as soon as they are out of office. Striking examples are Generals Douglas MacArthur and Omar Bradley, Field Marshall Lord Mountbatten, Admiral Hyman Rickover, and Presidents Dwight Eisenhower and Jimmy Carter.

Two related sets of forces seem to contribute to this strange behavior: leadership groups and bureaucracies. People do not gain entrance into either unless they already subscribe to the world view of the group, and once they are in office many forces conspire to keep them from reevaluating their basic premises.

In the realm of human relationships and values, people validate their judgments by comparing them with the judgments of other people who are important to them.[2] Leadership groups are essentially closed communication systems in which members are continually reinforcing each other in their beliefs. This behavior is intensified under prolonged or intermittently acute stresses, because under such circumstances members of leadership groups suppress individual judgments in the service of preserving group cohesiveness.[3] In both bureaucracies and small leadership groups, the penalties for opposing the group's consensus can be severe in terms of loss of favor with one's colleagues, including actual loss of office; and the longer one has been in the group and the greater one's influence, the more one has to lose.

As indicated in the text, bureaucracies screen information that reaches the leaders. In order to gain favor and influence, subordinates are inclined to give leaders information that supports their views and to withhold contrary information. This further reinforces the leaders' belief in the correctness of their policies.

Finally, leaders rely on bureaucracies for expertise, since they obviously cannot be masters of all the problems with which they must deal. Although each unit of a bureaucracy seeks to aggrandize itself, all unite to advocate policies that increase the power of the whole. Thus while the armed services compete with each other for funds under some circumstances, under others they support each other's demands as a way of increasing the power of all. It is difficult, if not impossible, for a leader to oppose policies that experts unanimously advocate. This further reinforces the nuclear trap.

In addition to these organizational obstacles to breaking out of the nuclear arms race, two general psychological ones deserve special attention because they may be more accessible to modification. One is the perception of nuclear weapons as simply larger conventional ones, to be handled as conventional weapons have been in the past. The other is the mutual distrust and suspicion engendered by nations with conflicting goals, especially when their ideologies also conflict.

A major psychological obstacle to perceiving nuclear weapons as fundamentally different from conventional ones is that they are psychologically unreal. Except for the few survivors of Hiroshima and Nagasaki, no living person has actually experienced the effects of a nuclear explosion and no national leader today has even witnessed one. Nuclear missiles poised in various countries to annihilate others cannot be detected by any of the senses—they cannot be seen, heard, felt, tasted, or smelled; hence they exist only in imagination. Furthermore, since 1945 all of the conflicts that continue to ravage the globe have been fought with conventional weapons, which has reinforced the old patterns.

Nuclear weapons have burst upon the world so recently that we have not had time to develop terms appropriate to them. As a result we have had to resort to language used to describe conventional weapons. Such words as superiority, inferiority, equivalence, margin of safety, defense, and so on correspond to real situations with conventional weapons. Once the "weaker" power can destroy the "stronger" power regardless of what the latter does, however, these words have no referents in the real world. Since our perception of reality, however, is shaped by the words we use to describe it, using the language of conventional weapons keeps us trapped in the perception that nuclear weapons are simply bigger conventional ones. Confucius put it very well: "If names be not correct, language is not in accordance with the truth of things. If language be not in accordance with the truth of things, affairs cannot be carried on to success."[4]

A second psychological force that keeps nations trapped in the arms race is the so-called image of the enemy that groups in conflict always form of each other, as discussed in the text. This image creates a self-fulfilling prophecy by causing enemies to acquire the evil characteristics they attribute to each other. Although the behavior of the enemy may be motivated by fear more than by aggressiveness, nations that fail to recognize that their enemies are treacherous and warlike would not long survive. Thus the image hostile nations form of each other more or less corresponds to reality.

Two aspects of the enemy image not adequately treated in the text are that it provides a convenient scapegoat for failures to solve domestic and international problems and that it blinds both sides to interests they have in common. By projecting the blame for political unrest on the enemy, each side protects its own sense of virtue. The rising tide of violence and disorder all over the world, for example, is caused primarily by collapsing standards of living resulting from increasing population pressure on limited resources and aggravated by the economic dislocations caused by huge military budgets. Yet both the U.S. and the U.S.S.R. blame turmoil in their client states mainly on the subversive machinations of the other, seeking to use unrest to their own advantage rather than address the basic causes underlying that unrest.

Finally, because by definition anything the enemy wants must be bad for us, the enemy image blinds both sides to interests they share—in this case, the reduction and eventual elimination of nuclear weapons. When either country suggests a move in this direction, the other dismisses it as a ruse to put it at a disadvantage. In this connection, the argument that a freeze on nuclear weapons at present levels would give the Soviets no incentive to pursue disarmament negotiations fails to recognize that reductions in nuclear weapons would free resources for coping with severe social and economic problems in the Soviet Union.

Two features of the Russian image in the American mind that are proven distortions are that Soviet leaders do not inform their citizens of the devastating consequences of nuclear war and that the Russians cannot be trusted to keep arms-control agreements. With respect to the first, the Russians have given extensive newspaper and television publicity to the conclusions of two conferences of the International Physicians for the Prevention of Nuclear War affirming that nuclear war would be a terrible disaster for all concerned. With respect to the untrustworthiness of the Russians, negotiators for SALT I, the American representative on the adherence to SALT I agreements, and the Department of Defense itself have all confirmed that the Russians have fully honored all the arms-control agreements they have signed.

A hopeful aspect of the enemy image is the ease with which it forms and dissolves, depending on the changing relationships between the groups involved. Thus Gallup polls have revealed that Americans view Russians, Germans, and Japanese as warlike and treacherous when they are enemies of the United States but that these adjectives disappear completely from their characterizations when they are our allies. The rapidity with which these adjectives can be applied or removed is well illustrated by American descriptions of the mainland Chinese. In 1966, "warlike" and "treacherous" were among the first ten adjectives used by Americans to characterize them.[5] After President Nixon's trip to China in 1972, these adjectives promptly disappeared and the Chinese were described as "hard-working," "intelligent," "artistic," "progressive," and "practical."[6]

Since humans will never forget how to make nuclear weapons, participants in future wars could always recreate them; hence the future of humanity depends on the ultimate elimination of violence as the final arbiter of international disputes. The achievement of this goal is, of course, very difficult and would require inputs from military scientists, politicians, economists, lawyers, and others concerned with the management of human affairs. From the strictly psychological standpoint, the immediate goals would be to bring perceptions into line with realities, notably by convincing leaders and the public that nuclear weapons are qualitatively different from conventional ones and therefore must be managed in different ways, and by substituting more complex and realistic appraisals by rival groups of each other for the mutual stereotype of the enemy.

To enter into activities toward these ends, we have to start with changes within ourselves. We must overcome internal obstacles to experiencing fully the immeasurable destructiveness of nuclear weapons. To open ourselves to this realization is inevitably painful, but, paradoxically, for many people the distress is somewhat assuaged by a mild state of exhilaration springing from the satisfaction of having finally faced up to the problem, thereby also overcoming our sense of powerlessness. In addition, we derive strength from the emotional support of those who have undergone the same experience.

At the individual level, becoming active means taking advantage of every opportunity to bring the topic of nuclear survival to the attention of others—in casual conversations, letters to the editor, communications with members of Congress, and particularly by participating in programs of organized groups. To be sure, we learn by unhappy experience that the topic of nuclear destruction is often unwelcome, especially at social gatherings and at the family dinner table, but it does not take long to develop a sense of when the topic can be usefully introduced and when doing so is inopportune.

In discussions, it is important to call things by their right names. Unfortunately, pending the invention of words adequate to describe nuclear weapons ("omnicide" is a promising candidate), we are forced to use the inappropriate words devised for discussing nonnuclear weapons. We can, however, continually challenge statements based on the perception of nuclear weapons as larger conventional ones. For example, in 1981 the United States Secretary of Defense stated that the Soviets could destroy 75 percent of American's land-based ICBM's in a surprise attack. Loss of three-fourths of a conventional weapons arsenal would indeed be disastrous. With the U.S. ICBM force such a loss would make no essential difference. The remaining one-fourth is sufficient to target every Soviet city over 100,000 people twice, not to mention missiles on bombers and submarines. Furthermore, a surprise attack with weapons never tested in battle fired over unfamiliar trajectories could not possibly succeed: "A one percent imperfection in performance, a level which experienced weapons engineers would call absurdly optimistic, would be intolerable to the attacker."[7]

Similarly, the argument that we cannot negotiate with the Russians because they would cheat on any treaty can be met by the reminder that, considering the huge superfluity of nuclear weapons, to make any difference at all in relative strength, the cheating would have to be on such a large scale that the risk of the consequences of being detected would outweigh any possible gains. In addition, as mentioned earlier, the Soviets' past performance is strong evidence that they would strictly adhere to arms-control agreements.

The creation of a world order compatible with nuclear weapons will be a long and arduous task requiring many lifetimes, but this goal will never be achieved unless we make a start. To slightly paraphrase the words of an ancient Jewish philosopher, "It is not incumbent upon us to finish the task; neither are we free to exempt ourselves from it."[8]

I am deeply grateful to Dr. James Muller for his initiative in making the arrangements for the republication of this book.

Dr. Jerome D. Frank
Baltimore, Maryland
June 1982

REFERENCES

1. H. Brown. Quoted in *Defense Monitor*, 9:8 (1980), p. 3.
2. L. Festinger *et. al.*, *When Prophecy Fails: A Social and Psychological Study of a Modern Group that Predicted the Destruction of the World* (New York: Harper & Row, 1956).
3. I. Janis, *Victims of Groupthink: A Psychological Study of Foreign Policy Decisions and Fiascos* (Boston: Houghton Mifflin, 1973).
4. J. Legge, ed., *Confucian Analects, The Great Learning and the Doctrine of the Mean* (New York: Dover, 1971), p. 264.
5. *Gallup Poll, Public Opinion 1959–71*, vol. 111 (New York: Random House, 1972), p. 2015.
6. *Gallup Poll, Public Opinion 1972–77*, vol. 1 (Wilmington, Del.: Scholarly Resources, Inc., 1978), p. 20.
7. S. Ramo, *Time*, March 29, 1982, p. 17.
8. Aboth, 2:16.

1 · *The New Predicament—*
Genocidal Weapons

THERE IS NO DOUBT that the dominant feature of life today is the explosive advance of science and technology, producing far-reaching changes in all the conditions of existence. To cope with these new circumstances requires not only acquiring new technical skills but devising new ways of getting along together to replace those rendered obsolete. Humans have an extraordinary ability to master new technical skills quickly— in the span of a few years we have learned to split atoms, dissect microscopic cells, fly supersonic jets, and navigate spaceships— but changing traditional values and ways of behaving is much more difficult. Humans must function by habit. Since we would be paralyzed if we had to evaluate and decide consciously how to meet every new situation, we rely on patterns formed during the plastic years of childhood, automatically assuming that the world will remain sufficiently unchanged so that they will continue to work.

When habitual ways of thinking and behaving appear to be failing, we become confused and anxious, so we try very hard to make new problems look like old ones and to cope with them in old ways. As a result science and technology plunge ahead with supersonic speed, but the necessary concomitant changes in human relations plod behind on foot. The widening gap between man's control of his environment and of himself, as many have pointed out, has become the greatest danger to human survival.

This danger has come into focus with the modern developments in weaponry. Human groups have always resorted to fighting as the ultimate means of settling their disputes and have expended endless ingenuity and effort to improve weapons of war. But suddenly we have succeeded all too well, and weapons now endanger victor and vanquished alike.

Information about modern weapons is boringly familiar to many, but since its implications keep slipping out of attention, a brief reminder of the salient facts is in order. Three types of weapons of war have been brought to fantastic levels of destructiveness: chemical, biological, and nuclear.

CHEMICAL AND BIOLOGICAL WEAPONS

Chemical warfare agents have been used for a very long time—around 400 B.C. the Spartans burned sulphur and pitch to form the irritating gas sulphur dioxide for use in their sieges of Athenian cities; aborigines still use poisoned arrows. World War I saw the introduction of poison gases, and World War II, napalm. Military chemists have not rested on their laurels, however, but have gone on to perfect two new classes of agents. The first, nerve gases, was invented by the Germans during World War II but not used. Far more lethal than any agent previously devised, nerve gases are odorless, colorless, give no warning, and are extremely deadly—a few good breaths or a few drops on the skin kill in a matter of minutes. Russia and the United States are known to be stockpiling these gases in huge amounts. (At this writing a plant in Newport, Indiana, with three hundred civilian employees has been operating twenty-four hours a day for over three years to make chemically filled rockets, land mines, and artillery shells.[1] * It has been reported that stockpiles of nerve gas at the Rocky Mountain Arsenal in Den-

* References will be found on page 293.

ver are sufficient to destroy mankind.[2]) Since these poisons can be made easily and cheaply, it is almost certain that many other nations are also stockpiling them.

Psychochemicals, also impossible to detect and effective in infinitesimal doses, alter states of consciousness and may produce panic and other violent emotional reactions. Their effects are transitory, but one is particularly dangerous when statesmen and military commanders control other weapons that are so deadly: they impair judgment and, worst of all, the victim may not realize that he is under their influence. There is a film in which troops under the influence of one of these agents were shown to be unable to follow simple commands, yet were unaware of their abnormal condition. It is not inconceivable that under the influence of such an agent a commander might give an order that would precipitate an irrevocable disaster.

As to biological agents, there are about thirty-five known bacteria, viruses, fungi, and toxins that could be used as agents of bacteriological warfare.[3] Nations have stockpiled huge quantities of familiar toxins and disease-producing organisms, some extraordinarily deadly. A large glassful of botulinus toxin, for example, contains enough single doses to kill everyone on earth. Societies like the United States, whose populations have lost their natural immunities because of efficient public health services, would be especially vulnerable to common epidemic diseases like anthrax and plague if health services broke down during war. New bacteria and virus strains have been developed which are highly resistant to antibiotics and to which there is no natural immunity. This creates a constant danger that such an agent might get loose accidentally and cause vast epidemics.

Since chemical and biological agents are cheap and easy to produce, small, poor nations can make them; and since poison gases chemically resemble pesticides and biological warfare agents can be made in any biological laboratory, their clandestine manufacture would be almost impossible to detect. But these attractions are currently offset by unsolved distribution problems —it will be a long while before they can be distributed widely enough to approach the damage potential of explosive weapons

—and by the dependence of their effectiveness on atmospheric conditions at the time and place of their use. Hence, although potentially devastating, they do not pose as immediately pressing a threat as nuclear weapons. They do, however, present some psychological concerns not raised by either high-explosive or nuclear weapons—there is something particularly repellent about incapacitating people by tampering with their minds or perverting life processes to destructive purposes—but these issues are subsidiary to the central one posed by the new dimensions of destructiveness, sufficiently epitomized by nuclear weapons.

NUCLEAR WEAPONS

Nuclear weapons are unique in two fundamental respects: their destructive potential is literally unlimited and their aftereffects are long-enduring. A responsible group of scientists stated some years ago that "with a stockpile . . . that now exists it is possible to cover the entire earth with a radiation level which for ten years would remain sufficiently intense to prove fatal to all living beings on land." [4] The absence of a ceiling on destructiveness means that, theoretically, any given level of defense could be overcome by increasing the level of attack—the attacker could always have the last word. Costs of delivery systems and the like may set practical limits and in any case the destruction of all mankind is highly improbable, but until now the possibility never existed at all.

Immediate Destructive Effects

The destructive power of nuclear weapons, so far outside ordinary human experience that the imagination cannot grasp it, is approached only by such major natural disasters as hurricanes or volcanic eruptions. When about six ounces of TNT can blow a hole six feet across and several feet deep or blast a two-foot stump, what does it mean to say that stockpiled nuclear weapons represent the equivalent of about twenty tons of TNT for every person on earth? Perhaps it is easier to imagine the damage one bomb would do by thinking of it with reference to your own town: a 20-megaton bomb exploded on the surface in the center of a town would blast a hole a mile across and eight hundred feet deep (about the height of the RCA Building in Rockefeller Center); the diameter of its fireball would be four and a half miles, and the blast would level everything over an area of about two hundred square miles (if the area were square, it would be about fourteen miles on a side); a deadly concentration of radioactive fallout would be showered over five thousand square miles—a square about seventy miles on a side.[5]

Another way of imagining the destructive power of nuclear weapons is to compare them with natural causes of death, particularly epidemics and famine. Weapons of war are thought of as deadly, but disease has killed far more soldiers; not until World War II did more fighting men die of wounds than of disease. A noted bacteriologist observed that ". . . soldiers have rarely won wars. They more often mop up after the barrage of epidemics. Typhus . . . plague, typhoid, cholera and dysentery [have] decided more campaigns than Caesar, Hannibal, Napoleon and all the inspector generals of history." [6] Famines periodically claim the lives of millions and disease decimates entire populations—it has been estimated that twenty-five million people, one-fourth of Europe's population at the time, died in successive waves of the Black Plague; as recently as the beginning of the twentieth century plague was killing over half a million people annually in India, and in 1918 the influenza pandemic claimed over ten million lives in six months.

Wars did not begin to achieve such lethal power until the First World War, which killed about eight and a half million soldiers, but took four years to do it, and then mostly by disease, not wounds. Fifteen million troops and about sixty-five million civilians died during World War II, but it took eight years (if one starts with the Japanese invasion of Manchuria), and again most of the deaths were due not to weapons but to famine, disease, and other secondary effects of the disruption of societies.

Now, suddenly, weapons have caught up with and far outstripped natural causes of death. Depending on where they fall, nuclear weapons can kill hundreds, even thousands of millions of people in seconds.

Long-term Destructive Effects

The damage caused by nuclear weapons continues long after the moment of impact, affecting the physical health of the survivors (with psychological repercussions to be considered in Chapter 8) and their descendants, if they have any. Many will not. Furthermore, it is well known that the fallout even from the atmospheric tests of nuclear weapons conducted so far has produced small but measurable genetic damage in future generations—just how much and for how long remains controversial, but previous weapons have produced none at all.

Nuclear weapons resemble forces of nature because they can permanently alter the environment. For example, the explosion in 1962 of a 1.4-megaton nuclear bomb—a relatively small one —250 miles up in the air produced radiation far exceeding expectations (it put three American space satellites out of commission) and its effects may last for a decade. Meteorologists have speculated that the increase in the radiation belt temporarily changed the climate—that was the year in which there were severe blizzards all over Europe and a heavy snowfall in Mississippi.

The effects of nuclear explosions cannot be predicted in detail, but a large-scale nuclear attack will certainly shift the balance of nature, thus making the environment permanently more hostile to man. Loss of forests, first through vast fires and later through deaths of radiosensitive trees like pines, will be followed by widespread floods, which will wash away irreplaceable topsoil. Insects, the only species that continues to challenge man for domination of the earth, are much more radioresistant than the birds which eat them. Many food crops are radiosensitive, while some weeds are highly resistant. And since exposure to radiation and disease lowers immunity, radioresistant disease-producing organisms and viruses would find the survivors easy prey.

Modern industrial societies are complex and delicately adjusted: very little disruption of their organization can bring them to a standstill—the 1965 power blackout in the Northeast following the failure of an insignificant bit of equipment is a case in point. Beyond the enormous loss of life during and following a nuclear attack, the sheer physical damage to industrial plants and the disruption of essential services could suffice to disorganize a society beyond the point of no return. The possible cumulative effects on the total system of concomitant breakdowns in many areas defies analysis.

Using computers, many scientists and mathematicians have been working out predictions of the amount of damage the United States would sustain under various sizes and distributions of nuclear attack. But there are so many unknowns in any such calculation that no one really knows what would happen.* Most experts would share the opinion of the chief of research of a large defense industry: "If [a nuclear exchange] did occur, the consequences would go so far beyond all our human experience as to be totally unpredictable. We cannot legitimately even guess whether civilization itself could survive such a disaster. We can be sure only that it would transcend any calamity that the world has experienced. . . ." [8]

Even in wars fought with bows and arrows, nations have always risked destruction if they lost, but a full-scale nuclear exchange would destroy both sides and perhaps all of civilization. Moreover, its delayed effects might make the earth uninhabitable for man. These contingencies are remote, but they have never previously existed, and one might think that with even the slightest chance of such an outcome, the abolition of nuclear weapons would be given top priority among the goals of all nations.

---

* Herman Kahn, after concluding that if all of seven optimistic assumptions were fulfilled, after a 1,500 megaton attack, "life would go on and the necessary adjustments would be made," adds in the next sentence: "But if all these things happened together and all the other effects were added at the same time, one cannot help but have some doubts." He observes that his optimistic judgment could not be made about recovery from a 20,000-megaton attack (now well within the capability of the U.S.S.R.) without more research efforts and "even then doubts may remain." [7]

Relation to National Security and the Abolition of War

Although nations are by no means ready for this step, the properties of nuclear weapons have had one profound effect on military thinking: nations now vie in the building of weapons whose purpose is *not* to be used, whose main function is seen as the deterring of other nuclear powers from using theirs. Military strategists are presently flirting with the use of tactical nuclear weapons in war, but the function of strategic ones is still viewed as purely deterrent.

Since psychological aspects of deterrence and its partner, civil defense, will be considered in Chapter 8, it suffices now only to point out that for the threat to use nuclear weapons to be plausible, a nation should be able to protect itself against nuclear attack while being able to penetrate its opponents' defenses. Some experts claim that the United States can achieve this goal, and they have worked out elaborate plans for its defensive facet;[9] (the psychological reasons for considering such activity to be pursuit of the will-o'-the-wisp will be presented in Chapter 8).

The most optimistic recent estimate of deaths in the United States from a full-scale nuclear attack, assuming that it had the best shelter and anti-missile system now available, was fifty million. It hardly seems worth it.

Until adequate defenses against nuclear weapons are invented, which I believe will not happen, their accumulation certainly increases the power of nations to destroy each other, but it does not make them one whit safer. Secretary of Defense Robert S. McNamara, whose vision about nuclear weapons is quite clear, has admitted that "even if we were to double or triple our forces . . . we could not preclude casualties in the tens of millions."[10] During the Cuban missile crisis our sixty thousand missiles did not suffice to reassure the United States against the prospect of Cuba's having forty.

In recent years, as our military power has been increasing, our security has actually been decreasing. Two military science experts recalled that early in the 1950s the Soviet Union could have launched against us bombers carrying atomic bombs and caused some millions of American casualties; in the later 1950s they could have used more and better bombers carrying hydrogen bombs, and the number of American casualties might have been in the tens of millions; in the mid-1960s, using intercontinental missiles and bombers carrying thermonuclear weapons, the Soviet Union could have inflicted American casualties in the neighborhood of a hundred million. The authors add: "This steady decrease in national security did not result from any inaction on [our] part . . . [but] . . . from the systematic exploration of modern science and technology by the U.S.S.R." They conclude: ". . . . the dilemma of steadily increasing military power and steadily decreasing national security . . . has no technical solution." [11]

The attempt to achieve nuclear superiority fosters the proliferation of weapons within and among nations and makes their control ever more difficult, thus further decreasing the security of all nations.

No nation really believes that another will risk its own existence to protect it, however solemn the promise to do so, and as a result the non-nuclear powers are demanding, with growing insistence, a share in the control of nuclear weapons or at least a guarantee against nuclear attack by the nuclear powers. Failing such arrangements, they will inevitably start manufacturing their own nuclear weapons, and as the cost of manufacturing nuclear warheads and delivery systems continues to drop, the temptation will increase.

Nuclear devices will soon be within the means of private organizations—many criminals and extremist groups have plenty of money and ready access to sources of weapons—and if they can get machine guns and antitank guns today, they can get "small" nuclear weapons tomorrow, most of which are considerably more destructive than the Hiroshima bomb. It would be easy to blackmail a city by hiding one of these devices, set to go off in a certain time, if their demands are not met. Since some nuclear weapons can fit into a typewriter case, finding a needle in a haystack would be a simpler task.

The nuclear powers now seem to be trying seriously to reach

a nonproliferation pact, although the effort would seem to be foredoomed by the unwillingness of China and France to participate. If the effort fails, a very rapid spread of these weapons can be anticipated, leading to a sharply increased danger of the precipitation of a nuclear exchange through accident or misjudgment, as will be discussed in Chapter 4.

Nuclear weapons and globe-circling instantaneous-delivery systems have rendered meaningless the concept of protection through military superiority. Like the frontiersman's revolver, nuclear weapons are the great equalizer—but the revolver enabled either adversary to kill the other, while nuclear weapons guarantee that both will be killed.

Almost everyone grants that a general nuclear war would be universally catastrophic, yet many believe that it will still be possible to fight conventional wars indefinitely because the mutual fear of nuclear destruction acts as a stabilizing force to keep such wars in bounds. There may be something in this assumption, but it rests on shaky psychological grounds, for in this interdependent world any war, no matter how limited initially, threatens to involve nuclear powers and escalate to a nuclear exchange. While the risk in any particular war may be small, the probability that one will trigger a nuclear exchange approaches certainty the longer they continue.

Furthermore, the knowledge of how to make nuclear and other weapons of mass destruction will never pass from the mind of man. Thus, even with disarmament of these weapons achieved, if a war should break out, the nation threatened with defeat could quickly reconstruct them, and mankind would again face the threat of total destruction.

The drastic conclusion that the only solution is the abolition of war is supported by a unanimous statement issued a few years ago by twenty-six experts in atomic, biological, and chemical warfare from eight nations who were trusted advisors of their respective governments—men who know better than anyone modern weaponry's destructive potential: "In the end, only the absolute prevention of war will preserve human life and civilization in the face of chemical and bacteriological as well as nuclear weapons. No ban of a single weapon, no agreement that leaves the general threat of war in existence, can protect mankind sufficiently." [12]

The abolition of war will be extremely difficult—perhaps impossible—but there is no other choice.

2 · No More War?

A SHARP EYE can detect changes in international relations that could be viewed as slight movements toward the goal of abolishing war. At least in the industrially advanced nations militant enthusiasm is being eroded by growing reluctance to engage in war. All wars since World War II have ended in stalemates; war has lost its glamour, its nature is changing, and wars are now justified more in terms of national security than national honor or the desire for more resources or territory. National leaders say they strive for peace, not the destruction of the enemy.

Concomitantly, the international organizations that could eventually develop into the means for peaceful resolution of international conflicts seem to be becoming stronger, despite setbacks. World public opinion is becoming a force that national leaders have begun to take into account, the United Nations is more effective than the League of Nations, and international organizations like the World Bank and the World Health Organization are becoming increasingly indispensable. Treaties for international cooperation in various spheres multiply, and there has even been some progress toward halting the spread of arms, although to do this it was necessary to go to Antarctica, the moon, and outer space.

Efforts to handle international problems in traditional ways are unfortunately being pursued much more vigorously. The enormous investment in weapons ostensibly built to deter rather than wage war is somewhat recent, yet many nations are caught in a gigantic arms race that threatens to suck more and more into its maelstrom. The United States is deeply involved at present in an escalating war in Vietnam, and trouble in such areas as the Middle East and Africa erupts periodically into violent conflict. The intellectual recognition that modern wars are too destructive to be tolerated obviously can make little headway against ingrained habits of national behavior.

After a brief review of certain psychological obstacles to appreciating or coping effectively with the dangers posed by nuclear weapons, we shall attempt to refute some of the apparently convincing arguments that the abolition of war is impossible, and finally indicate what would—and would not—be involved if one were to take seriously the challenge of trying to abolish it.

THE PSYCHOLOGICAL UNREALITY
OF THE DANGER

A few miles to the west of me, at Fort Detrick, is a biological warfare center, a few miles to the east, at Edgewood Arsenal, a chemical warfare center—in each is stored enough poison to wipe out the entire human race several times over, and if even a fraction of the materials at either installation escaped into the air over Baltimore, it would kill me. Yet this knowledge produces not the slightest anxiety, not because I have complete faith in safeguards against accidents—accidents have happened before and will happen again—but because these agents do not register on any of my senses.

Human sense organs are magnificently equipped to detect tiny changes in the environment—a few parts of illuminating gas in a million parts of air brings the housewife rushing into the kitchen; a match flaring a quarter of a mile away on a dark night instantly flags an onlooker's attention. Only the environmental events within range of our sense organs matter, and like our ancestors, we have no biological need to detect and respond to stimuli that do not impinge on any sense organ. With distant events becoming increasingly vital to our safety, this deficiency —"insensitivity to the remote"—is a particularly important source of the general failure to respond with appropriate vigor to the dangers of nuclear weapons. Nuclear missiles poised to kill cannot be seen, felt, tasted, or smelled, and so we scarcely think of them. We have evolved no sense organs for detecting radioactivity, a very new hazard in the history of man, and so it is hard to maintain concern about fallout or even about the growing deposits of radioactive strontium-90 nibbling at our bone marrow.

"Out of sight, out of mind" operates with respect to modern weapons, as illustrated by a finding in a 1948 public opinion survey: although 98 per cent of the respondents had heard of the atom bomb, the majority made no spontaneous reference to it in the course of intensive interviews about America's world role. When it was called to their attention, only a quarter admitted to any personal concern, half said they were not at all worried, and the others that they were worried very little. Their reasons—illustrating defensive avoidance and apathy—were that there was no use worrying over something you cannot do anything about, and that such problems must be solved by the government.[1]

Habituation, another property of our biological equipment, also impedes adequate appreciation of the nuclear danger. Survival in the wild requires the ability not only to detect tiny changes in the environment, but also to stop detecting them if nothing happens—if an animal kept on attending to every stimulus, his capacity to sense possible fresh dangers would be swamped. Therefore, continuing stimuli, except painful ones which represent a continuing danger, rapidly stop registering, thus freeing the sense organs to pick up new ones. The phenomenon is familiar to all of us—smoky, stale air, so suffocating as one enters a room, ceases to be noticed; a person moving to a busy street soon sleeps through the traffic noises that at first kept him awake. As long as it is not overwhelmingly unpleasant or dangerous, any persisting environmental feature gradually comes to be taken for granted. One is reminded of Alexander Pope's comment on vice: "a monster of such evil mien / as to be hated needs but to be seen / but seen too oft, familiar with her face, / we first endure, then pity, then embrace."

As a new form of destructive power the Hiroshima atom bomb, with an explosure equivalent of twenty thousand tons of TNT, created considerable apprehension. Since then, the size of available nuclear weapons has about doubled annually, until to-day the world's stockpiles total at least fifty-five billion tons. We should be terrified, but because of habituation and insensitivity to the remote, we are not.

THE TRAP OF WORDS

Man's one unique characteristic is his ability to use language. Among their psychological functions, words are the tools of thought and of problem solving. Words can lead thinking astray by arousing feelings that color thinking and by being imprecisely applied to the objects to which they refer. Man characteristically tries to apply past language to present events, and when the conditions of life are changing sufficiently rapidly, there may result a serious discrepancy between the words and what they stand for. Appropriate in the pre-nuclear era, the language describing present-day international conflict is now hopelessly dated, and in thinking about the problems of nuclear war, we may be committing ourselves to false conclusions by our choice of words even before we realize that we have begun to think.

Everyone misuses words, from partisans of world government to isolationists, and since the misuse is casual, it escapes scrutiny. For example, all nations refer to their nuclear arms policy as a policy of defense. But today "defense" means not "a state of being defended," but rather deterrence of an enemy attack through threat of retaliation. Yet since we automatically think of "defense" in its old connotation, we hear phrases like "massive defensive shield," when there is no shield against nuclear weap-

ons but only a precarious "balance of terror," at best a brief
reprieve in which, with luck, a better solution might be found.
"Nuclear stalemate," derived from chess, calls up an image of
static deadlock involving no threat to either side; "stabilized
mutual deterrence" is more militarily respectable; but "nuclear
umbrella" is the most remarkable of all. All conjure up a depend-
able, safe state of affairs. But they actually lead to faulty thinking and a false sense of security, for the arms race is far from
static: each day it continues the chances of mutual destruction
increase and the chances of peaceful accommodation decrease.

The American military speaks of "maintaining a margin of
superiority" over the Russians—a term which was meaningful
only as long as the destructive capacity of weapons was limited.
But once "saturation parity" has been reached and each country
then has the capacity to destroy the other, the whole concept of
superiority becomes meaningless.

If a psychiatric patient can see nothing wrong with the sentence "Bill Jones's feet are so big that he has to put his pants on
over his head," psychiatrists worry about the intactness of his
intellectual processes, on which ability to detect absurdities depends. Failure to take into account the changed meanings of
words leads to statements which are almost as absurd. A newspaper editiorial spoke of "the grim business of balancing power
against power as our only means of assuring peace." But balancing power against power has regularly culminated in war (although it may initially have postponed it); and what does it
mean to balance power against power when each side is able to
destroy the other many times over? An American military expert is quoted as saying, "The only solution . . . is for the
United States to get into this arms race with both feet and win
it" [2]—the implied comparison of the nuclear arms race with a
foot race needs no comment.

Words used to describe events are partly selected on an emotional basis, and the emotions they evoke in turn color perception of the events. Thus, the war that began in 1861 was referred
to in Massachusetts as the "Rebellion of the Southern States," in
Pennsylvania as the "Civil War," in Virginia as the "War Be-

tween the States," and in Texas as the "War To Repel Yankee Aggression." Each term obviously implies a certain view of the war, and its use intensified that view. Americans today refer to parts of Vietnam as "infested" by the National Liberation Front, leading to an image not of human beings but of vermin.

The language of military science has always been devoid of reference to killing people or creating suffering—soldiers are "effectives," the dead and wounded are "casualties." Nuclear strategists speak of weapons as "hardware," of "taking out" a city, and of those on the receiving end of the nuclear attack as "targets." The euphemisms are either emptied of emotional content or are implicitly reassuring, referring to familiar activities that have previously brought safety or victory and evoking images that suggest protection and stability. (What could be more protective than an umbrella or more cozily domestic than hardware?) Thus, they reinforce the other means of escaping from the unpleasant emotional tensions created by modern weaponry.

ESCAPES FROM ANXIETY

Although the emotional impact of nuclear weapons is dampened by habituation and remoteness, there is no doubt that they contribute to the emotional tension caused by the conditions of life today, and that people react to them as to other sources of unpleasant feelings. These reactions impede adequate recognition and response to the new dangers they present.

Defensive Avoidance

One way to deal with an emotionally upsetting topic is to put it out of one's mind, a process, termed "denial" when it occurs unconsciously, often seen in the mortally ill. For example, about one-fifth of a series of patients told that they had cancer flatly denied that they had been told.[3] Blotting a threat from consciousness is an extreme form of defensive avoidance. Several experiments have shown that a message urging action against a threat—for example, giving up cigarette smoking to escape lung cancer—is *less* effective if couched in strong fear-arousing terms than if put in milder ones, apparently because recipients of the more frightening message are impelled to find ways of avoiding its impact.[4]

The simplest type of defensive avoidance is not exposing one-self to the disturbing information. That some people deal in this way with the threat of nuclear weapons is suggested by the results of a 1963 public opinion poll: "persons who are very anxious about nuclear destruction . . . avoid relevant information and remain badly informed." [5] More typical is recognition of the existence of the nuclear threat but avoidance of its implications, as in the assumption: our nuclear weapons can destroy the enemy, but his cannot destroy us. In 1959 *The Wall Street Journal,* detailing our capacity to destroy Russia "in several ways and several times over," included in a long article only two brief references to what could happen to us—"either side can inflict painful destruction on the other" and Russia could "perhaps be able to pierce the country's defenses in part." [6] In addition to ignoring the fact that no country has anything approaching an adequate defense against nuclear weapons, the article failed to point out that piercing our defenses in part and inflicting painful destruction really means the destruction of our society. In similar vein, a senator was quoted as saying, "The first rocket to fall on the soil of our allies would be the signal for a rain of rockets on Russia . . ." [7] but one looks in vain for the remainder of the thought: . . . and a rain of Russian rockets on us.

Defensive avoidance is more reasonably expressed through taking refuge in the assumption that because nuclear weapons are so terrible, they will never be used. The self-imposed mutual restraint on the use of poison gas in World War II, offered in support of this view, may have some relevance, but is a rather weak basis for hope. The United States has not only stressed that it has signed no treaty barring use of biological and chemical weapons, but it has also steadfastly refused to enter into any pact that would commit it not to use nuclear weapons first and has admitted selecting nuclear targets in China should worse come to worst.

A more sophisticated form of defensive avoidance is a fallacious appeal to history: since alarmists have prophesied the destruction of mankind with the advent of each new weapon and have been wrong, those who say that nuclear, biological, and chemical weapons threaten humanity's existence are probably also wrong. When men killed each other with clubs and stones, a blow could scarcely kill more than one person, but half a million years later the destructiveness of weapons was so improved that an *average* firebomb raid on Japan in 1944 killed four thousand. A moderate nuclear raid today could kill fifty million people, an increase in destructive power over the most deadly non-atomic weapons of at least 12,500 times in a scant half-generation.

Those who believe the danger to be exaggerated point out that ever since Hiroshima, experts have been issuing dire warnings that destruction was just around the corner, and nothing has happened. These warnings have probably had an effect exactly opposite to that intended: fear of nuclear weapons has been reduced through a psychological phenomenon termed "extinction." If a stimulus that arouses anxiety is repeatedly presented to an animal without the feared consequence ensuing, the animal gradually ceases to react to it; humans have been shown to behave similarly. Yet there is no guarantee that just because there has been no nuclear catastrophe so far there will not be one eventually. The alarmists may simply have underestimated the length of the fuse to the powder keg, and those who prophesy disaster might eventually be right—when it is too late.

Apathy

Another response to a danger is a passive acceptance in advance of whatever lies in store. That apathy or fatalism is a powerful antidote for anxiety is illustrated by the account of an episode that occurred in 1959, shortly after Khrushchev set a deadline for the American evacuation of Berlin and caused a sharp rise in Soviet-American tension:

"Last week I was invited to lunch with a tall, smiling young man, happily married, who has risen in a very short time to one of the highest executive posts in American journalism. . . . 'My wife and children know what to expect, and they've accepted it,' he said. 'I've told them that there'll probably be an exchange of hydrogen bombs before the end of June and I've explained to them that it probably means the death of all of us.' His voice was calm . . . he was not arguing a case but regretfully defining a position.

"I said that while I recognized his right as an individual to commit suicide rather than live under alien rule, I could not understand his equanimity at the thought that the whole of mankind would perish with him. At this he smiled a deep, forgiving, historian's smile. Other forms of life, he said, had been destroyed; what was so special about the human race, which was doomed to ultimate annihilation anyway, by the cooling of the earth?" [8]

When death is threatened from sources beyond human control, denial or fatalism—which remove all incentive to act—may be as appropriate a response as any. But such attitudes can be disastrous when the death threat is of human making and can be removed by human action.

EMOTIONAL TENSION AND BEHAVIOR

Emotional tensions that lead one to avoid perceiving a danger or to block off its emotional impact also impede efforts to cope with it, especially if the danger is unfamiliar and demands a new solution. For the effect of emotion, to stimulate quick action, is incompatible with searching for new alternatives.

If an animal confronted by danger stopped to think, it would probably be dead. So the danger triggers ingrained, automatic emergency responses—freezing, flight, or attack, depending on the species and the nature of the threat—which must have coped successfully with most dangers faced by the species or it would not have survived.

In human terms, emotions reduce flexibility of thought and action, cutting down the number of perceived alternatives so the person has fewer choices to make and shortening time perspective so he tends to seize the first line of action that promises immediate relief. This is apt to be behavior, ingrained through familiarity, that has worked in the past, and since the hardest thing for an anxious person to stand is unclarity or uncertainty, he

automatically tries to make the source of his anxiety look familiar so that he can deal with it in a familiar way. Most behavior
patterns, developed in childhood, are often inappropriate for
handling the stresses of adult life. If they fail, the resulting increase in anxiety may reduce the person's ability to cope still
further, riveting him ever more firmly to the maladaptive pattern. This may partially explain the "repetition compulsion" of
some psychiatric patients, who keep trying to solve a problem by
the same inappropriate means. Like Hamlet, they prefer to bear
the ills they have than fly to unknown others.

A more powerful reason for holding to an unsuccessful way
of handling an emotionally disturbing situation is that it gives
temporary relief, even though at the cost of planting the seeds of
greater future anxiety. For example, most alcoholics, regarding
their personal problems as hopeless, respond to the lure of drink
because it quickly relieves their misery, and this outweighs their
knowledge that it will make them feel worse in the long run, or
even ultimately kill them.

Nuclear armaments have become for nations what alcohol is
to the alcoholic. Nations too regard their problems as insoluble,
and while arms afford no solution, no other course offers hope
of relief from fear. Nuclear stockpiles will probably eventually
be lethal, but this knowledge does not outweigh the short-term
relief of each increase in armaments. Nations, like alcoholics,
are reasonably sure that their addiction will eventually prove
fatal, but they cannot stop.[9]

Since we will consider the effects of emotion on thought and
behavior before and during war in Chapter 9, it suffices here
only to note that by reducing flexibility of thinking and behavior,
the anxiety generated by the new dangers of today's world impedes their solution.

THE LURE OF WAR

In addition to the negative obstacles to facing up to
the need for abolishing war—the fears created by contemplation
of the destructive potential of modern weapons—there are also

positive reasons for wishing to cling to the war system. Unlike alcohol and other self-defeating methods of assuaging anxiety, war and the preparation for it have been generally successful means for coping with a universal social source of fear—the presence of an enemy. It has also performed many positive functions for society and individuals.

War has been the medium of the birth and growth of modern nations. All major nations have periodically engaged in war, and the fact that they exist today means that they have won many of them; resort to war has been reinforced by success. Since the United States has won all the wars it has fought except the War of 1812 and the Korean War, it has particular difficulty in accepting the fact that war is becoming obsolete.

The demands of war have powerfully stimulated technological progress: the need for a more efficient way of making guns led Eli Whitney to devise mass production of standardized parts—the breakthrough that spawned modern industrial societies; World War II enormously speeded the development of earth-moving, radar, and rocketry; the need to guard the soldier's health spurred the development of public health services, and efforts to heal his wounds paced the development of surgery and antibiotics.

In every society war is sustained by very strong vested interests—"the military-industrial complex"—but there are no countervailing groups with equally strong vested interests in peace.[10] The preparation for and waging of war afforded a livelihood and paths to status and prestige not only for soldiers but for industrialists, engineers, and scientists. Investments in arms have been major temporary sources of economic prosperity. In a state of permanent peace influential groups would lose status and suffer a decline of living standards as well as severe economic dislocation.

War, or its anticipation, has had the attractive feature of stimulating a feeling of social solidarity. Thus, members of a society can ignore their differences in pursuit of their common safety, diminishing the burden of individual choice. War, like any disaster, strengthens each victim's feeling of identity with the others, but this sought-after and welcomed sense of group-belonging often dissipates in times of peace.

Finally, war has satisfied certain important psychological needs of men, especially young ones. The role of warrior, much esteemed in many societies, affords a means for establishing a feeling of manhood as well as an outlet for aggressiveness. Many young men seem to need to stretch themselves to the limit, including risking their lives, to achieve a sense of identity. War affords many opportunities for heroism or the altruism of self-sacrifice for others' welfare. It is a break in the humdrum routine of life, a means of supplying the excitement that everyone craves.

There are many reasons, therefore, why national leaders can hardly be blamed for clinging to war as the ultimate means of resolving international disputes, for having reached their positions through their ability to manage war-oriented societies, they cannot make decisions that run counter to the machinery of power over which they preside. Faced with a brand-new danger for which no readymade solution exists (nuclear weapons) and a very old one (the enemy) for which there is a tried-and-true antidote, they almost inevitably try to make the new threat look like the old one and handle it in the old way. Politicians and generals are practical men who would be unlikely to substitute some new and untried theory for a behavior pattern proven valid by millennia of experience. So the conviction that superior destructive force is still the final arbiter of conflict refuses to yield to the overwhelming evidence that in the nuclear age this will soon no longer be true.

War has been less a form of social pathology than an integral, if unpleasant, phase of a system of international behavior, of which the reciprocal phase was peace. Each phase depended on the other: in time of peace, ushered in by victory or defeat in war, the victor consolidated his gains and the loser recuperated from his losses and plotted revenge—and international tensions accumulated until they exploded in the next war. The conclusion thus seems unavoidable that war is an unalterable feature of human life, part of the very fabric of society, and that therefore the hope of eliminating it is a pipe dream. After all, one cannot change human nature.

Perhaps the elimination of war is impossible, but there is no alternative, and whether the enterprise of creating an international system of enduring peace is promising or not, it has to be attempted.

IS WAR INEVITABLE?

If the challenge is accepted, there are glimmers of hope that it can be successfully met without changing human nature. War is a form of social, not individual, behavior. It is a social institution, not a biological drive, and each new generation must be taught its patterns.

Other equally enduring and deeply ingrained social institutions are dead or dying out—human sacrifice in religious rites or India's caste system, for example: the former has virtually vanished, and in less than one generation Gandhi dealt a fatal blow to untouchability, although its death throes may last a while. Perhaps because it once served an important social function but died when the function disappeared, human slavery is war's closest parallel. The Industrial Revolution sounded its death knell because machines could do more work more cheaply than people, and though it lingers in non-industrialized parts of the world, slavery's days are certainly numbered. Analogously, since war's utility has been destroyed by nuclear weapons, its decline should be rapid.

While all social institutions satisfy certain individual needs, and war has been no exception, group standards and values determine the behaviors through which biological needs are expressed. Everyone must eat, yet one society's delicacies are revolting to another; many societies have such a strong taboo against eating human flesh that their members would starve to death rather than do so; other societies prescribe eating the flesh of one's enemies. Group standards can also counteract powerful personal drives. A mother's love is strong enough to cause her to sacrifice her life for her child, but mothers threw their infants under the wheels of the Juggernaut in response to their religion's demands. Self-preservation is a very powerful instinct, yet holders of certain religious beliefs have marched singing to the stake.

Social Control of Violence Within Groups

The impulse to violence shows a similar modifiability by social controls. Civilized societies have not eliminated violence, but they have steadily reduced occasions in which its display is considered permissible—a little over 150 years ago Aaron Burr killed Alexander Hamilton in a duel, a ritualized form of conflict that was still tacitly condoned in the United States then but in most areas has been outlawed today.

Society controls violence not only by social disapproval but also by providing machinery for settling disputes where violence had previously been the only recourse. Lawsuits, the modern equivalent of personal combat, are sometimes life-and-death struggles in that the loser may commit suicide; but only exceptionally does it occur to him to shoot his adversary.

The violence and bloodshed that typified industrial disputes two generations ago have become rare even in bitter and prolonged strikes. Today's workers and plant owners are certainly no less belligerent as individuals than their forebears, nor are the police stronger in the 1960s than in 1910. Part of the explanation may be that today's standards condemn the use of violence to settle industrial disputes, so that each party realizes that the cost of resort to force would outweigh the gains. Concomitantly the mere threat of strikes, whose results can be enormously costly, has become increasingly potent.

In the absence of legal institutions for resolving certain forms of conflict, group standards inhibiting resort to violence despite extreme provocation can be created in a very short time, as Gandhi in India and King and other civil rights leaders in the United States have shown, a matter that will be discussed in Chapter 12.

Societies Without War Patterns

If societies have succeeded in taming violence within their borders, there is no *a priori* reason why they cannot eliminate it in their dealings with each other. Hope that this might be possible is afforded by the example, rare to be sure, of societies that have no war patterns. Aggressive impulses can be channeled into less socially destructive forms: ". . . among the Hopi, competition is the worst of bad taste and physical aggression is rigorously suppressed. Outwardly a Hopi learned to smile at his enemies, to use 'sweet words with a low voice,' to share his property, and to work selflessly with others for the good of the tribe . . . but there remained another form of aggression open to him . . . with a tongue as pointed as a poison arrow, he carries on a constant guerrilla warfare with his fellows." [11] The Hopi are prone to nightmares as well as malicious gossip, but most people would be glad to pay an even higher price than this to be rid of the threat of nuclear war.

An apparently negative but nonetheless hopeful example is afforded by the Comanche, who as plains tribes seemed to live only for war: "The life story of the average old Comanche is nothing but a long collection of war stories. Other events—marriages, deaths—are mentioned casually as having taken place between such and such raids." But as plateau people they had been "completely without war patterns; they did not fight each other even over trespass." [12] The development of the warlike character may have been related to the fact that their new location was between the Spaniards and the Americans, which enabled them to steal horses from each group and sell them to the other.

If changes in its situation can cause a society to develop war patterns, by the same token other types of change—for example, the advent of nuclear weapons—could lead to the abandonment of war.

3 · *Why Men Kill— Biological Roots*

ONE WAY to view human history is as a long, intermittent blood bath. Always easily stimulated to torture and kill each other, men have killed—mechanically, furiously, pityingly, reverently, lustfully—for money, to avenge insults, in self-defense, to protect their countries, to impose their will on others, for the glory of God, and just for kicks.

Men's best talents and energies have been devoted to perfecting means of destroying each other, and societies continue to spend more of their economic and human resources on preparing for and waging war than on any other enterprise. Civilizations rise and fall, but the development of arms technology has never faltered.

The relationship between war and the human capacity to hurt and destroy is far from simple. In some wars the urge to kill seems to play a very minor part, but if this urge could not be aroused, war would be impossible: aggression—the human propensity to injure and kill—is a necessary though not sufficient condition for war. It is not yet possible to predict how more knowledge about the conditions that arouse and dampen aggression can be used to help eliminate war, but I am convinced that such knowledge will eventually prove to be relevant.

Its universality and the ease with which it can be aroused have led to the widely held conclusion that aggression—whether called Original Sin or the Death Instinct—is an unmodifiable attribute of human nature. Those who take this view hope that it can be checked by two other prominent features of human nature, reason and love.

Humans, as thinking creatures, might be able to see that they are embarked on a self-destructive course and to perceive the enormous potentialities for human welfare that could be exploited if they could get over their obsession with mutual murder. And the drive to love, protect, and cherish is certainly as strong as its opposite. The mobilization of intelligence and love holds out the best hope for human survival, but we have not yet learned how to utilize these powerful forces for the prevention of war. Between wars professors and clergymen continually exhort their compatriots to be reasonable and love their fellow men; but the martial spirit of many of them equals or exceeds that of their fellow citizens as soon as the next war begins. Thus, no matter how impassioned or eloquent, general appeals to reason or love are essentially counsels of despair. They never have succeeded, and there is no reason to think they ever will.

Science tries to understand natural phenomena by systematically investigating their causes through observation and experiment, and scientists have recently become bold enough to apply this approach to human behavior. Viewed as a scientific problem, then, the control of aggression may look a bit less insoluble, for if we can understand the conditions that generate destructive behavior and guide its expression, perhaps it can be controlled. To this end, and to gain perspective on its manifestations in humans, we shall look briefly at aggression in animals.

INTRA-SPECIES FIGHTING *

Since man shares anatomical and physiological features with the rest of the animal kingdom, there is no reason to

---

* In addition to the sources mentioned in the bibliography, I have drawn heavily on Konrad Lorenz's *On Aggression*.[1]

suppose that he does not also share certain patterns of behavior. These are buried under a huge superstructure of culture and are modified by the unique human capacity to abstract and symbolize, but recent studies of the behavior of animals in their natural state are rich sources of hypotheses about human behavior that warrant further consideration. Conclusions about humans cannot automatically be drawn from studies of animals, any more than the behavior of nations can be generalized from that of individuals—study of one suggests hypotheses about the other to be studied in their own right.

All animals apparently have innate patterns of aggressive behavior that are necessary to preserve the species, and these are directed either toward prey, toward predators, or toward members of their own species.[2] Fights with predators or prey are to the death, while fights between members of the same species ordinarily are not. Animals like rats that live in communities do fight to the death with rats from another colony if they should collide, and they will kill a strange rat introduced into their midst; but these contingencies seldom arise in nature because the colonies keep out of each other's territory.

Fights between members of the same species are ordinarily kept from getting out of hand by instinctive devices. One safeguard for animals capable of killing each other is the tournament-like ritualization of the fight: the combatants do not use their lethal weapons on their adversaries. Rattlesnakes, not immune to their own venom, never bite each other but instead indulge in a kind of Indian wrestle; onyx antelopes never spear each other with their long sharp horns, but simply butt their foreheads. Another safeguard protects such species as wolves and seals, whose fights are more in earnest, from disaster: the loser emits a signal that inhibits the victor from administering the *coup de grâce*. A defeated wolf will stand with head averted, his throat exposed to a fatal bite by the victor, but this posture makes the latter hesitate just long enough for the loser to run away, and the victor does not pursue him.

Animals who are not powerful enough to kill a creature their own size and whose main defense is flight seem to lack these inhibitory devices. If rabbits or doves, for example, get into a fight and cannot escape each other, as in a cage, they will keep at it until one is killed.

Far from being deleterious to the species, intra-species fighting is necessary for its preservation. Members of the same animal colony establish territories from which each fights to expel all intruders, and the psychological advantage always lies with the defender—the nearer he is to the center of his territory, the more successfully he fights; correspondingly, the intruder's efforts are weaker, the further he gets from his home base. Equilibrium is thus established, and families are adequately spaced out so that each has enough food. This species-preserving function seems to have human analogues in territorial defense and in the establishment of a dominance hierarchy, the other function of intra-species fighting that has survival value. Aside from maintaining order and peace within the group, a dominance hierarchy assures the strongest and most courageous specimens the preferred choice of mates and hence the most favorable opportunity to propagate; the losers—usually less mature males—are preserved for another day.

These biological stimulators and inhibitors of aggression can be faintly discerned beneath the complex behavior of humans. The bitter human struggles for power, prestige, and property are closely associated. Property rights have always taken precedence over human rights, and although this can be mitigated it is doubtful if it can be reversed, since possessions are a major source of psychological security, and no society, not even the most doctrinaire communist ones, have been able to dispense with them for long. An attack on one's home, and by extension, one's nation,* will call forth the most intense and obstinate resistance, as invaders have learned through the ages. In humans, as in animals, furthermore, status and property are powerful lures in helping the male attract a mate.

Certain human attitudes of prayer or suppliance may be analogous to those that inhibit aggression in animals, but their efficacy is at best uncertain, and they may fail altogether to in-

* See discussion in Chapter 6, pp. 107ff.

hibit an attacker from a different culture who does not recognize the signal. In fact, the most striking difference between humans and almost all animals is that, as we shall see, they lack adequate inhibitions against killing their own kind.

THE CENTRAL NERVOUS SYSTEM
AND AGGRESSION

Species obviously differ widely in their propensity to be aggressive, and each has characteristic ways of showing aggression, indicating some "programming" in the central nervous system.

Experiments on animals have yielded some information about brain centers determining aggressive behavior, and observations suggest the existence of similar ones in humans. Fight patterns can be elicited from animals when a very weak current is run through microscopic electrodes inserted into certain spots in the brain. It has been possible to locate separate centers in chickens' brains for the distinctly different attack patterns directed at other chickens and at predators. Each pattern includes its specific environmental releaser—that is, stimulation of these centers will elicit the attack behavior only when an appropriate target is also provided; otherwise the bird simply shows restlessness.[3]

In recent years some investigators have implanted electrodes in human brains in conjunction with efforts to heal illnesses like epilepsy. Predictably, the patients' subjective and behavioral responses vary a lot—depending on their personalities, their momentary mental states, and the specific situation in which the stimulation is given—but in general the findings are consistent with those obtained from animals. In one such study four out of five epileptics whose brains were stimulated in a certain area experienced "feelings of fear, anxiety, and at times a 'weird' or 'terrific' feeling in association with alterations in motor behavior."[4]

Clinical observations support these findings. Many patients with injuries or electrical abnormalities in certain deep areas of the brain concerned with emotions show a low threshold for aggressive behavior, intolerance of frustration, impulsiveness, and irritability. Epileptics with damage in these areas may have bouts of homicidal rage, and in this state, "if they are placed in a quiet side room after an attack so that they are free from distraction, they often remain quiet, but if someone enters they rise in a menacing fashion and if one is careless they are apt to attack in a blind fury." [5] With humans, as with chickens, stimulation of certain brain areas makes them more irritable, but they are not violent until presented with a suitable object to attack.

Finally it should be mentioned that one type of brain fever —encephalitis lethargica—can be followed by a personality change characterized by marked destructiveness and impulsiveness. Children who have previously behaved normally lie, steal, destroy property, set fire, and make serious, even murderous attacks upon others.[6] It is a plausible, though not proven, hypothesis that the malignant features of Adolf Hitler's personality were manifestations of a post-encephalitic state.[7] Descriptions of aspects of his behavior in his last years are compatible with this diagnosis, including a characteristic disturbance of sleep rhythm, extreme restlessness, staring spells, and wild rages accompanied by marked signs of deranged functioning of his vegetative nervous system. He also had tremors and disturbances of posture characteristic of post-encephalitic Parkinsonism. Hitler is said to have been proud of his ability to hold his arm in the Nazi salute longer than anyone else, and in view of subsequent developments, this may have been the motor rigidity that sometimes precedes Parkinsonism.

To support the diagnosis of post-encephalitic Parkinsonism, it would have to be established that Hitler had had encephalitis. According to school reports he was a model student until his twelfth year, when he abruptly became a "behavior problem" —restless, truanting, and quarrelsome. This change occurred shortly after a younger brother died of an illness diagnosed as measles encephalitis, but unfortunately for the hypothesis, measles encephalitis does not have such sequelae. The diagnosis may have been wrong, however, and it is possible, though it can never be established with certainty, that Hitler had a subclinical case of encephalitis lethargica. Even the possibility that his illness was post-encephalitic is chilling, for in a nuclear world a post-encephalitic might succeed where Hitler wasn't powerful enough—and achieve the *Götterdämmerung*. We shall return to the question of mental illness in national leaders in the next chapter.

THE MALE SEX HORMONES AND AGGRESSION

The relationship between heightened aggressiveness and hormonal level is very striking with the male sex hormones. Males of many species are much more quarrelsome during the mating season when their male sex hormone level is high. Young mice, for example, cannot be made to fight until they are thirty to forty days old, the age at which they start to produce these hormones.[8] Prepubertal castration of mice or of domestic animals increases their docility. Mice castrated before puberty do not fight, but those castrated in adulthood after they have learned to fight will continue to do so if they are given a daily opportunity.[9] The habit of fighting persists in the absence of male sex hormones, but dies out if not continually reinforced, and mice given a few weeks' rest can no longer be aroused to fight.

Mature male house mice ordinarily fight fiercely but briefly if placed together, but experience and training can drastically modify this pattern in either direction. Repeatedly stimulated to fight under conditions in which they always win, they become so ferocious that they even attack females and young, which males ordinarily will not do; on the other hand, inexperienced males kept with females for a few weeks develop inhibitions against fighting, and two such males, placed together in the presence of females, do not fight at all.[10] In short, male sex hormones increase an animal's readiness to fight, probably by stimulating the brain centers for this type of behavior, but his past experience and the features of the particular situation determine whether he fights or not.

In humans, too, sexual virility and aggressiveness are often linked. The killer hero in literature, from "shaggy-breasted" Achilles to James Bond, is always pictured as highly sexed. But training, life experience, and especially a person's philosophy of life are obviously far more important determinants of aggressiveness than the level of male sex hormones. Normally virile men like Gandhi and Martin Luther King, Jr., have refrained from violence under extreme provocation, while some men who appear to have been deficient in male sex hormones have been notoriously quarrelsome—the early American statesman John Randolph of Roanoke comes to mind.

Violence is not a male monopoly. Sexual sadism is not confined to men, and there are many accounts of violent behavior by women—dispatches from Indonesia during the slaughter of communists and their sympathizers in 1966 told of trained women torturers, there are historical accounts of Dutch *Hausfrauen* kicking the enemy soldiers' severed heads around the street, and there is an old adage concerning the fury of a woman scorned.

Sex Differences in Human Aggressiveness

By and large men are more aggressive than women. On the attitudes scales of all polls that raise the question, men express more warlike attitudes than women, scoring less pacifistic and more "toughminded"—a generally aggressive orientation;[11, 12] they are also more apt to say that pacifist demonstrations are harmful to American interests and to advocate nuclear retaliation against a non-nuclear attack on our allies.[13] Among college students asked to rate parallel statements, attributing actions that had been taken by both countries either to the U.S. or the U.S.S.R., the girls rated warlike, disapproving, or competitive actions by either country less favorably than the boys.[14] In experiments to be described in Chapter 5, witnessing an aggressive model elicited more subsequent aggression from four-year-old boys than girls.

It is impossible to determine the relative contributions to both attitudes and behavior of innate sex differences and cultural expectations concerning male and female roles. Experiments have shown that male college students are more angered than female by derogation of leadership or intellectual ability; but this may simply reflect stronger culturally determined drives in these areas, because men more often receive early training to fight back when attacked which creates stronger aggressive habits.

The major source of difference in aggressiveness may be that women are trained to have stronger inhibitions against direct aggression. When given an excuse to shock someone who had angered them, men and women gave the same number of shocks the first time; the women, however, showed a sharp decline the second time, as if they had felt guilty over their previous behavior.[15]

AGGRESSION AND TARGET SUBSTITUTION

A final feature of animal aggression that seems to have a human counterpart emerges when an animal is stimulated to aggression but no suitable environmental trigger is available. The animal becomes restless, like the hen whose brain center for aggression was electrically stimulated, or he may search actively for an appropriate stimulus—"appetitive behavior" that in humans would be called spoiling for a fight. If a target that arouses both aggression and inhibition presents itself, like a mate or a too powerful rival, the animal—exhibiting "displacement"—may attack a substitute object. An aroused fish might attack one of another species if the only available one of his own species were his mate; similarly, the man angered by his wife's criticism attacks his brother-in-law. Or the animal may indulge in substitute behavior, like preening or nest building, much as an angry man might take out his knife and sharpen some pencils.

If lower animals can express their aggressiveness in so many ways, the range of alternatives to humans should be very much greater.

IMPLICATIONS FOR HUMAN AGGRESSION

Since cultural determinants and human symbolic powers enormously influence the expression of biological drives, it would be a mistake to push the human-animal analogy too far.

But this quick look at our ancestors suggests implications—some hopeful, some alarming—with respect to aggression in humans.

Aggression in animals, even against members of their own species, is essential for survival. The same probably holds for humans, and even if such were possible, it would not be desirable to eliminate aggression from human life. Without rivalry and competition among their members, societies would stagnate; and moral indignation is the main spur to social progress.

Perhaps the most hopeful finding is that although internal factors influence thresholds for aggressive behavior, both aggression's threshold and its expression are under close environmental control. Animals can be trained to fight or not to fight: depending on the provocations, an animal may go through life never fighting or fighting every day. Sometimes, as when the male sex hormone level is high, the animal may act as if he is spoiling for a fight, but if no suitable target presents itself, the urge will eventually wane and the animal is none the worse. Rather than a need to fight that must be expressed, there are latent behavioral patterns that the environment may or may not evoke. Features of the animal's environment release or inhibit aggression and provide a large variety of alternative modes of expression for it—if some are blocked, the animal can find substitutes.

A lifelong student of animal behavior sums up his findings in these terms: " . . . the chain of causation . . . eventually traces back to the outside . . . there is no need for fighting . . . apart from what happens in the external environment"; " . . . an internal physiological mechanism has only to be stimulated to produce fighting . . . but it can be kept under control by external means." [16] Aggression, so readily modifiable in subhuman species by the environment, is probably even more so in humans.

The review of aggression in animals also suggests some less optimistic lines of thought. Like all other creatures, humans probably have fight patterns programmed into their central nervous systems that are sensitized by male sex hormones and stimulated by environmental provocations. Although the individual life experience and cultural expectations substantially modify the normal, intact human's triggers and modes of expression of biological fight patterns, the presence of these patterns probably explains why in both individual and group conflicts the party that first resorts to violence almost always impels the other to follow suit. Only intensive training and powerful group sanctions can prevent persons and groups from responding to violence with violence, as discussed in Chapter 12. From the biologist's viewpoint, the most disturbing feature of human aggression is that we don't know when to stop. In this we may resemble animals without attack equipment, rabbits for example, that rely on flight for protection and will massacre each other if confined to close quarters. This is in contrast to animals like wolves, that have strong attack equipment and specific inhibitions against killing their own kind. Perhaps because of our relatively ineffective native attack equipment, like rabbits we failed to develop these inhibitions because they were biologically superfluous. When we invented weapons, we took evolution by surprise, soon making ourselves safe from serious threat by members of other species and making other hostile groups the main sources of danger to each human group. This may have led to selective breeding that favored those temperamentally most inclined to attack their fellows.

A more important abolisher of inhibitions against killing our own kind may be the uniquely human power to symbolize, which enables us to regard each other almost at will as conspecifics, prey, or predator, and behave accordingly: with those whom we regard as like ourselves, we indulge only in such ritualized nonlethal fighting as games and lawsuits; but like rats, once we define someone as an enemy, no holds are barred—rats, however, lack nuclear weapons.

The human propensity for self-slaughter has become the greatest threat to survival. Perhaps the best hope of keeping it within bounds lies in fully exploiting ways of making all humans recognize that they are members of a single group—that is, by making the brotherhood of man not only a biological fact and a theological tenet, but also a political and therefore a psychological reality, a possibility more fully explored in Chapter 11.

In short, animal studies make clear that insofar as humans

still have traits of their animal ancestors, attempts to abolish war cannot ignore aggressiveness or suppress it by fiat or appeals to love one another; but perhaps it can be managed. Although it would be a questionable undertaking even if feasible, it may be possible someday to raise the internal threshold for aggression. Meanwhile, the goal must be to reduce environmental instigators to aggression, to strengthen inhibitions against its more destructive forms, and to develop satisfactory substitute outlets.

4 · *Unintentional or Unauthorized Destructiveness*

BEFORE CONSIDERING the psychosocial determinants of destructive behavior, we should examine accidental and unauthorized destructiveness, which are important precisely because they elude social control. Accidental or unintentional destructiveness—which like any accidental behavior is not consciously motivated—results from the inability to cope with the demands of a specific situation because of reduced alertness or energy, among other reasons. Without extending the concept too much, it can include a leader's failure of judgment resulting from ill health. Unauthorized destructive behavior is intentional but arises from aberrant perception of a situation or aberrant motives, as in insane persons or those with certain types of personality disorder.

It is virtually inconceivable that, acting deliberately and in full possession of all the facts, the responsible leader of a nuclear power would instigate a general nuclear war, because in any rational calculation both sides would lose. Furthermore, acts of aberrant individuals are unlikely to trigger a major nuclear exchange in peacetime. In complex societies—the only ones currently possessing these weapons—individual initiative is highly restricted: such major decisions as those involving the use of nuclear weapons require the concurrence of several people, and any aberrant person would probably be stopped by his colleagues. The less well organized the society, however, the greater the scope for individual misbehavior; so the hazard increases as nuclear weapons proliferate. The spread of nuclear weapons also exacerbates the danger, because the great powers' possible involvement in wars, whether nuclear or not, between smaller nations is the most likely path to a general nuclear exchange.

The danger that an accidental or unauthorized discharge of a nuclear weapon could trigger a nuclear exchange in peacetime has receded in those countries whose missile bases and nuclear submarines are hardened so that their retaliatory missiles cannot be destroyed by an enemy's surprise attack. A nation hit by a nuclear missile can take the time to investigate before retaliating, thereby reducing the chances of acting on misinformation. But if nuclear weapons spread to countries which cannot afford to protect them, the danger of sparking a nuclear war through a mistaken pre-emptive attack will again be important.

The danger of an accident or error of judgment precipitating a general nuclear exchange would rise sharply in time of crisis or war, because exhausted leaders in a state of great emotional strain might believe they had to make a quick decision on the basis of incomplete or false information. With mutual distrust at its greatest, each adversary would be led to place the most ominous interpretation on the other's inadvertent or unauthorized firing of a nuclear weapon. The danger would be increased if nuclear devices were armed, as in the Cuban crisis of 1962, or if tactical nuclear weapons had already been used in the course of a war.

It is improbable that the situation and the accidental act would coincide, but the risk of precipitating unintended nuclear war does exist; and since one such disaster would be too many, it seems worthwhile to look at the problem of preventing nuclear accidents.

ACCIDENTS

Each new form of power brings new hazards, and nuclear power is no exception. There have been literally hundreds of minor accidents in nuclear reactors and at least two serious ones, and more can be expected. While it would be catastrophic, the explosion of a nuclear power plant near a city would be very unlikely to lead to nuclear war, but the accidental firings or explosions of missiles through failure of safety devices are of greater concern. The Pentagon has acknowledged fourteen accidents involving nuclear weapons, the most spectacular of which was the release of four unarmed nuclear bombs from a B-52 following its collision with a jet tanker near Palomares, Spain, in January, 1966. Great publicity was given the dramatic, successful retrieval of the bomb that fell into the sea, but the two bombs that burst on impact, scattering radioactive debris and necessitating the removal of some sixteen hundred tons of slightly radioactive soil,[1] received much less notice.

American nuclear bombs and missiles are loaded with safety devices, so the chances of any one going off accidentally are very small; but even the most improbable event can happen sooner or later—tossing coins long enough eventually yields twenty heads in a row. Moreover, since the safeguards cannot be so elaborate that they interfere with intentional firing, there is an upper limit to the protection they can afford. Nor is it likely that all nations getting nuclear weapons will be as safety-conscious as the United States, especially since their safeguards make the weapons more expensive.

While mechanical problems are not our major concern, they too are sources of danger because of the possibility that the elaborate missile detection equipment could signal erroneously. The Greenland radar warning system once mistook the rim of the rising moon for a sortie by Russian bombers, and only his recollection that Khrushchev was in the United States at the time prevented one commander of the North American Air Defense Command from flashing the alert. Missiles allow much less time for such decisions, and such fortunate coincidences cannot be counted on.

Human failure is much more potentially disastrous. At the very peak of the Cuban missile crisis, for example, a U-2 pilot collecting air samples over the North Pole took a reading on the wrong star and headed straight for Moscow. As President Kennedy wryly remarked, "There's always someone who doesn't get the word." [2] The pilot was reached before any harm was done —but just how many such accidents will be harmless?

UNAUTHORIZED FIRING OF A NUCLEAR WEAPON

The possibility that a nuclear weapon could be set off through insanity or malice has been considered serious enough to warrant considerable attention by the Armed Forces. While the number of battle reactions is related to the amount of a soldier's combat duty, the number of soldiers hospitalized for insanity, in all nations that have kept records, seems unaffected by external events and is remarkably constant—ranging annually between two and three per thousand, occasionally rising a little higher or dropping a little lower, regardless of peace or war.[3]

As more and more persons get their hands on nuclear weapons, the probability increases that one of them in a position to fire a nuclear weapon will have an irrational impulse to do so. The risk is greatest not among combat personnel, who are carefully selected and whose weapons have safeguards, but among the military police guarding the missile bases and the mechanics who assemble and maintain the weapons: the police might give access to weapons to someone planning to cause a nuclear disaster; the mechanics have access to weapons before safety devices are installed.

The designer of the Air Force Human Reliability Program tells of a psychotically depressed maintenance sergeant who rigged a partly assembled nuclear missile so that firing a pistol at it would set it off; he was dissuaded with much difficulty from carrying out his plan to commit suicide in this spectacular fashion. The report published later stated that the missile could not have gone off, but the speaker said explicitly that it could.

A greater risk than the insane are the apparently normal people who delight in destruction or who are extremely hostile and suspicious. Many of these are experts at concealing their feelings and plans, and no brief screening method can detect them. Some years ago two young music school students were accused of plotting to dynamite the school; they had stolen over a hundred sticks of dynamite for the purpose. A psychologist who examined one of the girls at the request of the police said he "couldn't find a single symptom of insanity"; the dean of the school described the other as a good and truthful girl, a good student and well liked by her classmates.[4] How many such people, who must also exist in the Armed Forces, are patiently working their way up to positions in which they can do major damage? There are reports, like this one, of unauthorized acts by soldiers timed to cause maximum trouble: during the Algerian struggle for independence a French colonel ordered an Algerian village bombed just when a Red Cross mission was expected and rebel troops had been withdrawn; the reporter asks: "If one colonel can cause so much damage by one misguided decision involving only conventional weapons, what can other colonels commanding nuclear and missile detachments do to menace future world peace?"[5]

The American Armed Forces have taken the best steps they can to minimize these contingencies. The Air Force Human Reliability Program, for example, involves semiannual screening of all personnel directly or indirectly in contact with nuclear weapons (the first screening resulted in the replacement of about two per thousand), but such a program's effectiveness is limited because it is unlikely to detect either the skillful dissembler, who probably represents the greatest danger, or the person who becomes deranged between examinations. The pamphlet describing the program ruefully concludes that "Unauthorized destructive acts cannot be completely prevented."[6]

During actual war, when field commanders would be empowered to use their own judgment if communications with the central command broke down, the danger of unauthorized use of at least tactical nuclear weapons would be increased. And a field commander whose unit was about to be wiped out and who couldn't reach headquarters would be most unlikely to refrain from using them as a last resort. Once the psychological barrier has been broken by the use of even the smallest nuclear weapons, there is no clear stopping place before a full-scale nuclear exchange.[7]

The long-term isolation of the teams that man strategic nuclear weapons, notably in Polaris submarines, is a new psychological hazard.* As long as the missiles can be armed only by a signal from headquarters, there is no danger of unauthorized firing, but it seems likely that there is some provision for transferring this function to the submarine commander in the event of a wartime communications breakdown. More knowledge is needed about conditions promoting development of group psychoses or distortions of judgment under prolonged isolation and stress.[8]

Though it increases with the deployment of such weapons, the possibility of precipitating a nuclear war *in peacetime* by accidental or unauthorized firing of a nuclear weapon is probably still very small, and is even further decreased by periodic screening of weapons personnel and especially by the "hot line" between Washington and Moscow, an arrangement apparently being adopted by other nuclear powers.

INSANITY OR INCAPACITY OF NATIONAL LEADERS

A more refractory source of danger is a serious error of judgment by a national leader in time of crisis. Every organized group requires a leader to represent its values and to act as spokesman for and executor of its policies; and although he is

---

* A psychiatric referral rate of about four percent in nuclear submarine crews is reported by A. Satloff in "Psychiatry and the Nuclear Submarine," *American Journal of Psychiatry*, 124 (October, 1967), 547–49.

constrained by the demands of his role and by his function as a member of a ruling group, he has considerable freedom of action even in the most egalitarian society. His personality and the structure of the political system determine the degree to which he can be restrained from an unwise act—the advisors of a Roosevelt or a Churchill could probably speak their minds more freely than those of a Trujillo or a Hitler. In a crisis, when an error of judgment can do the most harm, a leader has greatest freedom. Subordinates can often assume some of the leader's functions and prevent him from making gross blunders when he is incapacitated—as did those of Wilson, Roosevelt, and Churchill—but they cannot take the initiative or make the crucial decisions. And in today's world failure to act may be as dangerous as making the wrong move.

The answer to "How does physical and mental illness influence negotiations between diplomats?"[9] is not particularly comforting. At least seventy-five chiefs of state in the last four centuries led their countries, actually or symbolically, for a total of several centuries while suffering from severe mental disturbances[10]—a not very surprising figure considering the inbreeding of royal families and the fact that the right to rule had nothing to do with competence. The passing of hereditary leaders has removed the dangers of an unfavorable roll of the genetic dice, but the present social and political forces that bring leaders to power do not necessarily assure a wise selection.

It is generally claimed, and it is probably true, that with its strict role demands and pressures to conformity, modern organized industrial society's bureaucratic structure will ordinarily filter out the emotionally unstable and elevate only the realistic, task-oriented, and well-integrated into leadership roles. Yet a nation like Germany—politically sophisticated and bureaucratized, and with a highly educated population—could entrust itself to a Hitler when sufficiently demoralized and embittered. It could happen again, and the probability is increased by the great number of new nations whose populations are as embittered as the Germans were and whose political skills are much less developed.

Furthermore, although many of the causes of antisocial behavior are still obscure, many more criminals and sociopaths—those who are self-seeking, impulsive, and seem to lack a conscience—come from broken homes than do good citizens.[11] Since millions of young adults spent their formative years in refugee camps or other socially disorganized settings and lost one or both parents in childhood, there is reason to fear that leaders with antisocial tendencies will be more common than usual in the near future.

The possibility of a national leader's becoming insane or incapacitated is a more pervasive and immediate danger. Even though the former contingency is rare, there is a notable example in James Forrestal, the first U. S. Secretary of Defense, who was frankly delusional when he was relieved from office and probably had been for many months before—for example, he thought that the sockets of beach umbrellas were wired to record everything he said, and at one point thought that some planes overhead were Russian bombers.[12] The thought that such a man might be in a position to order nuclear retaliation against an imagined attack is rather disquieting.

The Danger of Aging Leaders

Flagrant mental illness is rare in leaders of modern democracies, but creeping incapacity under the pressure of age and the strains of office is unfortunately much more common than is generally realized. In this century alone at least six British Prime Ministers and a very large number of cabinet officers were ill while in office;[13] the United States affords the examples of Presidents Wilson and Franklin Roosevelt who, during their last months in office, had advanced hardening of the arteries of the brain (Wilson had also suffered a severe stroke), and Eisenhower, who had a heart attack, a major operation, and a mild stroke.

Wilson's inability to exert effective leadership was undoubtedly responsible for America's failure to join the League of Nations. Roosevelt, whose powers had seemed to be failing at Quebec, was a dying man at Yalta, unable to brief himself ade-

quately for the conference, and ". . . no longer [seeming] to
take an intelligent interest in the war; often he [did] not seem
even to read the papers [Churchill gave] him." [14] Already after
the Quebec Conference the previous fall, when Secretary Henry
L. Stimson read him the statement he had signed that proposed
turning Germany into an agrarian nation, Roosevelt's reaction
was revealing: "Stimson tells us that the President was staggered
when he listened to this sentence. He had no idea, he said, that
he could have initialled such language." [15]

The characteristic manifestations of hardening of the arteries
of the brain are general loss of energy and adaptive capacity,
impairment of ability to concentrate, lapses of memory (as
seems to have been the case in the example just cited), periods
of confusion,* emotional liability, and irritability. A leader with
such disabilities is poorly equipped to meet the demands of
modern leadership, especially when he is apt to be faced with
prolonged crises in which decisions must be made under emotional stress and without sufficient sleep.

Many studies have shown that sleep deprivation and other
forms of stress interfere markedly with the performance and
judgment even of healthy young adults. The most common effect
of sleep loss is impairment of the ability to sustain intellectual
effort, and continuous wakefulness for three or four days can
produce the whole gamut of symptoms of severe mental illness;[17]
presumably, however, even national leaders in crises would
probably not have to stay awake for that long.

Studies of the effect of stress on performance are also of interest, but since the most common way of producing stress experimentally has been to lead college students to believe they have
failed on some task, the conclusions may be irrelevant. The studies do show, however, that the universal effect of this type of
pressure seems to be to increase the students' rigidity of
thought: they were less able, for example, to shift from one kind

---

* President Eisenhower described his mental state after his slight stroke
in 1957 as "a confusion of mind. I just couldn't pick up a pen. I
messed some papers off the desk. I went down to pick them up. I
didn't know where to put them." [16]

of problem solving to a more appropriate one when the task changed.[18,19,20]

Such inadequate responses to stress would be expected to be more pronounced in persons with cerebral arteriosclerosis, and while medicine is making great strides in repairing or replacing blood vessels, kidneys, and hearts, no way of replacing the brain is in sight. The result is predictable: an increasing proportion of national leaders with vigorous bodies and potentially failing minds.

The Problem of Removing an Incapacitated Leader

It is practically impossible to remove an insane or failing leader, for he is usually reluctant to admit that anything is wrong, and those around him have many reasons for humoring him. In an absolute monarchy or a dictatorship, the problem is insuperable since, in addition to other considerations, the subordinates fear reprisal. Thus, Caligula's and Nero's henchmen loyally executed their leaders' most bizarre and outrageous orders for years before finally assassinating them; Ludwig the Mad of Bavaria could not be deposed until he removed himself by suicide, taking his unfortunate psychiatrist with him; Hitler's subordinates remained faithful long after his cause was hopeless and continued to try to carry out his orders long after they were impossible to fulfill.

Democracies are little better: the mentally ill governor of Louisiana gained his release from a mental hospital by firing its superintendent; the United States was without a Chief Executive for eighty days while Garfield was dying from an assassin's bullet because the Vice-President did nothing. And his followers are generally the last to recognize a deterioration in their leader's health: the pretense that Wilson was functioning adequately as President was maintained for eighteen months after his stroke, and Roosevelt was elected to his fourth term when anyone not blinded by loyalty to a wartime leader would have seen that he was not strong enough for the arduous duties of the office.

There are various reasons for the "conspiracy" to pretend that a national leader is not subject to the ills of ordinary mortals: a leader's fall would cost his subordinates their positions, for their power rests on his; moreover, since he is his nation's representative to the world, public acknowledgment of his deterioration would weaken its international influence. Aside from these specific reasons for pretense, there is a universal human trait, probably springing from the fact that we are group animals: since members of all tightly knit groups have a strong emotional investment in their leader, they identify with him—feeling strong when he is strong, becoming anxious if he falters. Regardless of the circumstances or his personality, the death of a powerful leader, which forces recognition of his mortality, is almost always a severe shock to his followers, simply because he was the leader. The deaths of both Roosevelt and Kennedy elicited intense grief reactions, yet Roosevelt's death in wartime was the culmination of an obvious and prolonged physical decline, while Kennedy's in peacetime was totally unexpected. Both, however, were Presidents when they died, and it is this feature which is probably primarily responsible for the intensity of the emotional reaction to their deaths.

Partly as a manifestation of the need to believe in their mental and physical health, top leaders, unlike many ordinary civil servants, do not have to submit to medical screening before assuming office. Moreover, the pressures of the job may operate to prevent them, unlike their subordinates, from receiving adequate and prompt medical care or from taking leaves during minor illnesses.

All this was tolerable when a leader's wrong decision or failure to act could, at worst, ruin only his own country; but today civilization is at stake. Some countries now accept the necessity of regular medical examinations for their leaders, but something must be done to cover the contingency of a leader's becoming mentally deranged or incapacitated. The situation seems particularly hopeless in societies lacking the legitimate machinery for removing a leader, whether he be hereditary monarch or dictator, for a social system that permits a madman to gain power would be unlikely to provide for a psychiatrist to examine him.

The establishment of regular psychological check-ups for all national leaders can come about only when the stigma attached to mental illness is reduced. Once the need is recognized, however, it should not be too difficult to arrange for each leading policy-maker to unburden himself periodically to a carefully chosen professional confidant, analogous to a father-confessor, who would be empowered to bring his client's condition before a disability commission if he were convinced beyond reasonable doubt that the condition gravely endangered the leader or his country. The commission would, of course, have to be composed of such people as federal judges, who are barred from the political power struggle, and they too would be expected to undergo periodic evaluations.[21,22]

Mere mention of such a scheme raises many difficult questions: What should be the qualifications of the professional confidant and the members of the disability commission? How would they be selected? What safeguards would be needed against abuse of their powers? These and many others that appear virtually insuperable come to mind; yet the provision of institutionalized ways to protect a nation against the acts of a mentally incapacitated leader must eventually be taken seriously.

5 · Why Men Fight— Psychosocial Determinants

THE ULTIMATE ACT of war is killing: no matter how indirect the method, how complex the chain of command, how intricate the team cooperation necessary to launch a weapon, or how many of the enemy killed at once, the final act is that of a single person. The inquiry into the psychosocial causes of war should thus begin by reviewing the causes of aggressive behavior in individuals. I am well aware that the difference between a child hitting a doll or a college student administering an electric shock and the complex group activity called war is enormous, and that although there are connections between the two types of behavior, they are obscure. Not knowing what aspects of aggression in individuals are pertinent to war, I selected material for inclusion simply on the hunch that it will eventually prove to be relevant; when in doubt, I have preferred to risk including possibly irrelevant material rather than omit information that might be important.

Humans respond not to events but to their meanings and can read into any event an endless variety of meanings. In humans as in other animals a physical attack will incite aggression, but so too will a dare, an insult to one's wife, spitting on the flag, or a military command.

Aggression's forms are as varied as their instigators—verbal abuse, physical assault, a lawsuit, complaining to the police, releasing a nuclear bomb. Since this chapter deals mainly with psychological experiments, the behaviors used as indicators of aggression are rather mild—killing, needless to say, is not among them—but since they do involve the infliction of psychological or physical pain, it may not be too far-fetched to assume that if additional conditions were also fulfilled, some of their determinants could contribute to the impulse to kill.

Although aggression can be generated by such varied motives as hate, revenge, protection of self-esteem, obedience to orders, or altruism, fight patterns in themselves are morally neutral: to murder a man for pay is regarded as wicked but to kill someone who attacks your child or your country is considered virtuous, as is supporting your family by prizefighting. The purpose of aggressive acts, as defined here, is to make the victim suffer: the sight of his victim's humiliation, fear, or pain may be actively pleasurable to an angry person and incite him to further violence, while other of his opponent's acts will inhibit it—again the variety is immense. A human aggressor may be satisfied by any behavior that indicates submission, as long as it is the behavior he set out to elicit.

There is the story of a nursery school child who became angry with a playmate and started to hit him. The teacher, attempting to divert him, handed him a doll and suggested that he hit it instead. He hit it a couple of times, then disgustedly threw it across the room, saying, "I want it to say 'Ouch!' "

THE INSTIGATOR AND TARGET
OF AGGRESSION

Illustrated here is the failure of an aggression-discharging mechanism: if for any reason a person cannot attack the source of his anger, he may "displace" the attack to a substitute object, just like a fighting fish or a monkey. Displacement may be illustrated by another story, hopefully apocryphal: a blacksmith in a little Swiss village was convicted of murder and sentenced to be hanged. But since he was the only blacksmith and could not be spared, they hanged one of the village's seven tailors instead.

Humans have the capacity to displace their aggression to a remarkable degree, but a bit of experimental evidence suggests that they may obtain more relief by attacking the source of their anger rather than a substitute. The experimenter, who was also their teacher, angered some undergraduates by heckling them while they counted backwards from a hundred by twos as fast as they could, making sure that they could not finish in the allotted time. He then told them to ask a "victim"—either himself or a fellow undergraduate—to guess the number they were thinking of, between one and ten, and to shock him every time he missed, over a series of ten trials. The measurement of anger was a rise in blood pressure—readings were taken before and after the heckling, and then after shocking the victim—and the central finding was that blood pressure rose significantly after the heckling and stayed up after shocking the undergraduate, but fell significantly after shocking the teacher, who had caused all the trouble.[1]

An analogous finding was that experimental subjects directed more aggression to a person who had insulted them, the greater his resemblance to a person in a film who was the object of justified aggression.*

Unlike animals, humans can discharge their aggression on substitute victims by "projecting" onto the object their own unacceptable feelings and attacking him for harboring them. Projection justifies and intensifies their hostility, and relieves their own feelings of guilt. As will be seen in Chapters 7 and 9, the fact that enemies are particularly suitable objects for both projection and displacement may contribute to the ferocity of wars.

* This will be described more fully on pages 79 to 81.

HOW CHILDREN LEARN AGGRESSION

It seems reasonable to suppose that a person's child-hood experiences may affect his propensity to resort to violence in later life. The possibility that knowledge about early determinants of aggression may prove to have at least some remote relevance to the prevention of war thus justifies some consideration of the relationship to childhood aggression of individual and group methods of punishment, and of imitation.

Individual Punishment

Insofar as it is strengthened by rewards and inhibited by punishment, aggressive behavior, in humans as in animals, often seems to obey the regular laws of learning. In mice the relationship is straightforward, as described in Chapter 3. Analogously, prizefight managers and team coaches try to arrange for their protégés to meet weak opponents first; victory—the reward—presumably reinforces the behavior associated with it.

Because of its many possible meanings, however, the effect of childhood punishment on stimulating or inhibiting later aggressiveness is complex. In general, punishments range between two poles: infliction of bodily pain and withdrawal of affection. The latter is always involved, at least implicitly, and used alone, it seems more effective in causing the child to internalize the parents' standards and feel guilty when he does the disapproved act, even in their absence. Corporal punishment elicits compliance from the child when the punishing agent is present—actually or in his mind—but he is less apt to feel guilty and more inclined to feel anger and resentment at the frustrating parent, which may strengthen his tendency to be aggressive.

A comparative study of delinquent and non-delinquent middle-class adolescent boys has shown that children whose families freely use corporal punishment are more aggressive than those whose families do not. In humans, as in animals, the infliction of pain is a powerful stimulus to fighting. Two caged rats or monkeys, for example, will promptly attack each other if simultaneously given a painful shock, exhibiting an inborn response which takes precedence over more appropriate responses like pressing a lever to turn off the shock. If the same kind of reflex reaction can be seen as causing a spanked child to attack a toy or a playmate,[2] this would partially explain why physical punishment may make children prone to fight. Since they are not allowed to attack their parents, children must seek outside targets—an activity reinforced by the characteristic approval of physically aggressive parents.[3]

One subtle experiment illustrates a principle—termed the "strain toward consistency"—which is applicable, as we shall see, at the level of national as well as personal behavior. The study involved dissuading children from choosing to play with an attractive toy which they were shown along with others. Some were threatened with severe and some with mild punishment if they played with it, and all the children obeyed the prohibition. Asked to rate the toy's attractiveness three weeks to two months later, the children threatened with severe punishment still found it attractive, while those threatened with mild punishment derogated it.[4] The assumption on which the experiment was based, and which it therefore may be said to support (although the findings could be explained in many other ways), is that the child must be able to explain to himself why he behaves inconsistently by avoiding the attractive toy. The threat of severe punishment for playing with it is sufficient reason, so he can still regard it as attractive; but if the threatened punishment is too mild to justify his avoidance, the most readily available reason is that the toy wasn't attractive after all. In other words, the most effective way to change a person's attitude toward an act to be deterred is apparently a threat "severe enough to induce momentary compliance yet mild enough to provide inadequate justification for that compliance." [5] An ingenious statesman will perhaps find a way to apply this principle to deter his nation's enemies.

Group Punishment and Aggression

In keeping with the individualistic competitive orientation of American culture, educational methods, like those of child-rearing, apply rewards and punishments to the child as an individual. Each child is expected to be concerned only with his own advancement and with the success or failure of his performance, not with that of the rest of the class or group.

In the Soviet system, which stresses training for collective responsibility, each child is held responsible for his group's welfare and good behavior, and it is the group's responsibility to help the laggard and discipline the deviate. Rewards and punishments are meted out not to individuals but to the group as a whole for the good or bad behavior of its members.[6]

Does this method, and such similar ones as that of the Israeli *kibbutz*,[7] affect the children's patterns of aggression? As far as I can determine, they may change its direction but not its amount. There is no evidence that they lead children to be more kindly disposed to members of other groups, even though they inhibit aggressive behavior toward fellow group members. One might surmise, in fact, that these methods would foster uncritical acceptance of group values and attitudes, including those toward members of an "enemy" group. Because of a strong sense of group responsibility, children brought up this way are said to make excellent military officers. In short, insofar as individual aggression is relevant to war, collective education probably contributes fully as much to it as education based on individual competition.

Imitation

Imitation is a very rapid and effective method of learning, and this may be another reason why children of parents who use corporal punishment may be more aggressive than children of those who do not.

Imitation of aggressive parents can be enhanced by what psychoanalytic theory terms "identification with the aggressor": "By impersonating the aggressor, assuming his attributes or imitating his aggression, the child transforms himself from the person threatened to the person making the threat," thereby presumably counteracting the anxiety the aggressor has aroused.[8]

Children who do not have a parental model for aggression may develop the habit of not fighting—which in itself can be an aggression inhibitor. This principle has been used to explain why, if brought together before fighting patterns have developed, such "natural enemies" as dogs and cats grow up in perfect harmony, their innate patterns of fighting apparently either inhibited by other habits of not fighting or simply atrophied through disuse.[9]

The power of imitation to instigate aggression in children has been elegantly demonstrated by a series of experiments with nursery school children about four years old. In the initial experiment they watched an adult playing with some toys: half saw him attack a large inflated doll while the other half saw him play quietly with some Tinker Toys. The experimenter then mildly frustrated the children by permitting them to play briefly with some very attractive toys, then interrupting them and taking them into a room containing the doll and other toys. If they did what the model had done to the doll and used his words, their aggressive behavior was classified as imitative; if they did different things, attacked different toys, or used different aggressive expressions, it was non-imitative. Boys and girls alike who had witnessed the aggressive model showed more of both types of aggression than did those who had seen the non-aggressive one[10] —showing that an aggressive model stimulates both imitative and non-imitative aggressive behavior in young children.

In other studies filmed or cartoon models proved as effective as live ones,[11] thus making possible an experiment to test whether vicarious reward and punishment influences aggressive behavior. Three groups of four-year-olds watched a "TV show" in which a man was playing with some toys and another man, the aggressor, came in and tried to take them away from him. The first group saw the aggressor rewarded—he physically intimidated the owner, who retreated dejectedly to a corner; the aggressor played happily with the toys and finally left with them. Another group saw the aggressor punished—the owner thrashed him and he cowered in a corner while the owner walked off with the toys. The third group, for control purposes, saw the two adults vigorously playing together with the toys without attacking each other. When the children were allowed to play with the same toys, those in the first group (aggressor rewarded) showed more imitative aggressiveness toward the toys and said more often that they preferred to be like him than did those in the second group (aggressor punished);[12] in the control group (no attack) only the boys showed increased non-imitative aggression and increased aggression. It is noteworthy that the children were *not* frustrated—merely observing a victorious aggressor sufficed.

These experiments, which have made a beginning toward discovering some of the environmental determinants of aggression in children, show that filmed and live models are equally effective in instigating aggression.

Exposure to Violence in the Mass Media

The demonstration that young children will readily imitate televised violence raises disquieting questions about the possible effects of the extraordinarily rich and varied diet of violence dispensed by television and the comics. Since pandering to the American appetite for violence pays well, television, movies, comic books, and the press all do so.

Television, to confine attention to it, is a very powerful educational medium: ". . . the impact . . . is real. What the child absorbs while he is being 'entertained' he uses in the interpretation of his real life experiences, and is preparing himself for roles that he will play in the future, as well as for immediate action." [13] Surveys have shown that children between the ages of three and sixteen spend over four hours a day watching television, more time than is devoted to any other activity except school.[14] And they prefer "adult" programs, especially crime thrillers—it has been calculated that between the ages of five and fourteen the average American child sees some thirteen thousand televised deaths-by-violence.

In an extensive survey mothers confirmed the experiments by reporting that children under nine were especially likely to imitate what they saw on TV and that the younger the child, the more he reacted to particular incidents rather than the whole story.[15] The typical TV villain is abundantly rewarded until the very end, when he receives his just deserts, usually violent. Since young children do not grasp the story as a whole, they would be more likely to remember that violence is rewarded rather than that crime does not pay. The same study concluded that by presenting violence as an inevitable part of life and often a resort of good people, television altered children's social-ethical values.

The effects of televised and comic book violence differ somewhat, depending on the child, probably reinforcing existing antisocial tendencies (antisocial children are particularly addicted to television and the comics); overaggressive and disturbed children are known to have imitated crimes they saw in these media.[16] The violence may merely suggest a way of discharging rather than instigating aggression, of course—but the burden of proof is on those who maintain this.

A recent discussion about the effects of television advertising on viewers, however, suggests that repeated viewing without emotional involvement leads to latent learning: while the viewer is not necessarily persuaded of an advertised product's merit, it does become more salient in his mind, and when he next sees it on the shelf, he is more apt to buy it. Because it would be inconsistent to buy a poor product, his evaluation of it changes to accord with his behavior; it is as if he told himself, "Since I am buying it, it must be good." [17] Similarly, repeatedly witnessing violent behavior on TV, even without emotional involvement, might lower a child's threshold for indulging in violence in certain situations of daily life. Latent learning could influence all children, not only aggressive ones.

Finally, people may become inured to violence through constant vicarious experience. For example, during the summer of 1966 in Washington the Army staged a weekly open-air show called "Torchlight Tattoo," which featured demonstrations of strangling, stabbings, and other methods of killing used by soldiers; an announcer offered detailed explanations, often in a jovial tone. Over a hundred thousand people saw the show before someone protested; but that is less extraordinary than the especially revealing comment of an Army officer who when asked, "Is demonstrating how to strangle a man with piano wire and the best way to cut a man's throat . . . healthy for the public?"

replied, "I think the public is well versed in these subjects. They read it in these detective magazines and see it on TV. Why, my children saw this show and they just shrugged off the Ranger act." [18]

Two alarming features of American life today are the skyrocketing rise in crime, especially among juveniles, and the "bystander" phenomenon in which persons witnessing someone being violently attacked or even murdered don't raise a finger or, even worse, urge a suicidal person standing on the ledge of a building to jump. The diet of violence on television, in the comics, and in the other mass media may have nothing to do with these developments, but it certainly does nothing to counteract them.

IMMEDIATE INSTIGATORS OF AGGRESSION

Having reviewed some possible predisposers to aggressive behavior, we now turn to aspects of the immediate situation that can elicit it. The dominant theory holds that all instigators to aggression can be regarded as forms of frustration —that is, as events that block ongoing goal-directed behavior.[19] The subjective response to frustration is anger; the objective response, verbal or physical attack on the frustrating agent.

Rather than attempting to force all inciters to aggression into the procrustean bed labeled "frustration," we shall consider them under five headings—conflict, violation of expectations, boredom, contagion, and obedience—of which only the first three are clearly forms of frustration. Contagion and obedience could be subsumed under this concept only by considerable mental gymnastics; their major effect is to determine the form aggressive behavior takes, but they can also instigate it directly.

Conflict

Conflict is a ubiquitous and powerful form of frustration, one which frequently instigates violent behavior. Hostile feelings are especially likely to be aroused by some features of conflict between individuals. Actual or threatened bodily attack not only blocks one's progress toward a goal, including the universal goal of preserving life and limb, but can drive him further from it. Such a threat or attack arouses fear, which instigates flight or submission, but if these are perceived to be impossible, it becomes a stimulus to counterattack. The victim may perceive counterattack to be the best defense; or he may feel cornered although he is not physically trapped: the feeling that submission or flight would disgrace him in his own opinion or in that of persons who matter to him has the same psychological effect. Under these circumstances fear becomes a powerful motive for aggression, and with the change in behavior it becomes mingled with anger.

Perhaps because they involve infliction of pain, body-contact sports readily rouse the contestant to anger, resulting in the creation of elaborate machinery for controlling its expression. In an experiment on conflict in a boys' camp* five days of competitive sports sufficed to make enemies of friends.

Competition with no bodily component can arouse anger—think of the friendships and even marriages that have been broken at the card table. That the loser's anger in such situations is aroused primarily by the penalty for losing is suggested by the finding in an experimental competition: the loser not only became vindictive but saw his opponent as malevolent if he was penalized, but he did not become angry if defeat did not involve a penalty.[20] A possible explanation is that the loser, attempting to assuage his own feelings of guilt at being angered, blames his anger on his adversary's misbehavior. Since a penalty is a public confirmation of defeat, it may not be stretching matters too far to consider it a special case of attack on a person's self-esteem.

A more direct assault on self-esteem is insulting a person or a group to which he belongs, such as his family, school, or nation. Insults are widely used to arouse anger in psychological experiments because they are both harmless and effective.

Violation of Expectations

The most aggravating aspect of frustration may be that it violates expectations, in fact, even with chimpanzees: "When a chimpanzee in heat is introduced into the next cage, the male

* A full description appears in Chapter 11, pp. 250–51.

. . . comes as close as he can until he is stopped by the intervening cage wire. . . . At this time he shows no anger. . . . But the anger becomes highly predictable if the male is first led to expect, by the caretaker's actions, that he will be admitted to the female cage and then is not." [21] Analogously, the bridge player who loses through his partner's error gets angry not at his opponents but at the partner, whom he expects not to let him down; the motorist rushing to work is more annoyed by the man ahead of him who stalls at a green light than at the driver who stops at a red one.

That expectation-violating behavior creates more anger than the same behavior when expected has been demonstrated by an experiment that used pairs of college students who were strangers to each other.[22] After meeting briefly they were placed in separate rooms and ostensibly exchanged written messages—but the notes were actually written by the experimenter, who sent half the subjects friendly messages and half derogatory ones. When asked to rate the note-sender as friendly or hostile, their ratings, as might be expected, accorded with the tone of the messages. Then came the crucial maneuver: each subject received a second note, either duplicating the tone of the first or in sharp contrast to it. When the subjects rated the note-sender this time, the discrepant message proved to have a much greater effect than the consistent one—that is, after a friendly message, a hostile one caused the sender to be rated as more unfriendly than if the first message had also been hostile.

Conversely, a friendly message following a hostile one made a better impression than two friendly ones. This finding lends experimental support to the negotiating technique of suddenly making a concession after first being adamant—the unexpectedness of the concession seems to increase its ability to elicit a cooperative counter-move.

Both results were confirmed in another experiment in which each partner was first given a fictitious personality sketch of the other and then was sent a message either in accord with the expectation created by the sketch or discrepant from it. The magnitude of the message's impact proved to be a direct function of the size of its contrast with the expectation created by the personality description.[23]

Immediate circumstances as well as past experience determine the expectations concerning the behavior of others. Depending on whether the punisher has the right to inflict it and whether the person punished considers it to be deserved, punishment will or will not arouse resentment. Punishment by an authority figure for an admitted breach of the rules is expected and therefore usually accepted, while attempted punishment may be resented if it is for an unacknowledged infraction or comes from a non-authority, because it violates the victim's expectations.

Analogously, behavior accepted calmly in an equal or superior is "insolent," and therefore anger-arousing, in an inferior since it is not commensurate with what is expected from him. Air Force reservists, for example, were given orders over an intercom in a pompous, hostility-arousing way; given a chance to answer back after the speaker had finished, they directed more aggression at him when they believed him to be of lower rank than themselves than when they believed him to be of higher rank.

That the amount of aggression aroused or displayed depends also on an individual's personal qualities* is indicated by the fact that authoritarian subjects, who did not differ from the others in the amount of aggression they expressed toward the "higher-rank" speaker, were more strongly annoyed by the "lower-rank" speaker.[24]

An example of anger aroused by violation of expectations created by rules is the reaction to a foul in a game, infuriating because the opponent seeks to gain an "unfair" advantage by committing it. The unfairness lies not only in the nature of the act itself—like hitting below the belt—but also in its unexpectedness.

The power of disappointed expectations to arouse aggression is perhaps pointed up most significantly by the fact that members of a deprived nation or segment of society become violent only when, expecting to better their lot, they find themselves un-

* See Chapter 7, pp. 122–24.

able to do so. Calcutta slum dwellers are incomparably worse off than the Negro citizens of Detroit; yet the latter exploded with rage and frustration, while the Indians, who until recently lived out their miserable existences in apathetic resignation, are only now becoming restive.

What has happened is that the mass media have made the poor much more aware than ever before that they are not getting their share of the world's increasing affluence—their once absolute deprivation has become relative deprivation.[25] * And their sense of frustration is heightened because both democratic and communist ideologies hold out universal affluence as a legitimate expectation—nay, a right—and their hopes of achieving it are raised by the loosening of traditional social and political structures.

Boredom

The absence of certain stimuli can be as frustrating as the presence of others. Men, like rats, dogs, and monkeys, hunger for stimulation and excitement,[27] and when life does not offer enough, they are prone to make some. It has been suggested that boredom, which stimulates the human propensity for mischief-making, is a major source of delinquency: "The delinquent is stuck with his boredom, stuck inside it, stuck to it, until for two or three minutes he 'lives'; he goes on a raid around the corner and feels the thrill of risking his skin or his life as he smashes a bottle filled with gasoline on some other kid's head. In a sense, it is his trip to Miami. It makes his day. It is his shopping tour. It gives him something to talk about for a week. It is *life*. Standing around with nothing coming up is as close to dying as you can get. Unless one grasps the power of boredom, the threat of it to one's existence, it is impossible to 'place' the delinquent as a member of the human race." [28]

---

* "A generation or two ago the Colombian peasant was considerably more content with his lot in life. But the cheap transistor radio has changed that. Today the native of even the most remote Andean village is aware that a different way of life is available to some, if not yet to him. The result has been a new feeling of frustration and resentment." [26]

Because modern industrial societies have not found ways of keeping everybody busy, the ranks of the idle contain large numbers of young men—some unemployed, but others, their energies and abilities meeting insufficient challenge, for whom life is too easy. The reading about or viewing of violence, which enables such people to identify with the aggressor as well as with criminal acts, might be analogous to the appetitive behavior of animals whose environment contains no suitable target for aroused aggression. Bored young men thus constitute a reservoir of latent violence that national leaders can direct toward other nations.

Implicit in all of this is that it is far too optimistic to think that aggression would vanish if everyone were affluent and well fed, for it is not even theoretically possible to eliminate human aggression by removing all frustration. Frustration cannot be eliminated from life because humans, never satisfied, keep pushing until they come to a barrier—erected by the natural environment or by others who are also in process of aggrandizing themselves or their groups—at which point they become frustrated.

This analysis of frustration and aggression, however, does suggest two hopeful possibilities: it is possible to decrease frustration in a society by increasing the general level of well-being, providing channels for advancement, and the like; it is also possible to teach people to adjust their expectations to reality. And just as humans can always find targets for their rage, they can also find substitute ways of expressing it, including many which are socially useful—the social reformer who expresses his anger by fighting injustice probably obtains as much relief and satisfaction as the hoodlum who beats up an old man.

Contagion

Conflict, boredom, and other forms of frustration arouse aggressive impulses, but the aroused person's actions depend in part on the behavior of others in his environment. That the presence of others behaving violently seems to be powerfully stimulating is indicated by the fact that most senseless violence is perpetrated by gangs: the individuals, needing the support of their fellows, egg each other on and commit excesses as mob members that they would not dream of alone.

The contagiousness of any strong emotion, whether joy, grief, or rage, is probably one of the most potent causes of this phenomenon. While it would be difficult to manage these in a laboratory experiment, two other sources of contagion—imitation and the alleviation of guilt—have been experimentally approached. The power of imitation to instigate aggression in children has already been considered; and certain experiments with college students suggest that more than imitation is involved in the contagious effect of witnessing violence.[29] In these experiments, after an accomplice had angered the subject by insulting him, both then read one of two film synopses in which the hero, a prizefighter, was presented either sympathetically or as an unprincipled scoundrel. Accomplice and subject then viewed the film's climax, in which the hero was brutally beaten in a prizefight. Subjects who had read the first synopsis would presumably see the beating as unjustified, those who had read the second as justified. The accomplice left the room, ostensibly to prepare a floor plan as a solution to a problem, and this plan was then brought to the subject who was told to express his judgment of its quality by administering electric shocks to the accomplice in the next room—the more shocks, the worse the plan. The accomplice received more shocks after the subject had seen the justified aggression. A control series, in which the accomplice did not anger the subject before they watched the film, showed that witnessing the prizefight did not arouse aggression in itself (as measured by the number of shocks the subject gave), but merely made it easier for an angered person to vent his feelings.

Imitation cannot account for the results since the subject's aggressive behavior, administering shocks, bore no resemblance to the aggression he had witnessed. That he gave more shocks after witnessing justified aggression suggests that the releasing effect resulted mainly from alleviation of guilt. The subtlety of environmental control over aggressive behavior is further revealed by the fact that the more the accomplice was made to resemble the justly punished protagonist, the more shocks he received. This was true if he was introduced with the same first name as the actor and also if as a boxer rather than a speech major.[30]

The releasing effect of witnessing aggression has also been demonstrated in an experiment in which Naval enlisted men believed themselves to be overhearing two other men—A and B—through earphones. A and B, who were actually recordings, discussed six topics, on each of which B took a position that was unacceptable to the subject. After listening to a brief discussion between A and B, the subject was asked to say what he thought of B. The experimenter scored only those comments which were "extremely aggressive," including such epithets as "ass," "idiot," "nuts," and such recommendations for or threats of punishment as "locked up," "tortured," "beaten," and "shot."

The major finding was that if A attacked B vigorously, the subject became increasingly aggressive toward B, whether B counterattacked, held his ground, or retracted. By the sixth trial about two-thirds of the subjects were describing B in extremely aggressive terms. The subjects did not strongly attack B if A disagreed calmly or rationally, or if they could not hear what A was saying but only B replying. Finally, they did not express aggression, despite A's attacks, if B had expressed an acceptable position.

In short, subjects became extremely aggressive only if two conditions were met—B disagreed with their views and A offered a model of aggression. As was true of the children and the college students, an aggressive model seemed to reduce their own restraints.[31]

Obedience

So far it has been assumed that most aggressive behavior is an expression of anger or hatred. This may be true in civilian life and these feelings sometimes contribute to the soldier's aggressiveness in hand-to-hand fighting. But the combat soldier's main motive for killing—especially as methods of killing become increasingly impersonal—is obedience: soldiers go into battle, fire cannon, and drop bombs simply because they have been ordered to do so, and not primarily because they hate the enemy.

Obedience to legitimate authority is one of the strongest motivating forces in the life of all normal members of organized societies, a fact that American students of psychology seem to have systematically minimized, perhaps because it does not fit the image of the self-reliant, ruggedly individualistic American. Yet the most cursory glance at history reveals the virtually unlimited power of a duly constituted authority to control his subjects' behavior, and this holds for aggression, both toward self and toward others. Subordinates have been known to commit suicide on order from their chief; and Henri Christophe, an early dictator of Haiti, is said to have shown his power by ordering his soldiers to march over the edge of the citadel cliff.

The power of obedience as a motivating force was brought into sharp focus by the Eichmann trial: was this man who was instrumental in the extermination of millions of Jews a sadistic monster or simply an efficient bureaucrat carrying out orders? Rather than entering into this unresolved controversy, let us turn to an experiment designed to test the limits of the power of obedience to cause someone to inflict pain on an innocent victim.[32]

The subjects—normal American college students and adults —believed that the purpose of the experiment was to study the effect of punishment on learning. Each subject was to present a fellow subject (actually an experimenter's accomplice) with a simple learning task and shock him each time he made a mistake. Every detail of the setting was arranged so that the subject was completely convinced that he was administering shocks. The shocks were administered by a machine on which the voltage level was plainly marked, starting with 15 volts and increasing by 15-volt steps to 450 volts; the levels were also labeled: 300 volts was "intense shock" and 420 "danger, severe shock," with the two highest levels marked only "XXX." Before the experiment began the subject saw electrodes placed on the accomplice, who was then strapped to a chair in a neighboring room.

The actual experiment involved signaling a series of problems to the accomplice, who signaled his answer back. The accomplice made frequent errors in accordance with a prearranged schedule, and since the subject had been told to increase the shock by 15 volts after each error, he had to keep increasing the severity of the shock. At 300 volts the accomplice pounded the wall and thereafter stopped signaling answers; at this point the subject was told to regard failure to respond as an error and to continue to administer shocks. The accomplice pounded the wall once more at 315 volts, and then was not heard from again. Whenever the subject demurred, the experimenter told him to continue, with increasing urgency, the most forceful command being: "You have no other choice, you *must* go on."

The findings are disturbing: all subjects administered shocks up to 300 volts ("painful shock"), and 62 per cent went to the maximum—450 volts (two levels beyond "danger, severe shock").

Subsequent studies showed that the closer the victim was to the subject psychologically, the less likely the subject was to be obedient. But even when they had to hold the struggling, screaming victim's hand on the shock plate, 30 per cent of the subjects went on to give the maximum shock.[32]*

Over 90 per cent of the subjects would participate in giving the maximum shock if they were required to perform only one step in a chain, such as throwing a master switch that permitted someone else to give the shock.

The degree of psychological closeness of the experimenter influenced the subjects' obedience in the opposite direction. The number of subjects who gave the full shock was about three times as great when the experimenter was in the room as it was when, after giving the original instructions, he left and gave his orders by telephone.[33]

Although sadism may have facilitated an occasional subject's obedience (one or two were horrified to discover that they felt pleasure when administering the shocks), the main determinant seems to be that the experimenter mobilized habits of obedience ingrained in all members of organized societies and also absolved the subject of guilt, since responsibility rested with the experimenter. A person submitting to a legitimate authority

* In view of the ethical questions raised by this experiment, unusual care was taken at its conclusion to explain the procedure to the subjects and to give them ample opportunity to work through their feelings.

hands his conscience over, in effect, for since the authority de-
cides what is right and wrong, the subordinate's own conscience
is suspended.

Considering the intensity of indoctrination and training and
the power of military authority, the proportion of soldiers attacking an enemy under orders would be expected to be considerably greater than the proportion of subjects in the experiments
who obediently gave the full shock. Actually it was less—only
15 to 25 per cent of American soldiers in World War II fired
their guns in combat,[34] perhaps because the victims were psychologically closer and the authority more remote. Nuclear weapons are fired by a team against distant victims. The experiments
suggest that these conditions should elicit ready obedience, so it
is not surprising that when the commander of a Polaris submarine was asked how it felt to be the man whose act could unleash
the submarine's destructive power, he replied: "I've never given
it any thought. But, if we ever have to hit, we'll hit. And there
won't be a second's hesitation." [35] Fortunately obedience is as
powerful an inhibitor of aggression as an instigator of it. Military
authority forbids soldiers from killing except under very special
circumstances and, as we shall see in Chapter 12, obedience can
restrain normally aggressive men from resorting to violence,
even under extreme provocation.

GROUP ORGANIZATION AND
INDIVIDUAL AGGRESSION

In the process of becoming a member of any organized society each person must repeatedly block old habits and
attitudes in order to learn new ones, and members of the same
society are bound to collide as they struggle to find their niches
in the social structure. Thus, in humans, as in animals, social
living arouses a certain amount of aggression, necessary for the
group's formation and maintenance. In all societies internal conflicts are inhibited by each member's belonging to several groups
whose interests coincide in some respects and differ in others,
and strong pressure is exerted not to carry any given conflict too

far, for an enemy when one set of interests is salient may be required as an ally when another set comes to the fore.[36] Interlocking group memberships may suffice to keep the peace even in societies which lack officials with power to judge quarrels and enforce their decisions: "These societies are so organized into a series of groups and relationships, that people who are friends on one basis are enemies on another. Herein lies social cohesion, rooted in conflict between men's different allegiances." [37]

In stabilized societies that have developed adequate machinery for the peaceful resolution of disputes, the mere threat of physical violence is enough to secure redress of grievances. To gain concessions from their opponents, leaders of dissident groups, even those committed to non-violence, threaten that they will not be able to restrain their followers from violence. It has been suggested that since elections can be viewed as ways in which elites measure their relative strengths—analogous to choosing up sides in a game[38]—their effectiveness in such societies depends on their implicit threat of violence. The outcome predicts the winner in case of a violent showdown, which then becomes superfluous.

Group Disorganization and Violence

There seems to be an optimal degree of social control from the standpoint of minimizing frustrations. The frustrations of life under a rigidly organized, repressive system are too obvious to require elaboration. Since members of such a society cannot express their aggression toward their government, they displace it to external targets, as will be discussed in the next chapter.

But that too little social control can be equally frustrating is possibly a plausible explanation of why, in both human and animal societies, overt violence is most likely to occur before a firm social organization has been achieved or when it has broken down. In animal societies violence is at its peak while the social structure is forming—when territories are being staked out and dominance hierarchies established. The state of rapidly developing societies like the emerging nations may be analogous: individual citizens have not yet found their places or determined the limits of their powers, and the rules of the game have not been established. Under these circumstances there is bound to be much jockeying for power and wealth—sometimes by means which the adversary regards as illegitimate—and citizens constantly regarding each other as committing fouls. Furthermore, since individuals are prone to overestimate their capacities in comparison with their rivals', discrepancies between hopes and achievements are pronounced. Rapidly innovating societies, such as practically all industrialized nations today, could be expected to show similar characteristics, because their dominance hierarchies are constantly shifting and the rules changing to fit new circumstances.

The breakdown of social organization in an already established society has similar effects. In animal societies one source of this breakdown is overcrowding, such as characterized monkey colonies in zoos before its disastrous effects were recognized. Perhaps a similar phenomenon contributes to the high crime rates of densely populated city slums, although it is difficult to determine the relative contributions of overcrowding, poverty, poor education, and other factors. Part of the finding is attributable to attitudes of law enforcement agencies: since slum dwellers are booked for minor crimes more frequently than their better situated fellow citizens, there is a greater discrepancy between reported crime rates than between actual ones in the two areas.

One study has managed to adduce evidence that social disorganization in itself fosters delinquency. The investigators were able to locate two lower-middle-class neighborhoods in the same city, roughly matched in average educational and economic levels; but one had a crime rate three times the other's. The area with greater delinquency scored significantly lower on such indices of community integration as knowing five neighbors well enough to borrow a cup of sugar, having the same interests and ideas as one's neighbors, and attending church regularly. It is also interesting that although the adults of both neighborhoods gave the same relative ratings of "seriousness" to different kinds of juvenile misbehavior, adults in the low-delinquency area reported more delinquent acts and more of them said they would intervene if they saw such an act, in other words, taking more responsibility for enforcing group standards and seeming more aware of their violation.[39]

Socially Sanctioned Violence

All societies provide safety-valves for release of aggression in the form of permissible behavior, sharply limited in time and space and hedged by rules and customs that permit the discharge of aggression in ways that do not destroy the group.

Some of these safety valves permit actual killing. Some societies have sporadically allowed an individual to kill quite a few people before the fit passed or he himself was killed—the Vikings' *Berserkgang,* for example, possibly precipitated by eating certain mushrooms,[40] and the Malays' *Amok.* That even these behaviors are not entirely attributable to the psychopathology of the killers is indicated by the fact that both abruptly disappeared. Going berserk vanished in the twelfth century after having plagued the Vikings for about three centuries, and *Amok* disappeared when the Dutch, sensing that it was basically a dramatic way of committing suicide, prevented the *Amok* runner from being killed but instead sentenced him to life imprisonment at hard labor.[41]

Other societies have permitted or even encouraged the discharge of pent-up aggression by violence against minority groups. As in such examples as the Jews in Czarist Russia or the Chinese in Indonesia in 1965, since the groups chosen as scapegoats usually cannot adequately defend themselves, are suitable targets for projection and displacement, and are not fully integrated into the society, attacking them does not seriously disrupt the social structure.

Least damaging to society are such vicarious discharges of aggression as horror movies, crime thrillers, and certain spectator sports which are the lineal descendants of gladiatorial combats. Many people attend prizefights, wrestling matches, and automobile races in the more or less conscious hope of seeing someone get hurt or killed. For radio listeners, special microphones are used to pick up the thud of body against body in prizefights and professional football games.

Organized sports also afford a socially desirable expression of aggression for the participants. They teach the player to control his anger under strong provocation, since he "must mobilize at a given time and a given place all the skill and intelligence and courage he possesses, to do this in the face of the most strenuous opposition and to do it with a smile and a cool head." [42]

From the standpoint of group dynamics, team members gain mutual respect for each others' strength of will, physical prowess, and sportsmanship, improving the self-image of each and of the team as a whole. Insofar as spectators identify with teams, a successful team can improve the self-image of a city or, as in the Olympic games, even a nation.

Sports also have a beneficial effect on attitudes toward the adversary, for "good sportsmanship" requires that he be not turned into an enemy, or that if he is, friendship be reinstated after the match. It may not be too farfetched to suggest that if competitive sports may sometimes strengthen or actually create feelings of solidarity with the opponent, reflecting perhaps the close biological link between aggressive and affectional behavior patterns, international sporting events may help to promote international unity.[43]

While disapproving its direct expression, the American social system contains many instigations to aggression—the lifetime atmosphere of competition begins with competition for marks in school—but the social norms concerning how most conflicts should be conducted simultaneously demand that the competitors be smiling, polite, and considerate to their opponents, in short, good sports. Thus, it seems plausible that many Americans of all ages experience frequent instigations to aggression every day for which they are permitted no direct outlet, which is perhaps why Americans seem so drawn to forms of vicarious satisfaction.

A Note on Law Enforcement Agencies

Violence within societies is controlled by courts, police, prisons, and other institutions for making and enforcing laws. Although consideration of the social and institutional forces securing obedience to law lie beyond the scope of this book, a psychological component of law-abidingness warrants brief mention because, as will be seen in Chapter 11, it is central to the question of whether world government is possible.

It is often assumed that a world government's peace-keeping forces would have to be more powerful than the armies of any single state—a condition impossible to fulfill as long as nuclear weapons exist. This is based on the theory that police within societies secure obedience mainly through their monopoly of violence. Although this may be true in newly forming societies, in mature well-integrated ones their peace-keeping power lies primarily not in their guns but in the fact that they symbolize society's collective will. Someone has remarked that peace in American towns is maintained not primarily by the policeman, but by the postman, because he is the ever-present symbol of the federal government. Until recently in Great Britain unarmed police effectively kept the peace. On the international scene, the United Nations Emergency Force on the Arab-Israeli borders was a force for peace because it symbolized the concern of the international community.

Put in another way, within stable communities the main source of obedience to law is not fear of the police but voluntary compliance. Instances have been reported in which, despite a temporary collapse of law enforcement machinery, there was no crime—a fairly recent example was the interregnum for several days in Copenhagen between withdrawal of the Germans and reconstitution of the police force.

As the experience of the United States with Prohibition illustrated, no law can be enforced in the face of widespread opposition: voluntary compliance by at least 90 per cent of the population is usually required.[44]

Humans form communities because they cannot get along without each other, and communities cannot function without rules, some taking the form of social conventions and others of laws. Social conventions make dealings between members of the same community mutually predictable, just as grammar makes conversation intelligible.[45] Laws protect individuals from encroachments by each other or by the community. Perhaps the average citizen is law-abiding mainly because he recognizes intuitively that he is better off submitting even to laws that restrict his freedom or otherwise work to his disadvantage than he would be if there were no laws.

Development of effective organizations for creating and enforcing international law cannot proceed faster than the development of a sense of community to sustain them. As will be described in Chapter 11 many new and powerful ways for building an international community have been created by the conditions of modern life.

6 · *Why Nations Fight*

WAR, AN ACTIVITY of organized groups, can be understood only in the light of certain of their properties. Since conflicts between groups grow out of their interaction, their onset and course cannot be adequately predicted from the characteristics of their individual members or from their own internal properties.[1] Democracies that pride themselves on their humaneness have proved themselves capable of waging wars as savagely as the most brutal dictatorship.

Those conflicts that now pose a threat to survival involve nation-states—large, extremely complex groups—which have three major functions: creating internal integration, including management of intra-group conflicts; promoting their own growth and expansion; and protecting their members from external enemies.[2] These are discharged by a complex variety of subgroupings, class stratifications, codes of conduct, and institutions. Insights gained through the study of properties of groups less complex than nation-states, especially artificially formed groups, can be applied only cautiously to national behavior, but the data they provide are not entirely without relevance.

It is convenient to separate national motives for war into two classes.[3] The first, which plays a part in all wars, may be called success-oriented: the war is intended to achieve certain ends at the enemy's expense or to prevent him from achieving his. The motives of such wars may be quite diverse—from trying to gain control of disputed territory to establishing a greater capacity to win future wars by disposing of a rival—but their one common characteristic is that no value is attached to war for its own sake. The other class of motives may be termed conflict-oriented: they are satisfied by the struggle itself, although it is expected to end victoriously, of course. Certain ideologies, the most recent being Nazism, glorify the waging of war for its own sake and regard death in battle as the highest experience open to man. Since conflict-oriented war can also help to solve a society's internal problems, a nation may seek conflict; it needs an enemy.

WAR AS A MEANS OF SOLVING
INTERNAL PROBLEMS

War can help pull a country out of an economic depression, reduce unemployment, or enable a dictator to put down unrest. From the standpoint of group psychology the main purpose of conflict-oriented war is to increase the group's cohesiveness by diverting its members' aggression to an outside target, or to reinforce its self-image of its courage, sense of honor, and other necessary aspects of its sense of security.

Since all group living involves frustrations, all nations are faced with the problem of coping with their citizens' aggressions. Some arrangements for handling aggressions directed at other members of the same group were considered in Chapter 5. Now we shall briefly consider the relationship of intra-group tensions to aggression directed toward an external enemy.

The impression that an external enemy increases group cohesiveness is supported by a content analysis of radio broadcasts of nine communist-governed states which yielded a high positive relationship between an index of cohesiveness of the Communist bloc and the level of East-West tension.[4] Even when artificially formed groups are placed in competition, cohesiveness has been shown to increase, continuing high in the victorious group but decreasing sharply in the defeated one.[5] Societies that are too tightly organized or too disorganized may dangerously frustrate their members, so either type should be predisposed to seek war with an external enemy.

One would expect that the more strongly a society stimulates its members' aggressiveness while inhibiting its expression within the group, the more warlike the society would be. The unquestioning obedience that totalitarian regimes demand of their subjects and the harsh methods of control they use are profoundly frustrating because they do violence to individuals' self-respect and sense of personal autonomy. Much of the resulting anger and fear do not reach consciousness, but rather are counteracted by an identification with the leaders and the group that can derive its strength from any strong emotion.

The displacement of conscious anger onto subordinates helps to maintain self-esteem, but the need to maintain group cohesiveness limits this outlet. The most satisfactory target for displacing the dictatorship-generated aggressiveness is thus an external enemy on whose bodies and possessions the subjects of such regimes are promised the opportunity to slake their bottled-up destructive urges. Since victory powerfully strengthens group cohesiveness and defeat corrodes it, such societies require continuing victories in order to maintain internal stability, and usually cannot survive defeat.

Similarly, the harsh discipline and demand for complete obedience that characterize military establishments may contribute to the fighting spirit of soldiers.

In disorganized societies the situation is more complex. Some studies have found an inverse relationship between internal disorganization and external hostility. It is reported, for example, that before 1850 Teton Indian tribesmen frequently murdered each other in quarrels over unequal distribution of tribal wealth. For thirty years following the arrival of the white man, however, in-group homicide decreased as a united front was presented to this external enemy; it reappeared when peace with him was restored.[6]

On the other hand, studies analyzing newspaper contents to

obtain indices of internal and external aggression found a small positive relationship between riots and troop movements and riots and anti-foreign demonstrations, suggesting that internal disorganization predisposes to external aggression.[7]

One study found that war is more likely to result from arms races in countries with high suicidal and alcoholism rates than in those with high homicide rates. Assuming suicide and alcoholism to be self-directed expressions of aggression, this can be interpreted as suggesting that societies which do not permit outward expression of intra-group aggression are more likely to seek external targets.[8]

These findings are too sparse and too tenuous to afford firm ground for speculation, but they do support the relating of internal and external violence: the Tetons closed ranks against a common enemy; national leaders divert internal tensions to an external target; riots and troop movements are correlated. By only a slight stretch of the imagination the findings concerning suicide, homicide, and war could also be interpreted as evidence that when an intra-group target is unavailable, a group tends to seek an external target for aggression.

An odd if not fortuitous phenomenon concerning war may be explained partly in terms of an effort to resolve the intra-group tensions of members of different generations by attacking an external enemy.[9] Since the last quarter of the eighteenth century, the intervals between wars fought by European nations or the United States have been remarkably constant, ranging from eighteen to twenty-four years and averaging nineteen and a half years over all—just about the time required for the generation born during or just after the previous war to reach manhood.

The male sex hormone level is high, which lowers the threshold for aggression, but psychosocial characteristics of this age would probably be more relevant to war. Psychologically the young man is often at the peak of his identity struggle; internally he is a battleground of conflicting forces, much like a developing society in which the rules of the struggle have not been firmly established, but various factions are striving for dominance. Thus, seeking forms of behavior and social roles that will help him to achieve a strong sense of selfhood, he tests his powers to the utmost; and since adolescence is the age of reckless activities, this can include risking his life. In most societies the role of warrior admirably meets this need because it embodies the ideal of masculine courage and, especially in the past, afforded superb opportunities for personal heroism and demonstrations of loyalty to one's group and its ideals.

One aspect of the young man's social role—his emergence as a serious rival to his father—may have special significance for war. There has been much comment made in psychoanalytic literature about the welter of love, hate, loyalty, rebelliousness, and guilt that can be aroused in the rival generations. Perhaps war is one way through which the stresses are resolved: the soldier's combination of devotion and hostility to the "old man" is proverbial, and he, in turn, loves his "son" but sends him forth to be killed. War may also be seen as having an analogous psychological source in those *rites de passage* in which the older generation resolves its mixed feelings for the younger by subjecting them to severe punishments from which they emerge as full-fledged members of the group.

WAR AS A MEANS OF PROMOTING NATIONAL INTERESTS

Tensions within nations contribute to the outbreak of wars, but the aim of war is always to achieve victory over the enemy, and this is defined in terms of protecting or promoting the national interest. Many national interests are tangible, such as control of territory, human labor, natural resources or wealth; but intertwined with these are interests determined by the nation's particular view or image of itself and its place in the world,[10,11] and these are the legitimate concern of psychologists. Because he envisaged Italy as a great nation, and all great nations had colonial empires, Mussolini conquered Ethiopia long after colonies had become economic liabilities.

Nations seem to have a "psychological need . . . to prove

that they are bigger, better or stronger than other nations. Implicit in this drive is the assumption . . . that when a nation shows that it has the stronger army, it is also proving that it has . . . a better civilization." [12] Anything that threatens this drive toward power is seen as threatening the national interest. Expanding nations feel themselves threatened by an expansionist rival or by weaker nations that resist domination. Nations whose pre-eminence is established regard as endangering their national interest threats to the status quo, including internal revolutions, based on nationalist and economic aspirations, that might possibly unseat subservient governments.

The power of psychological as compared with tangible causes of war is well illustrated by the war in Vietnam. From a strictly materialistic standpoint, Vietnam is of minor strategic importance to the United States, and the North Vietnamese would be infinitely better off economically if they peacefully acquiesced to the American presence in the South, for not only would the progressive destruction of their hard-won factories and power plants cease, but the United States would probably pour millions into rebuilding them. But the issues at stake are colored by psychological considerations.

The struggle is desperately intense because each side sees itself as fighting to defend certain abstract concepts, the primary one being "freedom." But the National Liberation Front is fighting for "freedom" from a foreign, white, neo-imperialistic invader; the Americans are fighting to enable the Vietnamese to have "freedom" to choose their own form of government without foreign interference. For many on each side freedom is a component of a more comprehensive ideology, which they perceive as dangerously threatened by the opponent's ideology; thus, in 1966, 76 per cent of the respondents to an American opinion survey agreed that United States actions in Vietnam were part of its worldwide commitment to prevent the spread of communism.[13]

In addition, the United States is motivated by a determination to show the world that it is strong and steadfast and keeps its commitments. It perceives this as essential to the maintenance of its national prestige, even though the government to whom the original commitment was made has long since vanished and the current commitment bears only the faintest resemblance to the one the United States claims it is fighting to uphold. The major goals at issue in the Vietnam war are intangible, but the combatants perceive them as being in limited supply—as the Duchess in *Alice in Wonderland* put it, "the more there is of mine, the less there is of yours." The more freedom there is for the National Liberation Front, the less there is for the United States, and vice versa.

If the world does not destroy itself first, it is certain to move eventually into an economy of affluence in which there will be plenty of material goods for everyone. The Duchess' Law will no longer apply for goods, but it will still apply to such psychological values as national prestige, honor, and the like. And until nations learn to base their sense of power on attributes other than military prowess, these will continue to be sources of war.

FORMATION OF NATIONAL REALITY WORLDS

From the psychological standpoint, then, the hope of learning to resolve without violence the clashes of national world-views depends on understanding the contents of these views that lead to conflict, the reasons nations cling so tenaciously to them, and the process by which they are maintained and changed. Adequate exploration of this topic will require a rather lengthy detour.

Strictly speaking, of course, nations cannot have world-views since they have no sense organs or minds. The term "national world-view" is a convenient way to indicate the common features of the world-views of most of a nation's citizens, especially those who make and execute its policies. These questions are thus best approached from the standpoint of the contents, functions, and maintenance of individuals' world-views.*

* In addition to "world-view," the commonly used terms for the picture of the world, or aspects of it, that each person forms from his experience are "reality world," "assumptive world," "image," "belief

There is no such thing as human nature independent of culture.[14] The ethnic group into which a baby is born determines which person he becomes among the thousands he might potentially become; it fills the gap between what his biological heritage teaches him and what he needs to know.

From the moment the newborn infant enters the world as a member of a family in a particular culture, he is bombarded by stimuli from his body and the outer environment. Except for a few like pain and hunger, these stimuli in themselves do not contain any hints as to how he should respond to them, nor are they organized beyond the degree required by the structure of his nervous system, which classes certain forms of incoming energy, for example, as sights and others as sounds. In order to survive and function in his society, the growing child must categorize and arrange these stimuli, decide which are harmful and which beneficent, which require attention and which can be safely ignored, and he must discover how his actions affect things and people and how theirs affect him—in short, he has to create an orderly, predictable world out of virtual chaos.

A person's reality world develops through his interactions with his physical and social environment: he learns by touching it that a red stove is hot, or that if he cries, Mother will comfort him, and so on. Every act is based simultaneously on an implicit prediction of what it will accomplish and a check on the validity of the prediction. The creation of the reality world, therefore, is an active process, formed by filtering, arranging, and distorting incoming experience to make a consistent picture.[15]

These processes go on continually, and largely out of awareness. An example of perceptual filtering is supplied by an ingenious experiment in which a psychologist had Mexican and American schoolteachers look into a device that simultaneously presented Mexican figures and scenes to one eye and American

---

systems," and "ideology." Although it makes philosophers unhappy, "reality world" seems the most appropriate generic term for our purposes, since it conveys the idea that a person's world-view is the way the world really is to him. The other terms will be used as appropriate to refer to different aspects of the reality world.

ones to the other (one pair, for example, was a bullfighter and a baseball player); an overwhelming proportion of the Americans saw the pictures with American content first, and a similar preponderance of Mexicans first saw those with Mexican content.[16] That information coming through the ears is filtered in the same way was demonstrated in the New Deal days when some New Deal and anti-New Deal college students were asked to listen to a speech that contained an equal number of pro- and anti-New Deal statements. Immediately after it and again three weeks later they were shown a list of fifty statements; asked to identify which were in the speech, the pro-New Dealers said that they had heard a speech in favor of the New Deal and recognized more of the favorable statements; the anti-New Dealers said the speech was against the New Deal and recognized more of the statements consistent with this view.[17] The example illustrates that memory as well as perception filters information to accord with preconceptions.

Much of the physical reality world is formed by such direct individual experience as contact with a red-hot stove. But social reality has no existence apart from other people—those aspects of the world which mean most to us can be learned only from others. These include their feelings about us as expressed through conventions of social behavior, and the dimensions of experience that enrich and give meaning to life—truth, goodness, and beauty. In these realms the validity of an opinion is tested by finding out if others share it. The most significant environmental stimuli come to each person already packaged and labeled, as it were, first by his immediate family and later by the larger society and the subgroups to which he belongs.

Since no two individuals have identical experiences, and such temperamental qualities as energy level or anxiety threshold affect the individual's organization of his experiences, some aspects of everyone's reality worlds are idiosyncratic, while others are shared by families or larger groups whose members come from similar backgrounds. In the United States, for example, the reality worlds of a Negro sharecropper in Alabama and Governor George Wallace would differ considerably, and both would differ from that of a New York City department store owner. But because they are all Americans, their reality worlds would probably also have such features in common as holding that a man is innocent until proven guilty or that America's security depends on her possessing more weapons than any other country.

GROUP FORCES HARMONIZING INDIVIDUAL REALITY WORLDS

The process of coordination of reality worlds among members of the same group is self-reinforcing, because each member is continually checking his views and opinions against those of the others, and bringing them into line. At the national level the mass media are the homogenizers.

The press, TV, and radio simultaneously offer the same events, with the same slant, to everyone, emphasizing those features that they believe people want to hear.* Furthermore, they introduce slogans and ways of thinking that become part of the imagery and vocabulary of every citizen. Obviously, the tighter the control of information, the more widely it is disseminated, and the greater the penalties for dissent, the more uniform the reality worlds of a nation's citizens will be, even in a pluralistic society like that of the United States. The uniformity of news and the informal sanctions against dissent assure considerable

---

* The interpretation of news events to fit the reality world has been amusingly described as "wordfact": "The wordfact makes words a precise substitute for reality." An example was the forced cancellation of President Eisenhower's planned visit to Japan in June of 1960. This ". . . would seem, superficially, to have been an unparalleled disaster of its kind . . . however, the President was able to report on his return that the trip had been a success. A small number of Communists, acting under outside orders, had made things a trifle sour in Japan. But that was because they knew how powerful was the impression Mr. Eisenhower made on his trips to other lands, and they determined, as a result, that no such impression would be made on Japan. Two years earlier, Communists had been forced to take similar preventive action because of the overwhelming appeal of Mr. Nixon to the Latin populace." [18]

similarity of those aspects of reality worlds that are relevant to the nation's purpose. Because it conflicts with the high valuation they place on dissent and with their self-image as rugged individualists, Americans underestimate their conformity, paradoxically denying conformity out of conformity.

The more cohesive the group, the more similar the belief systems and attitudes of its members. Since shared beliefs are a basis for mutual liking, they strengthen the individual's desire to belong to the group, and the more he wishes to belong, the greater is the pressure to conformity that he will feel.*

The power of group norms to mold their members' perceptions in matters of concern to the group can be shown even in temporary groups. For example, in a public housing project in which families in each entry were relatively isolated from each other, attitudes toward a community-wide problem were found to be homogeneous within each entry but differing among them.[20] The more cohesive the group in each entry, measured by its attractiveness to its members, the more uniform was their attitude; and those within each group who expressed deviant views tended to be disliked.

Similarly, citizens of nations develop shared interpretations of international events that are relevant to their interests. Differing national perceptions of President Kennedy's assassination afford a good example. According to one of my colleagues who was visiting Nigeria at the time, Nigerians all took for granted that it had been plotted by the Vice-President, for transfer of power by assassination is common in their society, and the most likely

---

* That similarity or difference even of minor belief systems is a powerful determinant of like or dislike has been shown by a series of ingenious experiments, in one of which Negro and white applicants for a mental hospital job were led into a discussion with four other ostensible applicants, two white and two colored, who were accomplices. One of each race agreed with the subject and one of each disagreed about whether to be permissive or follow rigid rules in dealing with certain problems presented by mental patients. When the subjects were asked whom they would like to work with, they chose a person of different race who agreed with them fifteen times as often as a person of the same race who disagreed! The study was conducted in a Northern state, but there had been serious race riots in its largest city.[19]

instigator of such an act would naturally be the one to whom the power would fall. By contrast, students in Brazil were firmly convinced that the assassination had been engineered by a conspiracy of the CIA, the Pentagon, and the steel barons.[21]

FACTORS AFFECTING RESISTANCE OF
REALITY WORLDS TO CHANGE

The reality world has been portrayed up to now as continually trying to force new information into its mold; but the opposite tendency is also always at work: belief systems adapt themselves to new information. If many of a person's perceptions and beliefs did not keep adjusting themselves to fit actual circumstances, he could not remain alive for long; those unfortunates who give up trying to coordinate their images with the actualities can survive only if others care for them in mental hospitals. While "We are all motivated . . . to see reality as it actually is, even if it hurts," [22] everyone also has a vested interest in maintaining his reality world intact, because to admit that any features of it are wrong introduces an element of unpredictability. Giving up any belief involves a temporary increase in insecurity until a new, better belief has been found, and like the hermit crab in the process of changing homes, the person in the throes of changing a major belief is dangerously exposed.

The extent to which any particular belief system responds to situational changes depends on many factors. Individuals vary in their general rigidity or flexibility—their general willingness to tolerate the feelings of uncertainty concomitant upon relinquishing a belief—and in their capacities for independent thought and their relative accessibility to certain types of influence. Some readily accept the pronouncements of authority, for example, while others are especially prone to resist them.* More germane to our discussion is the importance of any particular belief to a person's sense of identity and security. The belief that one is mortal or that his name is what it is are practically immutable,

* See Chapter 7, pp. 122ff.

whereas the belief that toothpaste X is better than toothpaste Y will yield to the remark of a friend, dentist, or advertisement.

Furthermore, those aspects of the reality world formed by direct experience and leading to behavior that elicits immediate feedback from the environment probably change more readily than those largely formed and maintained by indirect information. Images of other nations fall into this category: new information about another country tends to be used to strengthen the recipient's image of it but not to weaken an opposing view. An example of this is afforded by a public opinion poll concerning a proposed loan to England in 1945. One sample of respondents was given full information about how England would repay the money and how the loan would promote U.S. trade; the control group was uninformed. Among those who trusted England the information group had twice as many as the control approving the loan; but among those unfavorably disposed to England the information had not the slightest effect.[23]

An extensive review of opinion polls findings concerning American images of other nations concludes: "Almost nothing in the world seems to be able to shift the images of 40% of the populations of most countries, even within one or two decades. Combinations of events that shift the images and attitudes of the remaining 50–60% of the population are extremely rare, and these . . . require . . . the mutual reinforcement of cumulative events and substantial governmental efforts as well as the absence of sizeable cross pressures. Most of the spectacular changes of politics involve a change in the attitudes of between one-fifth and one-third of the population." [24]

CONTENTS OF NATIONAL REALITY WORLDS
THAT CREATE INTERNATIONAL TENSION

Three features of national reality worlds can be distinguished that may create or enhance international tensions: enthnocentrism, national images, and ideologies.

Ethnocentrism and Social Conventions

Ethnocentrism,[25] the overevaluation of one's own group in comparison with other groups, especially those perceived as rivals, is virtually universal. Membership in a group is an integral part of an individual's concept of himself. The group's success is his success and its failures damage his self-confidence; its friends and enemies are also his. Many people's group identification is so much a part of their personal identity that they would rather die than be absorbed into an alien group. Since everyone wants to think well of himself, he thinks well of his group—as far as he is concerned, the nation, class, or ethnic group into which he was born is the best, and he judges all events by its standards. Its world-view is the only correct one, its way of doing things the only proper one.

Examples of ethnocentrism are legion. Many cultures, the Javanese for example, use the same word for "human" and members of their own group;[26] the Mundurucu of the Brazilian rain forest divide the world into themselves and *"pariwat"*—everyone else—whom they regard as game to be hunted and speak of "in the same terms that they reserve for peccary and tapir." [27] A less extreme manifestation of the same tendency is that people of eight countries asked to describe themselves all used the adjectives "peace-loving," "brave," "intelligent," and "hard-working." [28]

Within a society the same overvaluation of one's groups is readily demonstrated. In one study of fifty-five sets of six organizations, ranging from dance studios to Protestant churches, raters were found to overestimate the prestige of their own organization eight times as frequently as they underestimated it.[29]

Along with overvaluation of people like oneself—those identifiable as members of one's own group—goes a distrust of the stranger. But at least among adults he is not always perceived as someone to be avoided, and because he is a novelty may actually be enticing—as is borne out by the widespread urge to travel or to meet foreign visitors. When for any reason the stranger becomes frightening, however, then all the deeply ingrained attitudes tending toward the devaluation of strangers come into play, seizing especially on the stranger's unfamiliar ways.

Since members of all organized societies develop behavior patterns which avoid intra-group conflict by identifying group members to each other and signaling mutual recognition of roles and statuses, ethnocentrism is reinforced. Each society, and often each class within a society, has a "right" way to act and speak, a system of etiquette, and the person using the proper forms is "one of us," while he who does not may be the object of ridicule or suspicion. When members of different nations meet, failure to know or abide by each other's conventions is a source of misunderstanding and embarrassment, with results that are usually trivial but can be serious.

Mutual irritation arises so easily because the forms are so habitual as to be largely unconscious, and each person may come away from the encounter feeling annoyed, which he attributes to the other's "boorishness" or "unpleasant" personal characteristics instead of to its proper source. Thus, many Americans interpreted the visiting Premier Khrushchev's Russian gesture of friendship—hands clasped above his head—as the prizefighter's sign of victory. The normal conversational distance among Latin Americans is less than that among North Americans, so the former may keep trying to get closer while the latter back off, thereby creating mutual discomfort. In France boy-girl relationships are usually either completely platonic or fully sexual, and the French regard the American custom of petting as dishonest and immoral. "Thus a certain lack of international consensus might result if an American girl indicated her willingness to have her French date kiss her good-night." [30]

American behavioral scientists have paid particular attention to the differences between American and Russian culturally determined behavior. Because they can seriously impede useful communication between members of the two societies, two examples are worth reporting.

In the first, which illustrates the Russian's greater dependence on groups than the American's,[31] an American psychiatrist interested in interviewing Russian students found them to be severely constrained when approached individually, but much freer in groups, even those formed of strangers. The atmosphere within such a group was friendly but impersonal, there was little competition; it regularly pushed its most talented members forward, and all members seemed to take pride in their performance. Criticisms were not taken personally, and there was no shyness in speaking up. This group orientation was reflected in the Russians' attitude toward the visitor's motives: when he said he was a tourist interested in Russian education, they were uneasy and suspicious because they are unfamiliar with individuals doing things on their own volition; but when, sensing this, he said he was with a delegation of American educators, the distrust vanished.

The second example of impeded communications has been found by many visitors to Russia who have noticed what appears to be a bland disregard of facts that might indicate failure or threaten self-esteem. Over thirty years ago I was among a group of medical students being shown through a Russian mental hospital, and the superintendent, our guide, insisted that Russian methods of treatment had made disturbed patients a thing of the past. A psychiatrist in the party kept asking repeatedly that a locked door we passed be opened. The superintendent finally reluctantly did so, and when we pointed out that the agitated patients were indistinguishable from those in any American mental hospital, he said, with a perfectly straight face, "They're disturbed only because you opened the door." Recent visitors have reported a Russian's failing to keep an appointment and then berating the American for not appearing, or another boasting about the clean air in a textile mill when it was visibly full of lint.

Various explanations have been offered for this curious behavior—curious to American eyes, that is. Perhaps it is due to the fact that in Russia failure implies moral culpability and social censure, so one denies it as much as possible, and when it cannot be denied, tries to shift the blame.[32] Or it may be a function of the Russian's intense group-orientedness, so that the group perceptual filter is particularly powerful. A more entertaining speculation (which I have not been able to verify from a

Russian) is that the Russians have a pattern of half-serious lying, *vranyo,* that they distinguish from a deliberate lie. The *vrun* starts out knowing he is pulling a long bow, but gradually convinces himself with his own story. The proper response is not to humiliate him by confronting him with the facts, but to listen respectfully and indicate by subtle clues that one admires the performance.[33]

American sensitivity to Russian disregard of the truth in some circumstances finds a parallel in the complaints of foreign students about the "deceitfulness" of their American teachers: because the teacher is friendly, they think they are doing well, but suddenly at the end of the course the teacher tells them that their work has been unsatisfactory; American students are able to pick up subtle cues beneath a teacher's friendliness that indicate what he thinks of their performance. Similarly, Russians must be able to detect *vranyo* or they would not be able to run their complex society.

National Images

Characteristics of every nation's self-image that contribute to war are national sovereignty, territoriality, and strength.

Each nation believes it has a right to pursue its "vital interests," regardless of the effect on those of other nations. Advances in weapons technology, communications, and transportation have made this concept obsolete, however, and today no nation can be secure at the expense of the security of other nations. Yet such is the power of this group standard that nations cannot be persuaded to relinquish aspects of their sovereignty that in fact they no longer possess.

A second aspect of national images that requires modification is the equation of national identity with possession of a certain piece of territory. A nation's self-image has been identical with the territory it occupied, directly or as colonies, and since national growth was equated with territorial growth, nations have attempted to expand at each other's expense. Because this has been a major source of war, the abolition of war thus requires loosening of the link between national identity and territory. In view of territoriality's deep biological roots, it is unlikely that it can ever be completely eliminated—every nation will probably always require land it can call its own where its administrative machinery and symbols of nationhood are located.* Fortunately, many political units have largely been defined by some principle of association or adherence to a common belief system—being a citizen of Rome, a vassal of a feudal fiefdom, a Communist Party member—and therefore "territory" need not be synonymous with "nationhood."

Strength, the third troublesome aspect of national images, probably has its source in the individual's identification with his group which makes its strength part of his. The strength of small nations finds expression as a sense of unity of purpose and firmness of will in the face of a menacing world. The strength of great nations, probably because they have been formed through wars and must have won more than they lost or they would not be extant today, is additionally equaled with military prowess. Shared events as preserved by history form every national image, and "war is the one experience which is dramatic, obviously important, and shared by everybody." [34]

The martial aspect of national images is expressed and reinforced by glorification of military heroes, whose fame rests on their victories even if their other contributions were equally or more significant. The French revere Napoleon for his military genius, which in the end permanently damaged the nation, and not for the Code Napoleon, which is a source of France's strength. Flags that have been carried in battle arouse the strongest emotions of loyalty, and all national anthems dwell on the nation's defiance of its enemies.

National Ideologies

The third aspect of national reality worlds relevant to war is their view of the meaning of existence, including concepts of right and wrong, or "conscience values." [35] Since there is no ob-

---

* The gypsies and Jews may be exceptions, if they can be called nations. An aspect of the Jews' self-image that preserved their identity during the millennia of the diaspora, however, may have been the prophecy-based hope that they would eventually reoccupy their homeland.

jective test of their validity, there is no other way than a test of
strength to determine which among different conscience values
will prevail. One conscience value all nations share is, unfortunately, that war is the right and proper response to another
group perceived as threatening or hostile. All modern nations
have been created by war, and since they are by definition good,
then war in defense of their national interests must also be. The
morality of war also gains support from the equation of manly
strength with willingness to resort to violence.

The conscience value that war under certain circumstances is
right is far more powerful than the contrary one implied in
Christianity's pacifistic teachings. These teachings have been
reconciled with the waging of war by the doctrine of the just
war, according to which war is justified if the potential good
effects of a victory for "us" outweigh the war's harmful effects.
Christians of all nations seldom have difficulty persuading themselves that any war in which they were engaged was just, and
some even seem able to find ways to reconcile a nuclear war
with Christian teachings.

Conscience values are an aspect of ideologies—the sets of beliefs that give meaning to life and contain an explicit or implicit
program of action. The beliefs include convictions about the nature of the universe, the goals of life, the proper organization of
society, and the like.

An individual human life is a momentary flash of experience
squeezed between two oblivions in a universe that appears indifferent to human existence, or at least gives no universally
convincing sign of caring. Since the full recognition of one's utter
insignificance is intolerable, everyone has some way of shielding
himself from the awful truth. Most people accomplish this by
identifying with some enduring and larger group and, beyond
this, by viewing their lives as being in the service of some more
or less permanent abstraction—freedom, democracy, communism, human welfare, or a religious creed: ". . . the conceptual
order to which we submit ourselves . . . is the bark that holds
us above the sea of chaos in which we would otherwise drown.
This is why people give their allegiance so passionately, so unre-

servedly, and so irrevocably to the grand doctrinal systems that invite their adherence." [36]

So important are ideologies' psychological functions for individuals that they strongly resist change, but they are not completely impregnable. Strongly held beliefs can be changed if, for one thing, motives to change them are stronger than motives to cling to them—if holding on to an ideology is accompanied by enough misery and if giving it up promises enough rewards, it may change.

Persons susceptible to religious conversion illustrate some psychological prerequisites for ideological change and the forces producing it. Characteristically, they feel that their world-view has failed them and they are filled with feelings of despair and isolation;[37] their conversions are typically precipitated by personal contact with someone whose ideology promises new hope and acceptance by a new group. Revival meetings supply these conditions, as does Chinese thought reform, but potential converts seek out the former because they are already miserable, while the latter's procedures are calculated to create the suffering that the conversion relieves.[38] Statistically speaking, neither is actually very effective. A follow-up study of a series of Billy Graham's revival meetings found that only 2 to 5 per cent were converted and of these only half were active a year later.[39] Thought reform was effective only in those immersed in a group supporting the new ideology after their release—the great majority of apparently successfully "brainwashed" American prisoners of war in Korea and Americans in Chinese prisons reverted to the American world-view on returning home.

Just as an ideology is essential to an individual's psychological well-being, so a shared ideology is a powerful cement holding a group together, and ideologies of groups, therefore, also strongly resist change. Other things being equal, a nation's capacity to survive depends on its morale, which in turn depends largely on its sense of shared purpose and destiny, and the conviction that its way of life will ultimately prevail. When the citizens of a nation lose faith in its ideology, it eventually disintegrates. Intra-group ideological revolutions occur only among peoples who, suffering widespread demoralization and despair, come under the spell of a magnetic leader who offers them a new way of organizing their reality worlds and promises great re- wards in terms of material welfare and renewed group solidarity if they follow him.

Violent efforts by one group or nation to force members of another to accept their ideology, so-called holy wars, are espe- cially bitter and prolonged, a matter to be considered more fully in the next chapter.

THE STRAIN TOWARD CONSISTENCY— A HOPEFUL ASPECT

To an intellectual and moral giant like Ralph Waldo Emerson a foolish consistency may be the hobgoblin of little minds, but few human beings can dispense with the need to maintain the consistency of their reality worlds. "Dissonance" between different aspects of the reality world creates anxiety, and efforts to reduce it account for many phenomena of human thinking and behavior.[40]

The strain toward consistency is a powerful force in human affairs which has been invoked already and will appear many times again. People filter and interpret incoming experiences to fit their preconceptions, and because belief systems are suffi- ciently abstract to allow almost unlimited room for redefinition of events to fit them, people also reinterpret their own behavior to make it consistent with their beliefs, which is one of the hope- ful aspects of the strain toward consistency. A national image is not shaken by day-to-day changes in policy and can accommo- date an extraordinarily wide range of national aims and behav- iors. A striking example is England, which maintains in the twentieth century the symbols of a medieval monarchy, having identified them "successively with most of the political and eco- nomic transactions known to Western man." [41]

The strain to consistency may lead nations with incompatible ideologies to exaggerate differences in their actual behavior—

each interpreting its behavior as consistent with its world-view, so the behaviors appear more incompatible than they are. It may well be that people of capitalist and communist nations, for example, actually behave in a much more similar fashion and have more similar aspirations than they have been prepared to admit, which raises the hopeful possibility that although national belief systems resist change, rival ones need not actually change very much in order for their adherents to coexist. In a study of Russian and American value systems it was found that despite the apparently irreconcilable differences in their national world-views, both regard as desirable free private enterprise, helping the underdog, and political freedoms: "[The] 'American capitalism' [Soviet citizens] have been taught to fear is not actually so very different from the Good Society that they themselves would like to see evolve in the U.S.S.R.—and . . . both are comparatively modest variations on themes that represent the great common aspirations of the human race." [42] Thus a promising way to reduce international conflict based on or fed by conflicting reality worlds would be to do everything possible to make visible the fact that the actual behavior and aims of adherents of rival world-views are much less discrepant than their programmatic statements.

To the extent that a person's culture filters and classifies incoming information, it supplies the raw material or building blocks for his reality world, limits the range of alternatives, and also supplies strong hints as to which are preferable. But in stressing how each person's world-view is determined by the group to which he belongs, I do not mean to imply that it cannot be modified by reflection. Progress and change depend on individuals in every society who can transcend the limitations its reality world imposes. In fact, human survival now depends more than ever on those who can appreciate if not adopt world-views of other cultures and societies.

For the first time the potential destructive consequences of national belief systems have become so great as to threaten civilization. To escape this calamity will require that citizens of every nation learn to "empathize" with those holding different views. Each nation is convinced that those who claim to see things differently or whose faith is in a different sociopolitical system are either misled or deluded. To recognize that each frame of reference is just as relative as the others, men will have to surmount this tribal outlook—that is, they must become more self-conscious about national images, which at present are "the last great stronghold of unsophistication" [43]—and then they will discover that many of the issues that propel nations to war are largely illusory.

7 · *The Image of the Enemy*

TO FORESTALL misunderstanding, it must be stressed that the psychological analysis which follows assumes the reality of enemies. Enemies exist; they are real and very dangerous to each other, they often possess the malevolent qualities attributed to them, and as they continue to interact their images of each other come to fit them more and more closely. In any given case certain aspects of the image may correspond more nearly to the realities than do others, but the degree of distortion is hard to determine, and those distortions that are introduced intensify conflict and impede non-violent resolution of mutual enmity. The chief danger of the enemy image is that it makes false perceptions as resistant to changes as if they were true ones. Only by becoming highly self-conscious about it can one hope to dispel its erroneous aspects, and to this extent reduce the likelihood of war.

SOURCES OF FORMATION OF THE
ENEMY IMAGE

The relationships of different groups largely determines how their members perceive and act toward each other, and these perceptions in turn influence the further development of their relationship. In this sense behavior and perception are part of an interacting process, a consideration especially pertinent to the image of the enemy which initially arises because two or more nations find themselves in conflict resulting from clashes of national interests. Because of the innate distrust of the stranger, the sense of threat is easily aroused on both sides, and once the opinion-makers have singled out and labeled the chosen foreign target, the distrust immediately focuses on it.[1] Regardless of their actual characteristics, the two nations now view each other as a threat.

The degree of fear of the enemy depends on each nation's perception of both the other's ability to harm it and the firmness of its intent to do so. These are shrouded in uncertainty for several reasons, including the adversary's behavior and obstacles to communication with him. When their interests conflict, part of each nation's strategy is to keep the other guessing as to its next moves and simultaneously try to convey the impression that it is powerful and indomitable. Since the unknown is an especially potent source of fear because one does not know how to combat it, to the extent that the exact scope and form of a threat is unclear, its capacity to arouse anxiety is increased.

This was clearly shown in an experimental study that included deliberate attempts to make subjects anxious by means of a half-hour "stress interview" that dwelt on their weaknesses and embarrassing experiences. In a pre-experimental session in which some simple measures of physiological functions involved placing electrodes on the subjects' arms and legs, the experimenters found to their surprise that on the average the subjects were made more anxious by these simple, painless procedures than by the stress interview. They were apparently frightened by the strange room full of equipment and by uncertainty as to what was going to happen to them.[2] Similarly, it has been suggested that mutual anxiety at the international level is greatest when each country knows enough about the other to recognize that it has the power to inflict harm, but does not know enough to be sure of is intent or of how much power it actually has.[3]

In any case, the effort to combat this anxiety by reducing uncertainty leads to progressive oversimplification and polarization of thinking—grays give way to blacks and whites. Those elements of each nation's national image that contribute to its morale and sense of security generally become more prominent, notably its perception of itself as moral and strong, and at the same time the first of these virtues is denied to the enemy.

THE "MIRROR IMAGE" OF THE ENEMY

The progressive mutual distortions lead to what has been termed the mirror image of the enemy. Enemy nations' reciprocal images differ, of course, in some respects, including the relative salience of varying features and the actual correspondence to reality of any particular perceived feature. But to a surprisingly large extent, the opponents attribute the same virtues to themselves and the same vices to each other. Data concerning the mirror image come from two sources: direct observations made by visitors to the Soviet Union, and content analyses of publications there and in the United States.

During a visit to the Soviet Union in 1960 a Russian-speaking American psychologist did some informal but careful interviewing of people in different walks of life, avoiding such obvious sources of bias as confining his talks to Russians who spoke to him first. The people he interviewed considered the Americans the aggressors, believed that the United States government exploited and deluded the people and the people did not fully support the government, and felt that American leaders could not be trusted and that their foreign policy bordered on madness—all of which many Americans say about the Soviets.[4]

The findings were similar in a quantitative study that compared Russian and American views of themselves and each other as revealed by statements in some of their mass media and elite publications. In the following presentation of selected items, the totals on which the percentages are based are the number of items which refer to the issue in question.[5]

Each nation's media portray the other as aggressive and

treacherous. Thus, 63 per cent of the American and 88 per cent of the Soviet items attribute war to one state's aggressiveness; and virtually 100 per cent of those in both describe the other's national goal as domination or expansion and its military doctrine as including a pre-emptive or preventive strike. Neither accepts self-preservation as the goal of the other's operational code. Consistent with their views of each other as aggressive and untrustworthy, two-thirds of the relevant items in the press of each say that negotiations are most likely to succeed when it is stronger.

Each nation sees as altruistic its own motives for offering foreign aid but the other's as in the service of expansion, and both nation's media are in virtually unanimous agreement that the other offers foreign aid not to help the recipients but to strengthen its own position and weaken the opponent's. Of the Soviet Union's items, 95 per cent assert that the primary purpose of their aid is to enable other countries to remain neutral or to help them, while the American items are more realistic, admitting in 42 per cent that foreign aid was given to strengthen their own side and weaken the other.

Further evidence for the self-image of each as peaceful is that practically no items in either country's media state that its own forcible measures will bring about the other's eventual demise— 87 per cent of the American items and 53 per cent of the Soviet place their main faith in the internal weaknesses and contradictions of the other's system.

The reciprocal images were sharply discrepant in one interesting respect—the degree of planning of the other's foreign policy. Of the relevant Soviet items, 74 per cent described American foreign policy as a haphazard response to events, while only 10 per cent saw it as masterful and thorough; the corresponding American figures were 8 per cent and 56 per cent.

Strangely enough, each sees the other's behavior as contradicting its own view of the general lawfulness of international relations: 69 per cent of the Russian items regard the predictability of national events as highly possible and none as almost impossible; the corresponding figures for the United States are 7 and 57 per cent. We believe that international events are unpredictable but that Soviet foreign policy is masterful; they believe that events are predictable but that our foreign policy is not. It is hard to know whether it is more alarming to view each move of an aggressive, powerful, and treacherous enemy as part of a deep-laid plot or as wild and unpredictable behavior.

The attribution to others of more competence and planning than is actually the fact may be a general American trait. Many Americans regard every communist maneuver as well-planned and deeply thought-out in the service of a worldwide conspiracy, although the Sino-Soviet split has made this view more difficult to maintain. While other nations may plan further ahead than the United States (I share the Soviet perception that United States leaders often seem to react from moment to moment), their control over events is obviously far from perfect.

The tendency to attribute greater control over events to others than oneself has been noted in free-discussion groups. Patients in therapy groups universally admit to astonishment at finding that behind their façades of self-assurance, others have similar problems; and the same experience is reported by industrial and business executives after participating in sensitivity training groups, small groups whose ground rules require revelation of feelings as a means of enhancing their members' ability to recognize others' feelings and attitudes. Similarly, in a series of studies of experimental bargaining situations each group was found to see the opponent as more purposeful than themselves: "They see their own disorganization but all they see [about the other group] are messages, proposals and counter-proposals, and these make it easy to presume some organized, shrewd causal agent at work." [6]

Americans are apparently especially prone to be taken in by each other's masks of competence and poise, and while one would suspect, knowing their own inner insecurity, that they would expect it of others as well, some other psychological principle seems to be operative here—as it is in those confidence men who easily fall victim to each other.

A striking aspect of the mirror image of the enemy is the perception that the leaders are their real villains—which assumes either that the rank and file are well disposed to one's own nation or that if they are not, it is because their leaders have intentionally misled them.

This is well expressed in the report of an American scientist who had an opportunity for long, informal conversation with his Russian counterparts: "The Westerner regards the Russians as controlled, for the most part without their knowledge, by an oligarchy of rapacious and malevolent men who seek constantly to foment world revolution. The Russian is equally convinced that the West (which means really America, for in Russian eyes all other Western countries are American satellites) is being victimized by a small group of profit-mad 'monopolists' who pull the strings that control government, press, and radio and who try to instigate wars in order to sell munitions. On the level of informal conversations such as ours it was impossible to resolve this difference in viewpoint. Each of us was repeating what he had read in his own newspapers, and each was suspicious of the other's sources." [7]

Concomitant with the view depicting the leaders as villainous oppressors and exploiters is the belief that the masses are disaffected. This belief feeds on reports of tourists who tell of speaking with people who expressed their discontent, but these reports are untrustworthy on several counts. Like everyone else, tourists perceive and remember selectively those experiences that accord with their expectations. The nationals who seek out foreigners would probably not be making the contact if they were not discontented, and furthermore they might have ulterior motives for telling the foreigner what they think he wants to hear. The psychologist who interviewed Russians found that those who had sought him out expressed considerable discontent, but that over 75 per cent of those with whom he had initiated the conversation spontaneously expressed pro-Soviet sentiments and identified fully with its way of life and world-view.

The belief that only the leaders of an opposing group are evil is practically universal. It is similar to "the American public's focus on the Kaiser as the villain of World War I, the complacent employer's conviction that his employees are contented and loyal but misled by union agitators, the Southerner's belief that Negroes in the South would be contented if it were not for 'nigger-loving agitators' from the North. It is a wonderfully consoling conception. It simultaneously eliminates the guilt of feeling hostile to a large number of people, creates a positive image of oneself as saving the underdog-masses from their conniving and oppressive leaders, provides a personal, visualizable Devil on whom to concentrate all hostility, and sustains hope that, once the leaders have been firmly dealt with, the battle will be over." [8]

Placing all the blame on the enemy leaders reinforces two aspects of a nation's own image, its goodness and its strength. People seek support from others to sustain their images, and the failure of people in an enemy nation to appreciate one's own nation's good intentions can be explained away by assuming that they would be appreciative if they were not being deceived by their leaders. Furthermore, anxiety is allayed by the belief that although the enemy appears strong and united, the people would overthrow their leaders if they could.

INDIVIDUAL DIFFERENCES IN THE ENEMY IMAGE

Whether citizens of one nation perceive those of another as enemies depends primarily on the nature of the relations between the two countries, but individuals seem to differ in their readiness to see foreigners as enemies.

Those at one extreme may be characterized as xenophobic, as well illustrated by a quotation from a published letter: ". . . Communist Dobrynin is a key member of a force which holds together in one gigantic conspiracy the largest and most vicious group of murdering, self-serving, power-seeking, ruthless megalomaniacs the world has ever known." [9]

At the other extreme are the xenophiles, perhaps most concentrated in pacifist groups, who while rejecting communism as a philosophy, take at face value the communist protestations of peaceful intentions and their interpretation of international affairs, and attribute all international tensions to American aggressiveness, duplicity, and stupidity.

Psychologically, the two extremes probably resemble each other more than either resembles a middle group, whose members try to differentiate various aspects of their own and the enemy image and weigh them in the light of available evidence. This group might be classed as open-minded in contrast to the extremes, which are close-minded in the sense that they defend themselves against new information that might call their opinions into question.[10] Both types of extremists are probably hostile toward authority figures, but the former displace the target to the enemy while the latter focus on their own leaders.

In this connection, most of the studies that have attempted to relate personality attributes to international attitudes have assumed an authoritarian character pattern whose dynamic core lies in repression of strong hostility originally aimed at parents and other severe but close authority figures. Those with this type of character pattern exaggerate the importance in human affairs of power, force, domination, and submission, and displace their own aggression to safer targets than authority figures at home. Greatly valuing conventional morality they express their bottled-up sexual and aggressive feelings indirectly through condemnatory over-concern with "immoral" behavior of foreigners and other out-groups, and they are similarly prone to externalize their fears, attributing their problems to external enemies rather than inner conflicts. Such people would be expected to over-value their own group and derogate others—that is, they would be ethnocentric.[11]

People with authoritarian personalities score high on the so-called "F-Scale," which consists of a series of such statements as: "What youth needs most is strict discipline, rugged determination and the will to work and fight for family and country"; "People can be divided into two classes, the weak and the strong"; "Most of our social problems would be solved if we could somehow get rid of the immoral, crooked, and feeble-minded people." The greater the number of such statements to which the person assents, the higher his score.[12] And it is scarcely surprising that several studies have found high F-Scale scores to correlate negatively with world-mindedness and positively with jingoism.[13]

Other investigations have found that tendencies toward certain personality attributes go with general attitudes toward foreign nations. Thus, one interview study found more world-minded persons to be less stereotyped and more likely to view various personal problems as internal rather than external in origin,[14] while a study of college students found that high "status concern" was associated with a militant foreign-policy stance and that anti-intellectual students favored a heavy-armament policy.[15] One study is of special interest because it was done not with American college students but with Norwegian military and naval students whose ways of responding to conflicts of daily life and whose attitudes toward international conflicts were classified by the experimenter as either threat- or problem-oriented; each type was further broken down into passive or active, and, if active, into inward- or outward-directed. The students were found to be self-consistent—there was some correspondence between how they scored on these scales with respect to the two types of conflict. An additional finding suggests that information relevant to international attitudes can be obtained from so-called projective tests—which tap feelings a person does not express directly and may not be aware of—for latent hostility revealed on such tests correlated in this study with manifest aggressive attitudes in foreign affairs.[16]

It might be of value if clear-cut relations could be established between national leaders' personality attributes and their attitudes toward foreign affairs, but this is very difficult since information about national leaders' personal characteristics can be obtained only indirectly, from speeches and autobiographical writings. Nevertheless, there has been one not entirely unpromising attempt involving analyses of United States congressmen's speeches with respect to evidences of personal insecurity or security and tolerance or intolerance of ambiguity on the one hand, and nationalism or internationalism on the other (the latter being also revealed by voting behavior). Nationalism was found to be related to personal insecurity, intolerance of ambiguity, and negative orientation to people.[17]

RESISTANCE OF THE ENEMY IMAGE
TO CHANGE

While people's personal characteristics may affect their readiness to form the image of the enemy, certain dynamic properties of this image—among them its resistance to change—seem remarkably similar regardless of who holds it or to which nation it is applied.

Since an enemy is seen as a threat to national survival, to change his image involves dropping one's guard—that is, acting as if he could be trusted. All life experience teaches that in the face of a serious conflict of interest, real or illusory, this is very risky, especially when there is no one to turn to for protection or redress should one's trust prove to have been unjustified. The enemy may be frightening, but the thought of dropping one's guard is more so. Once the enemy ceases to be dangerous, as after a massive defeat, the image is more amenable to change—suggesting that mutual fear is the chief source of its fixity—but two additional types of factors contribute to its rigidity. First, an enemy mobilizes certain feelings that increase a nation's sense of solidarity and strength; he is a convenient scapegoat for the release of internal aggressions and solves other internal problems, as discussed in Chapter 6. Second, the image of the enemy elicits behavior from him that not only makes the image increasingly difficult to correct but, as will be described in Chapters 8 and 9, actually reinforces it.

The image of the enemy as treacherous and warlike maintains itself through various psychological means, including restriction of communication, denial of the relevance of contrary evidence (selective filtering), and interpretation of the evidence to fit the image.

Restriction of Communication

The temptation to break off or restrict communication with an enemy is strong for many reasons. At the simplest level, one does not enjoy contact with someone he dislikes and the lack of communication may then intensify the dislike. These phenomena are illustrated by an experiment in which male undergraduates were angered by insulting notes, supposedly from a peer, and were then asked to write first impressions of him; in addition, half were permitted to send return notes, while half were prevented from doing so by immediately being given another task. In the first group, the more dislike expressed in first impressions, the smaller the volume of communications; but at the end of the experiment they wrote friendlier descriptions of their peers than did those in the second group. Furthermore, almost all said they wanted to continue note writing, while fewer than two-thirds of those who had been prevented from communicating wanted to continue the experiment, and the more unfriendly they felt, the greater their expressed unwillingness to continue.[18]

Since an enemy is untrustworthy, if we let him communicate with us, he may trick us, learn things about us that we do not want him to know, or reveal some good features that might undermine our will to resist him. Any increase in communication is therefore resisted by both parties. For example, in 1959 the Senate Internal Security Committee vigorously objected to Soviet-American cultural exchanges: "Soviet hoaxers are playing us . . . for suckers"; "This is a poisonous propaganda offensive which, if successful, could well be a prelude to sudden military attack." [19] At virtually the same time the Chairman of the U.S.S.R. State Committee for Cultural Relations with Foreign Countries accused the United States and other Western countries of regarding the exchange program as a "Trojan Horse whose stomach could be filled with anti-Soviet material." [20] In 1966 Peking blasted Secretary of State Dean Rusk's proposal for wider unofficial contacts between China and the United States as a mixture of hostility to China and deception: ". . . the real aim is to launch aggression against China. . . ." [21]

Leaders on each side fear that their people are so naïve as to be easily misled by the other's propaganda, and that their side could not use the contacts as effectively as the enemy to further its ends. Unfortunately, when two nations are hostile, both freely yield to the very great temptation to use visitors as spies, thereby supplying justification for the distrust of free communication—another example of a self-aggravating state of affairs.

Selective Filtering

When competing groups cannot break off contact, as when they live in close proximity, their mutually derogatory images maintain themselves by selective filtering and emphasis, in accordance with the strain toward consistency. A good example is the reported discrepancy in perceptions of Hindus and Muslims in a Hindu city whose influential Muslim minority suddenly lost status and became very insecure after the partition of India, which was followed by widespread unemployment. Seventy per cent of each group vigorously rejected the other; 85 to 90 per cent of both groups portrayed the situation in moralistic terms, with themselves as innocent. That the information filter also screens out information incompatible with the image of one's own group as blameless is illustrated by the Muslims' failure to realize that the Hindus had the same proportion of unemployed and suffered as much as they from inadequate police protection, and by the Hindus' failure to understand why the Muslims were upset (not one Hindu mentioned that eighteen Muslims had been killed in the previous year).[22]

Similarly, at a small international conference some years ago Russian scientists insisted with apparently absolute conviction that the spread of communism to satellite countries after 1946 was achieved entirely by peaceful means, in all cases expressing the free will of the vast majority of the people. Recently an English boy living and going to school in China informed me that no Russian or Chinese troops were stationed outside their own borders; but since I had just seen Russian troops in Hungary, I was able to fill in this gap in his information.

If information incompatible with a view of another nation as an enemy cannot be ignored, it is sometimes handled by being rejected as irrelevant, as is especially obvious in the area of race relations. The member of a despised group who does not show the unpleasant traits attributed to that group is an exception: "Some of my best friends are. . . ." Similarly, on the international scene, a Russian ovation given an American pianist, or vice versa, is dismissed as irrelevant to their political attitudes and feelings.

Interpretation of Evidence—the Double Standard

A more active way to maintain a derogatory image of another group is to reinterpret disconfirming or ambiguous evidence to fit it. Examples of this process abound in studies of race prejudice, of which the following is representative: "In Rhodesia a white truck driver passed a group of idle natives and muttered, 'They're lazy brutes!' A few hours later he saw natives heaving two hundred-pound sacks of grain onto a truck, singing in rhythm to their work. 'Savages,' he grumbled. 'What do you expect?' " [23]

The same behavior is seen as in the service of good motives if performed by our side and bad if performed by an enemy. A psychologist showed some American fifth- and sixth-graders photographs of Russian roads lined with young trees. When he asked why the Russians had trees along the road, two answers were: "So that people won't be able to see what is going on beyond the road," and "It's to make work for the prisoners"; but when he asked why some American roads have trees planted along the side, the children said "for shade" or "to keep the dust down." [24]

The double standard of evaluation was illustrated by a formal study conducted in 1965 in which a large number of college freshmen were presented with fifty statements concerning belligerent and conciliatory actions that had been taken by both the United States and Russia; for half the students the acts were attributed to the United States, for the other half to the Soviet Union. They were asked to indicate their feelings about each statement by marking it from +3 (most favorable) to −3 (most unfavorable), and as might be expected, an action was scored more favorably when attributed to the United States than when attributed to Russia. For purposes of statistical analysis the scores were transformed into 0-to-6 scale, so that scores above 3 would be favorable and those below 3 unfavorable. For example, the average score for "The U.S. (Russia) has established rocket bases close to the borders of Russia (the U.S.)" was 4.7 for the United States version and 0.5 for the Russian one. "The U.S. (Russia) has stated that it was compelled to resume nuclear testing by the action of Russia (the U.S.)" was scored 4.2 in the United States form and 1.0 in the Russian one.

The double standard, most extreme for warlike and competitive actions like those cited, was less obvious for conciliatory behavior and virtually absent in items concerning free dissemination of information. A statement that one nation had made several proposals concerning East-West disarmament, for example, was rated 4.7 in the United States version and 3.2 in the Russian one. The statement that the government of one nation had made it easier for tourists, students, and professional delegations to visit the other was scored about 4.9 in both versions. Statements rated over 5 in both versions concerned contributions to medical research and the warm receptions given the other nation's musicians.[25] Thus, the double standard was not absolute and the American students, not completely indiscriminate, were willing to give Russia credit for behavior that advanced scientific knowledge or indicated a friendly attitude.

In this they may have been more discriminating than the late John Foster Dulles, whose basic premise as Secretary of State was the inherent bad faith of the communists. A detailed analysis of his public speeches made between 1953 and 1959 reveals that he interpreted all their actions as confirming this premise,[26] seeing any apparent decrease in their hostility as a sign either of their increasing frustration or decreasing capacity, while attributing any increase in their hostility to their success and strength. Thus, he saw the Austrian treaty as evidence that the Soviet Union's policy with respect to Western Europe had failed and that the system was on the point of collapse, and ascribed their 1956 cut of 1,200,000 in armed forces to economic weakness and bad faith, in that the released men would be put to work on more lethal weapons. It followed that in either case the United States should increase the pressure—to hasten the collapse of the foe or to defend itself against their growing strength.

It should be stressed again that the question of how closely the interpretations of enemy behavior correspond to the truth is being left open. The point is that their dynamics make any erroneous intepretation as hard to change as if it were correct.

CONSEQUENCES OF INADEQUATE OR DISTORTED COMMUNICATION WITH THE ENEMY

A progressive hardening of the enemy image results from the actual difficulties of communicating with him and from the distortions and misinterpretations of information that does get through. These also reduce opportunities to learn about changes in the enemy since the impression was formed that might decrease initially justified fears or suggest new possibilities for resolving the mutual antagonism.* To the extent that fantasy fills the gaps left by insufficient information, the enemy image becomes colored by hopes and fears; and either type of distortion can make matters worse.

In accordance with the anxiety-arousing effect of unclarity, the enemy arouses fears to the degree that his capabilities and intentions are unknown. The effort to reduce emotional tension by eliminating ambiguity contributes to picturing the conflict increasingly in black-and-white terms, with our side becoming whiter, the enemy's blacker, and the gray area progressively shrinking.

* Experts about an enemy nation often show particular reluctance to modify their image to fit new, more favorable information. This apparent paradox is easily understood if it is remembered that they have a vested interest in maintaining their original impression intact, since it was the source of their prestige and influence.[27]

Under such circumstances it is easy to yield to "possibilistic thinking," characteristic of the paranoid person[28] who views others' behavior in the light of the worst behavior possibility instead of the probabilities. He may conclude, for example, that his psychiatrist is secretly a member of the Communist Party or the FBI, assigned to get him into trouble; indeed possible, it is not exactly probable. The mythical missile gap with which Americans frightened themselves in 1957 seems to have been based on similar thinking: instead of considering the probabilities, United States planners based estimates of Russian intercontinental missile production on their largest possible capacity and assumed their worst possible intentions, thereby overestimating their production by about thirty times.

A further source of overestimation of the enemy's evil characteristics has been termed the "mote-beam phenomenon." [29] Individuals are especially sensitive to undesirable traits in others that they too possess but try to hide from themselves—an aggressive person, for instance, is usually much quicker to recognize aggression in others than in himself. Analogously, Americans who seem especially oblivious to the degree of the Negroes' civil disabilities are acutely sensitive to restrictions of freedom in the Soviet Union. (This can be also viewed as an example of projection, described in Chapter 5.)

To the extent that fantasies about an enemy are colored by fear, they lead to overestimation of his evil intent. To the extent that they are colored by hope, they foster underestimation of his actual power. Before a war breaks out, military overconfidence is usually characteristic of both sides and is based on wishful thinking, supported by the image of one's own nation as strong and united and the image of the enemy as irresolute and internally divided.

IDEOLOGICAL DIFFERENCES AND HOLY WARS

If the issues over which nations find themselves at odds include ideological differences, the enemy image is apt to be especially powerful and threatening. Ideological differences contribute to the "dehumanization of the enemy," a process that comes to full fruition in actual war, in which context it will be considered more fully in Chapter 9. A group must be wicked or even diabolical if it considers something to be bad that one's own group ideology regards as good. For example, since communists have no use for theistic religions, which most American citizens consider to be good, communists are immoral and untrustworthy in the eyes of these Americans.

The mere existence of another group professing a different ideology is threatening to the true believers because it suggests that their own may be wrong—an atheistic society that survives and prospers is, by this very fact, a threat to a theistic one, and vice versa. The mutual sense of threat is sharply increased if each of the rival ideologies requires that its adherents convert or destroy believers in the other, as has been true of Islam and Christianity, Catholicism and Protestantism, and more recently, capitalism and communism. Holders of incompatible ideologies each demand that the others surrender their beliefs, "precisely the sort of change that most terrifies men and leaves them rootless." [30]

Because it would deprive their lives of meaning, the loss of their ideology would be for many individuals a kind of psychological death, one harder to contemplate than biological death. Furthermore, to suffer and die for a holy cause raises one's esteem in the eyes of fellow believers, encourages them to fight harder, and may convert some of the infidels by demonstrating the power of one's faith; it may even be a short-cut to heaven. Holy wars have no such natural end-point as control over a disputed piece of territory or group of people.

Thus, wars initiated wholly or in part by ideological conflicts are usually especially bitter and prolonged, sometimes terminating only when the holders of one belief system are exterminated. For example, the political power of the Albigensians—the members of a heretical sect that flourished in the south of France in the twelfth and thirteenth centuries—was destroyed after a bitter war, but this did not content their adversaries; for the next century they were hunted down by the Inquisition relentlessly, until they were wiped out so completely that practically all extant information about them comes from their enemies' writings.

Holy wars have more commonly ended in mutual exhaustion after tremendous carnage, with the survivors still clinging to their respective beliefs. Combatants on each side are convinced that they will never yield, no matter how much suffering they have to endure, but simultaneously, each believes it can punish the other into submission. The persistence of this belief, which in the face of all the evidence should have died in Rome with the Christian martyrs, is one of the unsolved mysteries of human behavior.*

It is debatable whether the propensity of humans to commit themselves absolutely to certain ideals has been good or bad for mankind in the long run. Certainly, the world would be a poorer place were it not for the religious, national, and intellectual heroes who sacrificed their lives for their convictions. But this propensity has also led to endless, catastrophic wars over differences in world-views that seemed vital to the protagonists but now seem hardly worth bloodshed—as, for example, whether God is unitarian or trinitarian.

Modern weapons, moreover, have drastically changed the consequences of dying for one's ideals. Patrick Henry's "Give me liberty or give me death" made sense in his day because his death in battle could help to win liberty for his compatriots and did not endanger other people. But today, when the slogan is

---

* World War II has been cited as an example of the successful use of force to make nations abandon their ideologies. But since neither Nazism nor Fascism had had time to become deeply rooted, their abandonment meant little more than that the Germans and Italians returned to former world-views. There may be more justification for the claim that their overwhelming defeat caused the Japanese to adopt permanently some aspects of the American reality world. The Japanese had long admired and emulated the American technological ability that made possible the military victory, and the United States offered massive material rewards for adopting its way of life and outlook on the world. It may also be that in the Japanese scheme of things, failure was in itself a sign that the belief system leading to it had been wrong, and finally, since they were strongly authority-oriented, the Emperor's public submission to General MacArthur's authority may have played a part.

"Better dead than Red," one must ask: for whom is the choice between Redness and death being made?* It is certainly legitimate—many would consider it noble—for a man to decide that he personally would rather be dead than Red and to act accordingly, and some might say he even had the right to make this decision for his nation. But does he have a right to make it for, let us say, the South Vietnamese or for that matter people in the rest of the world? A person could not die for his ideals in a nuclear holocaust without taking millions of innocent bystanders with him; nor could his sacrifice promote realization of the ideals for which it was made, since the necessary social organization would have been destroyed.

Past ideological wars often ended with mutual exhaustion, but today they are more likely to end in mutual total destruction. The world can no longer afford holy wars.

Since nations, like individuals, cannot survive without ideologies, periodic holy wars might seem to be inevitable, but two considerations mitigate this gloomy prospect. It is more satisfying psychologically to convert than to kill adherents of a rival belief system, because by his conversion the convert confirms the superiority of one's own world-view, as his death does not; and many forms of pressure and persuasion are at least as successful as violence in winning converts. Moreover, to meet their adherents' psychological needs, ideologies need not be exclusive. Many religions, like Hinduism, affirm that all religions have grasped some aspect of the Truth, and some secular ideologies, like the American one, highly value diversity, at least in some areas. Holders of world-views like these can coexist indefinitely without their beliefs becoming sources of armed conflict.

---

* Some Americans who use the slogan really mean it, but the seriousness of others' commitment is questionable. Only 40 per cent of a sample of college students asked to agree or disagree in writing with the statement "Death is preferable to living under a Communist regime" said they would rather be dead, and additional data suggest that they did not see this alternative as an immediate or realistic possibility; most believed that no one would be mad enough to start a nuclear holocaust and that war was improbable within the next decade (a very long time for a college student), while the great majority of the

THE STRAIN TO CONSISTENCY AND
MODIFIABILITY OF THE ENEMY IMAGE

The strain toward consistency, which in many ways tends to reinforce the enemy image, can also facilitate its demolition when for any reason an enemy is needed as an ally. This can be viewed as a special case of the generalization that the way another person is perceived depends on his context.

A simple experiment illustrates the old adage that a man is known by the company he keeps, or better, that he is believed to keep. Two groups of members of a chamber of commerce were shown the same photograph of a middle-aged man and asked to describe him; one group was told that he was the local manager of a small plant that was a branch of a large manufacturing corporation, the other that he was treasurer of his local union. The first group described him as a solid citizen, trustworthy, responsible, and thoughtful; the second saw him as opinionated, argumentative, and undependable.[32]

The effect of context on national perceptions is illustrated by how citizens of one nation change their perceptions of citizens of another to accord with a change in the two nations' positions vis-à-vis each other, as apparent in repeated public opinion polls concerning American characterization of peoples of other countries.[33] In 1942 and again in 1966 respondents were asked to choose from a list of adjectives those that best described the people of Russia, Germany, and Japan. In 1942 the first five adjectives chosen to characterize both Germans and Japanese (enemies) included warlike, treacherous, and cruel, none of which appeared among the first five describing the Russians (allies); in 1966 all three had disappeared from American characterizations of the Germans and Japanese (allies) but now the Russians (no longer allies, although mere rivals than enemies) were warlike and treacherous. Data were reported for the Main-

---

"better Red" respondents admitted to a fear that a madman might start a war at any moment.[31]

land Chinese only in 1966, and predictably, they were seen as warlike, treacherous, and sly. It is interesting that "hardworking" rates high for all these countries, whether friends or enemies, for besides being true, it reinforces the images of both enemy and friend: a hardworking enemy is more to be feared, a hardworking ally is a greater source of strength.

The adjectives applied to the Japanese and Germans as wartime enemies no doubt accurately described their behavior—as they do that of all nations at war, including the United States—but it is noteworthy that Americans did not apply these adjectives to the Russians when they were allies, although the Germans undoubtedly saw them as warlike and treacherous, and that Americans now use these terms for the Russians and the Chinese although there is no direct evidence that they apply. The Russians have been talking and acting with great restraint and Chinese bellicosity is restricted to words; neither nation has shown any particular signs of treachery.

It should be added that, consistent with the general inertia of national images, shifts in the frequencies with which the different adjectives were used at different times were rather small.

The postwar change in the American view of the Japanese and the Germans followed upon their total collapse, which was inconsistent with a view of their citizens as menacing; and the United States believed it needed these nations to help combat the spread of communism. The strain toward consistency required that their citizens become good.

Thus, in American eyes the bloodthirsty, cruel, treacherous, slant-eyed, buck-toothed little Japs of the Second World War have become a highly cultivated, charming, industrious, and thoroughly attractive people. The American image of the Germans is remarkable for having swung to opposite extremes twice within scarcely half a century. Before World War I the Germans were widely admired for their industry, culture, and scientific ability; during it they became the hated "Huns"; between wars the Weimar Republic, as a democracy, was looked on with great favor; then came the loathed Nazis; and now the Germans are again admirable chaps, even though a large number of government officials, including the current Chancellor, are former Nazis. The Germans whom Americans like today are by and large the same ones they hated yesterday, liked the day before that, and hated still earlier. The last change from hostility to friendliness has, of course, been made easier by the Germans' formal abandonment of the Nazi ideology. But if they really were convinced Nazis, the change is suspect, and if most were not, they did not warrant the hatred they received at the time. In either case their belief system would not have changed as much as American perceptions of them while the two nations oscillated between the roles of enemies and allies.

8 · Preparation for Nuclear War—the Nuclear Arms Race, Deterrence, and Civil Defense

IN THE INTERNATIONAL arena, states continually struggle to increase their power and influence or to protect themselves against other states trying to achieve more power at their expense. The struggle is waged in a great variety of ways, including such peaceful ones as secret and public negotiations, international conferences at various levels, and utilization of permanent international institutions like the United Nations. All involve bargaining and other forms of persuasion, but behind them all is the universal conviction based on millennia of experience that the nation which, alone or with allies, can mobilize the greatest military power will win.

The psychological aspects of negotiation and bargaining will be examined later; our present consideration is only of nations' efforts to intimidate each other through displays of military might and martial resolution. In the past if these efforts failed and they had to fight, each entered the war with some hope of winning, but the advent of nuclear weapons has introduced the possibility of both sides' being destroyed, should there be a nuclear exchange. The possibility has not eradicated the hope of winning, but it has led nations to attempt to confine fighting to limited wars fought with conventional weapons.

More significantly, modern weapons of mass destruction have forced into military thinking the new concept of weapons constructed for the purpose of preventing rather than winning certain types of war. The central power conflict between the major nuclear powers—the United States and the Soviet Union—currently is in the form of a competitive accumulation of arms that each views as the only way to forestall aggression by the other.

Unfortunately, unless nations stop building nuclear arsenals a major nuclear exchange seems inevitable—and the only questions are how and when it will be precipitated. It is safe to make this flat statement because nothing is more certain and inexorable than the law of chance. Present policies involve a continuing risk of nuclear war; the longer the risk continues, the greater the probability of war; and if the probability continues long enough, it approaches certainty. Despite its professed aims, therefore, I believe that the policy of deterrence, including civil defense, should be viewed as an aspect of preparation for war.

As far as can be foreseen, two paths to a nuclear holocaust are the most probable. It may be the final step in a series of small wars between non-nuclear nations that have involved nuclear powers more and more deeply, until finally one or the other believes it can do nothing except to press the button. These could start in Rhodesia or South Africa, where local racial struggles could expand to a racial war involving all of Africa, or in the Middle East, as the major nations line up behind Egypt or Israel; the United States and the Soviet Union may presently be in the middle stages of such a process in Vietnam. Alternatively, a nuclear holocaust may reflect the sudden failure of deterrence —that is, one of the powers, mistakenly led to believe that the other is about to strike, thinks it will have more chance of survival if it seizes the initiative.

General nuclear war will come in either case at the end of a period of intensifying mutual hostility and emotional tension that increases the chances for accident or failure of judgment.

PSYCHOLOGICAL PITFALLS OF DETERRENCE

Deterrence strategies are intended to achieve a posture that without heightening international tensions or provoking the adversary into further arming, clearly signals determination to retaliate if he attacks.* Once this happy state of affairs has been achieved, the argument goes, nations could proceed gradually toward disarmament.

Inherent in policies of deterrence, unfortunately, are components that aggravate tensions and lead to a permanent state of instability, creating irresistible pressures for weapons proliferation. The more widely nuclear and other genocidal weapons are diffused, the greater the degree of randomness introduced into the situation. The resulting heightened emotional tension is further increased by the fact that as long as "defense" really means "retaliation," a distinction cannot be maintained between offensive and defensive weapons. The Russians insisted that the missiles they tried to install in Cuba were defensive, but the United States certainly reacted to them as if they were offensive; the United States claimed that similar missiles it had installed in nations bordering the Soviet Union were defensive, a view the Russians did not seem to share.

The strategy of deterrence relies on the rationality of the opponent, and its success depends on the deterrer's ability to convince his adversary that an attempt to gain his objective would cost more than it is worth, and that the cost to the deterrer of applying the deterrent would be less than conceding the objective. Emotional tension impedes this type of rational calculation of relative costs and gains, increasing the likelihood that deterrence would fail in a crisis.

---

* The psychologically ideal deterrent might be just strong enough to deter the enemy but not strong enough to be an adequate reason for his being deterred, thereby inducing him to find his own reasons for doing as the deterrer desired. (See Chapter 5, pp. 69ff.)

Two other destabilizing features of deterrence—the problem of credibility and the pressure toward research and development —require more extended comment.

The Basic Paradox—How to Make the Incredible Credible

Since strategic nuclear weapons can have only one purpose— deterring their use by other nuclear powers by threatening to use them oneself—the nuclear powers are in the predicament of trying to convince each other that they are spending huge sums to build weapons that they would never use unless their purpose had failed. This paradox leads to the kind of double-think well illustrated by the following news release:

> Adm. Arleigh A. Burke, Chief of Naval Operations, told the crew of 100 (of the nuclear-powered submarine "George Washington") in a radio message they will have proved the deterrent value of their task only "if the need to fire your missiles never arises."
>
> He added that if the need to fire should arise, "your ship and the missiles it carries will contribute to the salvation of civilization, for you man the most powerful weapons system ever devised." [1]

Similarly, the statement of a high government official some years ago implied the absurdity that to defend human dignity and freedom we must be prepared to risk wiping out Western civilization, if not mankind: "credible deterrence in the nuclear age lies in being prepared to face the consequences if deterrence fails—up to and including all out nuclear war." [2]

In short, each nuclear power is faced with the extraordinary task of convincing the other that in a showdown it would prefer a nuclear exchange to yielding, while at the same time knowing, and knowing that the other knows, that after a nuclear exchange each would probably be worse off than if it had yielded. Thus, the problem posed by the policy of nuclear deterrence is how to make credible an essentially incredible threat.

Since in all mutual threat situations the worst thing one side can do is show irresolution or weakness, because this stimulates the other to increase his pressure, each side seeks to intimidate the other while simultaneously demonstrating that it cannot be intimidated. The more the threat's inherent incredibility, the greater the need to make this posture convincing, leading the United States and Russia to indulge in essentially irrational gestures in the effort to demonstrate their resoluteness.

Two examples may serve to illustrate this point. After Russia's verbally belligerent reaction to the U-2 incident in April, 1960, a House Appropriations Committee subcommittee reauthorized previously canceled funds for a nuclear-powered bomber, giving the reason that it would be a psychological mistake not to do so. What they had in mind is only conjecture, but it is reasonable to suppose that the counter-threat response was an attempt to show the Russians that their bluster did not intimidate the United States. In any case, no more has been heard of the nuclear-powered bomber. Psychological motives must also have contributed to Russia's building and detonating a 50-odd-megaton bomb. Expert opinions lead to the conclusion that from a strictly military standpoint, the same resources invested in a number of smaller bombs would have made more sense; in addition, in announcing its detonation, Khrushchev said, "We will not be intimidated."

A reviewer of two biographies of President Kennedy states that in his dealings with Russia, he was preoccupied with the need to avoid giving the *appearance* of weakness, and that many of his moves can be interpreted in this way. One of his main reasons for resuming atmospheric tests after the Russians did (which his advisers had told him were not militarily essential) was that he feared that the Soviets would be likely to attribute to weakness rather than good will a decision not to do so. Similarly, he regarded it as vital to force Russia to remove her missiles from Cuba, even though their presence would not have markedly changed the military balance of power (which depended on the ICBMs in both countries) because "it would have appeared to, and appearances contribute to reality." [3]

If pushed to its extreme, this logic asserts that the effectiveness of deterrence depends entirely on the adversary's belief in the opponent's weapons and will to use them. Cardboard ICBMs would be as effective as real ones if the enemy believed that they were real and would be used under certain provocations.

The Impetus to Weapons Research and Development

If all nuclear powers were content to accept being deterred by each others' stockpiles, some stability might conceivably be achieved. But each nation is impelled to try to free its own hands by simultaneously developing a defense that will escape the adversary's deterrence by intercepting his missiles and an attack that will keep him deterred by penetrating his defenses. Each contestant is spurred on by fear that the other might succeed even temporarily in the same endeavor and thereby achieve an opportunity for a knockout blow without danger of successful retaliation.

The devotion of the nuclear powers' major scientific and technological resources to weapons research and development has resulted in a rate of innovation vastly more rapid than ever before. The state of the art in the past was such that there were never major revolutions in weaponry more than once in a generation. Today the development of weapons partakes of the general acceleration of technological advance, with the result that in the two decades since Hiroshima there have been three weapons revolutions—the atom bomb, the hydrogen bomb, and the guided missile—and more are predicted for the near future.[4]

The runaway development of weapons technology may create the chief danger of a major nuclear exchange, for if either side believed itself or its adversary to be on the verge of a major breakthrough in attack or defense, *both* would be strongly tempted to launch a pre-emptive strike. Nation A, fearing that Nation B had achieved or was about to achieve a decisive advantage, would be strongly tempted to strike before Nation B could exploit it; Nation B would be tempted to strike while it had a chance or more probably because it feared that Nation A might strike in fear that it would do so.[5]

Self-Perpetuating Features of Deterrence

Despite the built-in sources of instability in mutual deterrence, it is possible that the power of the United States and the Soviet Union to inflict huge destruction on each other has had a stabilizing effect on the international scene—there has been no major nuclear exchange so far, and the prospect of one may have prevented the escalation of the smaller struggles in which they have been directly or indirectly involved. On the other hand, in the past, even without nuclear deterrence, some intervals between major wars have been longer than the time elapsed since the end of World War II.

All programs designed to prevent an event from occurring have properties that tend to perpetuate them after they are no longer necessary. The resulting major psychological problem arises because the programs provide no way of determining whether the action supposedly being deterred would have occurred in the absence of the deterrent, or if a threat that existed when the deterrent was established has ceased to exist.

Deterrence and Aversive Conditioning

In an important respect deterrence resembles aversive conditioning—teaching an animal to perform an act to avoid an undesirable stimulus. Animals must first actually experience the stimulus in order to learn to forestall it; humans need only imagine it. For example, a dog taught to press a lever every five minutes to avoid an electric shock will continue to press the lever at just under five-minute intervals almost indefinitely after the shock has been turned off—that is, by continuing to forestall the shock, he cannot discover that it no longer exists. The deterrent acts in somewhat the same way, for it is based on the assumption that the other side would attack if there were no deterrent. Many hard-headed and well-informed students of foreign affairs are convinced that Russia's occupation of the satellite countries and her other belligerent acts were responses to fear of the West, not precursors of an intended attack on Western Europe, but the United States could find out for certain only by removing the threat of retaliation, and this it is afraid to do.

Deterrence, Commitment, and the
Strain toward Consistency

Unnecessary deterrents are maintained not only because of continuing fear of a no longer existing threat, but equally or more important, because of the need to justify one's act by believing in its efficacy. When someone does something to prevent an undesired consequence, he is strongly motivated to regard its non-appearance as evidence for the correctness of his action, for if it really was unnecessary, it would have been foolish. There is an old story of a man who, when found busily tearing up newspapers and scattering the pieces about in a railway car, was asked what he was doing. He replied, "I'm keeping the elephants away." To the observation that there didn't seem to be any elephants about, he answered, "You see, it's working already!"

The greater the commitment to deterrent action, furthermore, the greater the reluctance to abandon it—once a belief has been made the basis for a public act, admission of error would be humiliating, so the leader or nation clings to it all the more strongly. That public approval of a policy rises after it has been put into effect is a regular finding of public opinion polls. At this writing this has been true in the United States with respect to sending large numbers of ground forces to Vietnam and to bombing Hanoi, both of which were strongly opposed before they occurred.

This can be seen as another manifestation of the strain to consistency. If actions deviate from beliefs, one or the other must yield; often it is the belief. One starts doing something under external compulsion or on the basis of an erroneous judgment, and then the fact of his doing it becomes evidence that it must be right.*

---

* Modern totalitarian regimes have exploited this phenomenon by requiring that their citizens continually behave as if they approve the system. It is not enough to avoid open dissent: they must march, demonstrate, attend mass meetings, and otherwise prove their support —a striking example was the compulsory Nazi greeting "Heil Hitler." For anti-Nazis, the contrast between their enforced public behavior and secret beliefs set up strong dissonance, and sometimes the beliefs

If a course of action has been embarked upon in response to a perceived threat, the greater the commitment to it and the sacrifices made in its behalf, the more its correctness must be defended. The very costliness of the nuclear deterrent thus becomes a strong motive for believing in the reality of the danger it is built to prevent.

The ultimate cost of deterrence to society as a whole has been a gain for certain of its influential segments. Deterrence has increased the wealth and influence of the American military establishment and that segment of the economy dependent on it, and since their position and affluence depend on the reality of the communist threat, they have a strong vested interest in continually affirming and even magnifying it. Similar vested interests in deterrence have presumably developed in the Soviet Union.

Deterrence as a Self-fulfilling Prophecy

Even if the threat of nuclear attack were originally nonexistent, the dynamics of the deterrence process would generate a belief in its reality, and eventually make the threat real. This irony reflects the operation of a self-fulfilling prophecy,[7] a familiar concept worth considering in some detail. Human behavior is a process of interaction—one person's acts influence another's, which in turn influence his—but actions depend in part on expectations, and these affect what actually occurs. Sometimes they lead to actions that prevent their realization. If everybody expects the beach to be too crowded on a Sunday, for example, they will all avoid it and the beach will be empty. In the area of our interest, a similar self-disconfirming expectation that a nuclear weapon would go off accidentally led to intensive efforts to improve their safety devices, thereby reducing the danger of accident. Conversely, some prophecies are self-fulfilling. The predictions of depositors in 1929 that their banks would fail, for example, led them to withdraw their funds, bringing about the very catastrophe they had expected would occur.

---

yielded.[6] An effective component of Chinese thought reform was its insistence that its victims continually defend the communist system and express their allegiance to communism.

A vivid and hopeful example of a self-fulfilling prophecy has been the change in hospital patients' behavior resulting from changed expectations of psychiatrists. For many years psychiatrists expected patients in mental hospitals to be violent and unmanageable, so they put them in isolation rooms, locked them in chairs, and wrapped them in strait jackets—and sure enough, the patients were violent and unmanageable. Recently psychiatrists have changed their prophecy and expected mental patients to be able to control themselves, and the patients have fulfilled these expectations.*

Deterrence policies grow out of mutual distrust and increase it every step of the way. In an effort to counteract the other's supposed hostile intentions each side acts in such a way as to confirm the other's fears and thereby his hostility. Because the United States fears Russian attack, it rings Russia with nuclear bases, which increase Russia's fear that the United States will attack it, and so it tries to plant missiles in Cuba as a deterrent, which only serves to confirm American fears of Russian hostility and treachery. Enemies finally become what they imagined each other to be, whether they started out that way or not; some enemies are warlike and treacherous to begin with, but all become so in time. Despite an undoubtedly genuine distaste for this sort of thing, the United States has performed its full share of skullduggery in the back alleys of the world, has broken its solemn treaties (as in the invasion of the Dominican Republic), and has murdered the enemy on as large a scale as any other nation, perhaps larger. None of these actions indicate that the United States is more wicked than other nations—in fact, Americans

---

* The administrator of an admission ward in a Naval hospital created strong group expectations that patients would not become violent and that restraint would never be necessary; of nearly a thousand patients admitted over a ten-month period, not a single one had to be ordered to be restrained or isolated.[8] Though tranquilizing drugs facilitated the change, it was by no means due solely to their direct influence on patients, but lay also in the change brought about in the staff's expectations of how patients would behave. Moreover, in an earlier century, long before these drugs, mental patients behaved as well as they do today because their physicians expected them to and treated them accordingly.

generally deplore such actions if they penetrate the domestic information filter. All nations are forced to be wicked by the dynamics of international conflict.

DETERRENCE AND THE GAME OF "CHICKEN"

The painful urgency of the dilemmas of deterrence coupled with the fascination of the intellectual problems it presents have mobilized the analytic efforts of experts in many fields. Games theorists, systems analysts, historians, economists, political scientists, and military analysts have produced a vast literature exploring every conceivable combination of weapons systems, how to survive in various hypothesized post-attack environments, and the like. Much of the literature is recondite and no one knows just which parts of it are most relevant to the actual predicament.[9]

Fortunately, beneath all the complexities and uncertainties of deterrence, a few relevant psychological principles are discernible that apply to types of conflict termed "mixed-motive games."[10] The antagonists are interdependent—each player's moves depend partly on what his opponent does, and while the interests of the antagonists coincide in some respects, they differ in others. On the international scene, each nation's acts are partly determined by what the others do; they have a common interest in avoiding nuclear war, but conflicting interests with respect to specific issues. Analysis of mixed-motives games also applies to negotiation and bargaining, but in this chapter only their relevance to deterrence will be considered.

Because it resembles the nuclear arms race, it is instructive to examine "Chicken," the mixed-motive game involving threat: with their gangs and girl friends looking on, two young men in cars head for each other at high speed on an open road, each straddling the white line in the middle; the one who swerves first to avoid collision loses.[11] Chicken is based entirely on mutual threat. The victor is the driver who intimidates his opponent, and if neither can do this—if deterrence fails—they crash. Their common interest in avoiding this outcome creates such possibilities for collaboration as working out a signal at which they swerve simultaneously and thereby avoid both disaster and defeat. The basic resemblance of Chicken to the arms race is obvious, but two important differences should be noted: it lacks the destabilizing effects of technological advance; and since it involves individuals, it does not encompass those aspects of international conflict that depend on relations between leaders and groups. The first of these problems has been discussed earlier in this chapter, and we shall come to the second in Chapter 9.

In games of chance like poker or roulette the odds for any given outcome are predictable, but in Chicken, as in international conflict, the amount of unpredictability is itself unpredictable. The unpredictable elements involve not only the drivers' intentions but the condition of their cars; and if each carries passengers, one might jog the driver's elbow at a crucial moment, or scream, or reach for the brake. In international affairs the complexity within each country of the decision-making process and the transmission of the decision to its final executor through bureaucratic channels involving human and electronic communications, as well as uncertainties in the command and control of weaponry, introduce considerable randomness—a randomness, moreover, whose amount fluctuates from moment to moment.

The element of unpredictability in Chicken and an arms race means that both involve competitive risk-taking. Since victory depends only partly on superior skill, and such qualities as courage and resolve or even recklessness are more important, the participants' behavior will lead their opponents, friends, and bystanders, to draw conclusions about their characters—it takes two *not* to play. If a person refuses to accept another's challenge without a valid excuse, he has lost—he has tacitly agreed that the challenger is braver than he, and has encouraged others to challenge him in the future. The United States has given reasons for fighting in Vietnam that fit this formulation closely: it claims that if it had refused to go into Vietnam, the communists would have been encouraged to try similar tactics elsewhere, and that the faith of those nations who rely on the United

States to maintain their independence, as well as the faith of its allies in its determination to resist communist aggression, would have decreased.

Avoiding the game is not as difficult if both parties see themselves as having been trapped into it against their own inclinations by "fate" or the maneuvers of a third party. Under these circumstances there is a better chance that they might find ways of collaborating to avoid playing the game but without loss of face for either. It is to be hoped that the nuclear arms race more closely resembles this state of affairs than does Vietnam.

Because of their built-in uncertainties, Chicken and international conflict both involve the protagonists in attempts to outguess the other. Each bases his conclusion as to what the other will do in part on how he thinks the other perceives his own intentions, leading to an infinite regress. In Chicken, driver A's decision on when to swerve is based on his estimate of when B will do so, based on A's impression of what B thinks A will do, and so on, until the whole calculation vanishes in a haze of uncertainty, intensifying the anxiety produced by the mutual threat.

Each driver's estimate of the other's intentions depends in part on objective appraisal of their relative capabilities, and capability involves components of attack and defense. If one has a jeep and the other a VW, unless the latter is a consummate bluffer, it is clear who will swerve first, since the jeep can do more damage and is more resistant to damage than the VW. If both were to drive VWs but one wore a crash helmet and padding, the credibility of his intention not to swerve first would be increased.

If neither driver knew for sure just how sturdy and powerful the other's car was and if each was also trying to strengthen his own up to the moment of the contest, estimation of relative capabilities would then be too full of uncertainties to be decisive. More weight would obviously be placed on each driver's ability to bluff and intimidate on the one hand and accurately to appraise his opponent's intentions on the other, thereby increasing emotional tension in both. This is more analogous to the nuclear arms race. When a player's capabilities are not obviously superior, he may be able to intimidate his opponent by referring to games he has won previously—the ability to point to a series of earlier victories is a clear psychological advantage.

It is harder to make credible a threat that has never been used, like the threat of a massive nuclear strike, and in such circumstances nations increase the credibility of their threats by responding harshly to acts analogous to those the threat is aimed at deterring. The atom bombings of World War II and the use of napalm in Vietnam probably add to the credibility of America's nuclear deterrent.

Finally, a contestant in a mixed-motive game can sometimes strengthen his position relative to his opponent by tying his own hands. The rationale behind this paradox is that the strategy of deterrence relies on the rationality and prudence of the person being deterred, and since he is simultaneously relying on your rationality to deter you, if you can convince him that you are more reckless than he, you may gain an advantage. One may have to appear a little mad in order to make deterrence credible.

In Chicken one driver could successfully convey this impression by arranging for the other to see him throw the steering wheel out of his car after the game starts, forcing on the other the last clear chance of avoiding disaster. Analogously, since it would be irrational to order a retaliatory nuclear attack after one's own country has been desolated, and since the enemy may count on this to restrain the leader of the devastated country from giving such an order, deterrence theorists have toyed with the idea of making retaliation automatic and irrevocable.

A less extreme and more plausible way of creating a situation in Chicken in which the last clear chance to yield rests with the opponent arises from the possibility of exploiting the large element of uncertainty. Thus, if one contestant used a car with considerable play in the steering wheel or unreliable brakes, or took along as passengers the most emotionally unstable members of his gang, perhaps crowding three into the front seat with him, the other would be under pressure not to wait too long before swerving because the first might not be able to swerve in time even if he wanted to. Analogously, going into a state of full-combat alert—that is, removing safety catches from nuclear weapons in a crisis—adds to the threat by increasing the chances that a missile will go off inadvertently.

Since uncertainty inhibits action, increasing the element of uncertainty in one's own behavior may increase the opponent's caution and indecision. This works both ways, unfortunately, reducing the opponent's ability to make a firm decisive move but simultaneously heightening his emotional tension, lessening his control of his own behavior, and thereby increasing the general instability of the situation.

Chicken and current deterrence policies are similar in important respects. In formal terms, both are mixed-motive games for very high stakes involving reciprocal threats and with a large but unspecifiable element of uncertainty. This puts a premium on outguessing the opponent as well as on trying to increase one's actual offensive and defensive strength and to present a greater appearance of strength and resoluteness. Each player's strategy is based on the assumption that his opponent's will be based on rational, prudent calculations, but that he can convince the opponent that he is more reckless—an aspect that becomes particularly important when, as in the nuclear arms race, the threat of precipitating mutual annihilation is not rationally credible.

DEFENSIVE COMPONENTS OF DETERRENCE—
ANTI-MISSILE MISSILES AND SHELTERS

So far we have dwelt mainly on the intimidating aspect of deterrence—the effort to prevent another country from attacking one's own by threatening to destroy it. The success of such a threat depends on its credibility, and one set of measures for increasing this is to convince the opponent that our side is more foolhardy.

But a better way to preserve the credibility of deterrence would be to build an effective defense against his weapons, so that our side could survive his retaliatory nuclear strike if we had to make good our threat. An effective defense system, moreover, would reduce tension by diminishing the fear of another nuclear power's surprise attack or his opportunities for nuclear blackmail—that is, it would make the threat of nuclear attack less effective. Such considerations may lie behind both the U.S.S.R.'s apparent decision in 1966 to deploy anti-missile missiles around its larger cities and the growing pressure in the recent decision of the United States to embark on a multibillion-dollar anti-missile program.

Defensive measures have an active and a passive component: the anti-missile missile and shelters to protect from the blast, fire, and fallout of nuclear explosions. Neither is much use without the other, and certain psychological considerations strongly suggest that both are unworkable.

The Anti-Missile Missile Mirage

Since there is no upper limit to the potential power of a nuclear attack, it would seem that building anti-missile missiles would only impel the enemy to increase the size of his attacking force and that the attacker would always have the last word. American proponents of a massive anti-missile program agree that this is theoretically correct but pin their hopes on building so extensive and effective a defensive system that the cost of building enough nuclear missiles to overcome it would be prohibitive for other nations.[12] Perhaps, but considering human ingenuity the many ways of delivering nuclear warheads, and the decreasing cost of missile production, this seems a rather shaky hope, especially since the United States is prone to underestimate other nations' technological capacities and the amount of sacrifice they are willing to make.

There are two major psychological obstacles to the creation of an effective active defense to nuclear weapons. First, as a result of the fantastic pace of weapons innovation, defense systems are obsolete almost before the ink is dry—Sage and Nike-Zeus, for example, were obsolete even before they were fully installed. Furthermore, since the designer of a defense cannot start work on it until he has some idea of the nature of the attack, he starts a lap behind the attacker.

But the main psychological reason for skepticism about the anti-missile missile is that the very mental processes that devise defenses against a weapon simultaneously devise means of circumventing it. As two leading nuclear scientists put it: "Work on defensive systems turns out to be the best way to promote invention of the penetration aids that nullify them," [13] and one Secretary of Defense observed that our missiles could penetrate our own defenses. No defense against a weapon has ever been very good, although this hasn't mattered too much because of the inefficiency of past weapons—after five hundred years no one has devised a very good defense against the bullet, but one bullet can kill only one person; British air defense gained the victory even though no more than 10 per cent of the Luftwaffe was intercepted. But since a single nuclear warhead can wipe out a large city, a useful defense would have to be virtually 100 per cent effective.

If these considerations are valid, nations will continue to be able to build missile systems that can penetrate each other's defenses. And the efforts to achieve a defense against the other's missiles will keep the deterrence system from stabilizing while constantly increasing its cost.

Psychosocial Effects of Shelter Building and Civil Defense Drills

Since some enemy missiles would be bound to penetrate any anti-missile defense and some of the defending nation's missiles might explode over its own territory, an anti-missile program would have to be coupled with a large-scale civilian shelter program.

Most proponents of such programs agree that while no society could survive the largest conceivable nuclear attack, a shelter program might save lives that would otherwise have been lost in the event of a smaller attack. Shelters are said to be like insurance, but this attractive-sounding analogy is weak in several respects. An effective shelter program offers protection. while insurance, which merely indemnifies against loss, does not—life insurance does not postpone death and a fire insurance policy will not put out a fire. On the other hand, insurance does not create new dangers, nor does it ordinarily increase the probability of the event against which it is taken out (although, to be sure, fire insurance sometimes tempts a person to burn his property). On both counts, however, serious doubts have arisen about shelter programs from some experiments, observations, and speculations of behavioral scientists—although any definitive answers are precluded by the enormous number of unknowns involved.

Even the modest efforts undertaken so far to afford protection against a nuclear strike may have adverse effects. Although it is indeterminate, there is some emotional cost to schoolchildren subjected to civilian defense drills.[14] These differ psychologically from fire drills in their implication to the children of indefinite separation from their families, and to the extent that they are aware of this, it is particularly stressful, as the study of children evacuated from London during the blitz has shown.[15] The possible emotional toll of civil defense drills would be a small price to pay if they enhanced prospects for survival in the event of a nuclear attack. But most such drills are exercises in futility. Children march to a part of the school as far away from windows as possible where there may be some protection from fallout but where there are neither provisions nor equipment for the necessarily long stay following a nuclear strike. An increasing number of schools, at least in Baltimore, have shelter areas equipped and stocked for a two-week stay, but none protect against blast and fire, the main hazards of a nuclear attack on a city.

Civil defense drills for schoolchildren are one aspect of a program which, if drill became reality, could set citizen against citizen and favor some groups and classes over others. These evils were highlighted by the home shelter program proposed by President Kennedy in 1961—who can forget the man standing outside his shelter, ready to shoot others who tried to enter?*

---

* In 1961 civil defense officials in some California and Nevada towns were reported as having advised the local citizenry to arm themselves against refugees from neighboring areas who might try to seek sanctuary in case of nuclear war. Although their authenticity was later questioned, the fact that the reports appeared to be widely believed indicates the state of mind at the time.[16]

American society has never really faced up to the vast changes in social organization that would be necessary if any shelter program were to have a reasonable chance of success, for merely to get people into them quickly would require regimentation to a degree far beyond anything America has experienced. The carnage that can ensue after someone stumbles on the exit steps when there is a sudden shower during a baseball game or when a theater exit door sticks during a fire scare would be multiplied many times. Actually, the shelter system might be feasible only if at all times a portion of the population lived in shelters, in rotation. And the suggestion was not entirely facetious that they should be reserved for honeymooning couples, so that at least some of the breeding population at any given time would escape destruction.[17]

The general state of confusion about shelters a few years ago was illustrated by findings of an interview study of eighty employees in a veterans hospital. The county's official fallout shelter areas could accommodate only 10 per cent of the population, yet 65 to 70 per cent of the employees planned to head for them although, according to the author's estimate, even the most realistic had perhaps one chance in four of finding adequate shelter. All but one said they would sanction killing of persons to prevent overcrowding, from which the author concludes: "Citizens in shelters *will kill to stay in* and others . . . *will kill to get in*. . . . The struggle for control of public shelters may be the only nuclear war area where killing would occur on other than an impersonal, scientific basis." [18] There is little reason to think that attitudes have changed.

An interesting subsidiary observation was that one aspect of the interview, reading survivors' accounts of Hiroshima, precipitated many symptoms of emotional strain such as stammering, sweating, headaches, and anger which in some respondents lasted the rest of the day. One wonders how they would fare in an actual holocaust.

Pamphlets have been prepared by the United States government to win public support for shelter programs. In a study to determine the pamphlets' effects on a group of eleventh-grade schoolchildren, half filled out a questionnaire about nuclear war without reading the pamphlet ("Ten for Survival"), the other half after reading it. Its persuasiveness is suggested by the finding that about two-thirds of those who had read it but only about one-fifth of the controls agreed strongly that a shelter program might save most of the lives that would otherwise be lost in a nuclear war. For our purposes, however, the interesting finding is that the pamphlet never mentioned nuclear war, yet with varying degrees of certainty almost all of the readers (compared with only about 60 per cent of the controls) believed that nuclear war would occur, probably reasoning that if war were not expected, the government would not go to the trouble of distributing the pamphlet.[19]

If reading about shelters increases the expectation that nuclear war will occur, so does actually building them. The flurry in 1961 over home fallout shelters was used to good advantage by some alert social scientists who interviewed shelter-builders and non-builders about their attitudes. One study compared the answers of eighty builders and eighty non-builders drawn from respondents to a large national survey and matched with respect to home ownership, educational level, and estimated income.[20] The two groups held similar views and were equally well informed about the hazards of nuclear war, but they differed in interesting ways: the shelter-builders relied on military strength as the major deterrent to war, while the non-builders favored diplomacy and foreign aid; the builders believed that America's position relative to the rest of the world had become stronger during the preceding year, but the non-builders that it had become weaker; finally, the builders believed that shelters would reduce the probability of war but also felt that war was more of a certainty than did non-builders. Note the inconsistency: if, as the shelter-builders believe, military strength deters war and the country has become militarily stronger, why is war more certain to come? Again, the answer probably can be found in the strain toward consistency—the need to justify oneself, to keep beliefs and acts in line: having built a shelter as protection in the event of war, one must believe that war is probable. A subsidiary finding along the same lines was that the shelter-builders were critical of the dilatoriness of local civil defense officials, as if they wanted more effort spent on getting other people to build shelters.*

These findings offer no comfort to those holding the view that a shelter program, as an implicit constant reminder of nuclear war's catastrophic consequences, would make people less likely to risk it. If anything, it supports the contrary view that even if it made the probable effects of nuclear war more vivid, such a program would increase the likelihood of nuclear war by strengthening expectations of it. In this connection a public opinion poll found no relation between awareness of the consequences of nuclear war and the propensity to endorse aggressive policies.[21]

The available scraps of information suggest that Americans have neither a real awareness of the requirements of an adequate civil defense program nor, insofar as they have thought about or actually built shelters, a lessened willingness to risk a nuclear exchange. And the program has had a socially disruptive effect.

Life in Shelters

In the event of a nuclear attack those able to reach shelters would have to live in them until the radioactive fallout level had lessened to a point that permitted survival on the earth's surface. Conditions of life would be so unprecedented that no one can be sure how the shelter-dwellers would fare. Londoners' reactions to their brief sojourns in underground shelters during World War II air raids, for example, cast no light on the psychic effects of a long and indeterminate period of underground living, under conditions of high emotional tension and with the prospect of eventually emerging to an environment changed beyond recognition.

Crowded together for an indefinite period in a confined space under conditions of mounting discomfort, those in community shelters would be for the most part strangers to each other or

* This is similar to the finding that when a prophecy of the world's end is not confirmed, those who made the prophecy try to make converts as a means of bolstering their own faith. See Chapter 9, pp. 176–78.

fragments of families (even for those with family shelters the odds are slim that the whole family would be present and could get in at the time of an alert). To these stresses would be added the anxiety and grief induced by separation and by fear of radiation sickness. An imperceptible threat or danger—like ionizing radiation—is particularly anxiety-producing; and radiation sickness, real or imagined, causes vomiting and diarrhea. Added to these miseries and anxieties, the shelter-dwellers would face uncertainties as to when they could safely emerge and anticipations of returning to a world whose desolation was indeterminate.

No real-life or experimental situation has ever remotely resembled this combination of stresses. Isolation is known to reduce a person's capacity to adapt to his environment, and if prolonged, even to precipitate psychotic states in some,[22] but most shelter-dwellers would not be alone. Experiments on shelter living have used volunteers, who have lived in a shelter in no danger and for predetermined periods of confinement. For example, one family—parents and two boys in their late teens—spent thirteen days in a fallout shelter; they were in constant contact with a local radio station, and the wording of one passage in the report implies that their words were broadcast, indicating that psychological isolation was far from complete. Yet even under these relatively ideal conditions, they became increasingly depressed, and on emerging, "the family mood . . . [was] characterized by a depressive bleakness and a diminution of vitality." [23] Since there was also some disruption of spatial perception, it may not have been entirely coincidental that the father had two automobile accidents in the weeks immediately following. There were all kinds of equipment breakdowns in the shelter, the worst being the overflow of the chemical toilet, which they managed to control with the plastic water containers. Another family—parents and three children, two of preschool and one of grammar school age—endured two weeks of shelter living without any apparent adverse psychological effects.[24] Reactions would vary widely, of course, depending on special circumstances and adaptability to stress. But if some families showed adverse emotional reactions under relatively favorable conditions, many more would do so under the actual conditions of shelter living.

One study relevant to community shelters used self-selected "families" in four groups of thirty individuals who lived in a community shelter for one or two weeks. The major reported finding was that the absence of adequate leadership led to a breakdown in established standards of conduct; but good leadership was able to cope with "sleeping difficulties, sexual tensions, hostility to other shelter occupants, claustrophobic reactions and depressions." [25] The researcher concludes that the serious problem areas are competent management, provision for sleep, and minimization of conflict over social, moral, and ethical values— although how the latter would be accomplished if members of different classes and races found themselves sharing a shelter can only be conjectured. Shelter living would open a Pandora's box of psychological stresses that these studies have barely tapped.

Psychosocial Effects of a Nuclear Strike

In weighing the effectiveness of civil defense, it is necessary to evaluate the survival prospects of those who eventually emerge from the shelters. The effects of a nuclear strike on the physical and biological environment would be compounded by the concomitant psychosocial disruption.

Among the many historical accounts of catastrophes, the Black Death of thirteenth-century Europe is comparable to a nuclear strike in the deaths it caused, although it was not as sudden and did not also destroy the physical environment. According to one historian, "the horror and confusion . . . brought general demoralization and social breakdown. [The period after the crisis was marked by] a mood of misery, depression and anxiety." [26]

Many other disasters—earthquakes, fires, floods—have been studied, and one symposium reached the conclusion that social disorganization is generally greater, the more rapid the disastrous force, the shorter the period of forewarning, the less familiar and less clearly perceived the disaster agent, and the greater its physical destructiveness and duration[27]—a conclusion supported by the immediate psychosocial effects of the atomic attacks on Hiroshima and Nagasaki. Though tiny by today's standards, they possessed the elements of surprise, speed of destruction, and unclarity of the disaster agent, and they detroyed social organization, incentive, and morale.[28, 29] Both rapidly received outside help in rebuilding both the physical cities and their social organization. But where would this aid come from after a widespread nuclear attack?

Since unlike other disasters, an atomic attack has continuing long-term effects, it permanently changes the lives of the survivors. A psychiatrist who interviewed survivors of Hiroshima seventeen years later has written a perceptive account of their enduring psychological damage.[30, 31] Vague knowledge of radiation effects, an increase in leukemia and other blood disease deaths, and an increase in cancer deaths have created in the survivors "a permanent encounter with death"; in addition, they have been forced to assume an unwanted identity—that of *"hibakusha"* ("survivors")—that sets them apart. A largely unjustified fear of genetic effects in their offspring discourages many from marrying or, if they are married, from having children, and handicaps those who wish to marry in their search for a spouse—in short, they are regarded by themselves and their society as having been somehow contaminated. They also suffer from guilt at having survived and from other unpleasant psychological states. One brief encounter with an atom bomb has permanently damaged them—more spiritually, perhaps, than physically.

Compounding these problems would be those of adjusting to a world in which familiar physical landmarks and social institutions had been drastically altered or destroyed, and there is considerable evidence from psychological studies that the loss of stable anchoring points in the environment enhances the effects of other stresses. A summary of an extensive study of American soldiers' behavior in combat states: "personality integration and the development of regularized patterns of behavior are strongly conditioned upon the existence of stable referents for activity." [32] And a clinical psychologist bases this conclusion on work with projective tests: "as the stimulus field becomes more and more unstructured—there is a tendency for the anxiety level to increase markedly." [33]

An experiment that initially appears to have nothing to do with civil defense may serve to illustrate this point. To study the "stability of the ego" as measured by the "autokinetic phenomenon"—the apparent movement of a point of light in a totally dark field (one, that is, without external landmarks)—the experimenter varied the degree of spatial and social anchorages in the subject's environment *before* he had to judge the light's movement. At one extreme a friendly experimenter showed him to his chair in a small room and allowed him a brief glimpse of its interior; at the other an impersonal experimenter turned the subject loose in a large pitch-black area, telling him only the direction in which he was to go, which also required him to go up and down a small flight of stairs. Even the relatively slight reduction in anchoring points produced greater apparent movement of the light and greater variation of movement between different subjects and the same subject from trial to trial, as well as a greater subjective sense of uncertainty and stress. The experimenters conclude: "As the physical and social anchorages become more unstable, more uncertain, the individual's personal bearings become more unstable, more uncertain." [34] The degree of possible extrapolation from this situation to the massive loss of anchorages and abolition in shelters and in the post-attack environment of customary life patterns is, of course, undetermined, but it is disquieting that even a small reduction of familiar landmarks produces measurable changes in personal security.

From the psychological standpoint, a civil defense shelter program, to be workable at all, would entail massive changes in social organization, and life in the shelters would be replete with emotional stresses. Many of those who finally emerged would be emotionally as well as physically ill-equipped to cope with the unpredictable stresses of the anarchic postwar environment. Civil defense might reduce casualties during the attack and the immediate post-attack periods, but the number of deaths would be far greater than is suggested by estimates based on blast, fire, radiation, starvation, and disease—for to these lethal agents would have to be added hopelessness (which can be literally fatal),[35] suicide, homicide, and panic.

Civil defense might still be worthwhile if it reduced the likelihood of a major nuclear war, but pertinent information suggests that, if anything, it would have the opposite effect. As a form of insurance, therefore, civil defense is a gamble whose odds are impossible to calculate but include the possibility that it would not prevent the destruction of the United States as a nation. I do not know how to weigh this unprecedented possibility against the possibilities of more optimistic outcomes, but it does not appear to have received adequate consideration by most proponents of civil defense.

IS "POSITIVE" DETERRENCE POSSIBLE?

The pessimistic conclusion to which this analysis of psychological factors in the nuclear arms race leads is that although it is motivated by the desire to prevent nuclear war, deterrence creates conditions that increasingly favor its outbreak; the process is self-aggravating and contains few features that could lead to its modification. Some hope can be placed, however, in the fact that nuclear policy is, after all, a mixed-motive game—so there are always opportunities for collaboration, if national leaders are ingenious enough to find and exploit them. And in this connection it is worth remembering that the concept of deterrence includes not only threats but also implicit assurances that if the nation being deterred refrains from certain acts, it will not be punished.[36, 37] Perhaps the assurance aspect of deterrence could be broadened to include open or tacit promises of rewards for carrying out desired actions—an example of this "positive" deterrence[38] was the sale of wheat to communist countries which tacitly encouraged them to divert some resources from arms to food. Carried further, it might be possible to devise a way to reward more rapid progress in certain internal reforms now under way in the United States and the Soviet Union which both would like to encourage in the other. The

United States, for example, would feel more comfortable if political liberties expanded more rapidly in communist countries; perhaps communist nations would feel less uneasy if the public sector of the American economy, including social and medical services, grew more rapidly.

Some encouraging possibilities for introducing into the international system rewards for actions promoting peace will be considered later, but first we must look at some psychological features of the most likely outcomes of present policies—crisis and war.

9 · Psychological Aspects of Prewar Crises and War

IT HAS BEEN possible until now to overlook important distinctions between national leaders and the nations they lead, and to treat nations as if they were people. In considering crisis and war, however, this crude level of analysis no longer suffices, for the factors that influence national leaders' decisions in these situations differ from those operating on the nation as a whole. Decisions must be based on specialized, rapidly changing information, much of which could not be understood by the average citizen even if it were accessible to him. Since the leader's personal qualities, his perceptions of the often conflicting interests of his various constituencies, the constraints and demands of his role, and the complex organizations through which information reaches him and his orders are executed all presumably affect his actions, they will be examined before considering some specific psychological aspects of crises and war.

PERSONAL QUALITIES OF LEADERS
RELEVANT TO DECISION-MAKING IN CRISES

Leaders' personalities, of course, are as varied as those of everybody else, but their achievement of power (inherited power is becoming increasingly rare) implies possession of certain personal qualities—charisma, for example, the mysterious personal magnetism that inspires loyalty and submission but defies adequate psychological analysis, possibly because it resides in the leader-follower interplay rather than wholly in the leader.

In practically all modern societies leadership positions can be gained only through a person's own persistent efforts, implying a strong drive for power in those who reach the top. The gaining of power need not be an end in itself—power can be used for any number of purposes, from the most selfish to the most altruistic. Since all human behavior has complex motives, not all necessarily fully conscious, there is no reason to think that the striving for leadership is an exception. But since power is in limited supply, it seems safe to surmise that all important leaders must have a certain degree of ruthlessness. To inspire confidence in others, moreover, they must have considerable self-confidence, at least at a superficial level.*

Leaders must have won more conflicts than they lost on the way up, or they would not have reached the top (there are always, of course, such rare exceptions as Abraham Lincoln), hence, whatever the initial basis for self-confidence, faith in their own powers and judgment would certainly have been reinforced. They must have been able simultaneously to shield their self-esteem from the effects of the failures and defeats that are the lot

---

* The apparent self-assurance of some national leaders seems to be an overcompensation for self-doubts. Maintained at the cost of considerable personal strain, great pressure may cause their façade to crack, leading to erratic behavior or even a mental breakdown—notable examples are Wilhelm II and James Forrestal. And it is perhaps worth noting that neither had to fight his way up through the ranks in which process their weaknesses might have been exposed.

of any rising leader no matter how skilled; hence, they would be expected to possess well-developed techniques for maintaining their public and private images as resolute and successful, which would also be necessary to hold their followers' allegiance in periods of adversity. Thus, national leaders would be expected to be adept at denying errors, explaining them away, or shifting blame to others. In short, they would be expected to dwell on their successes and minimize their failures to buttress their optimism about their ability to prevail in any conflict.

That leaders have generally been victorious in their domestic contests suggests that they have more than average courage, energy, and determination. Since all political conflicts involve competitive risk-taking, they probably have a high tolerance for uncertainty and a greater than average capacity to persevere in an apparently lost cause. Because of the conspiratorial aspect of politics, successful leaders must also be adept at sensing and forestalling or counteracting plots, so their suspicions of others' motives must be easily aroused, while at the same time they are probably skilled at dissembling when necessary. Leaders would be expected to be men of action rather than contemplation, more concerned with the short-term than the remote consequences of their decisions, since the path to power requires endless decisions about immediate practical issues. Although national leaders are skilled at expressing high ideals, it is safe to suspect a large underlying streak of hard-headed realism and practical shrewdness. Most are probably expert manipulators of their countries' political and bureaucratic processes.

Ruthlessness, overweening self-confidence, energy, and suspiciousness as exemplified by a Trujillo or a Sukarno would be expected to be more prominent in leaders whose countries do not have firmly established and well-defined legitimized paths to power, and whose populations are illiterate, impoverished, and embittered. As genocidal weapons spread, such leaders will pose an increasing danger because some will inevitably get into their control.

The surmise that national leaders tend to be energetic and optimistic on one hand and suspicious on the other gains tangential support from a study of democratically elected leaders in a mental hospital where patients governed themselves to some extent. The slight relationship found between how fully patients participated in the hospital's political life and how mentally healthy they were corresponds to a finding in the civilian population that the number of organizations to which a person belongs is unrelated to his mental health. Compared with the rest of the hospital population, paranoid and manic-depressive patients were over-represented in elective leadership positions,[1] probably because of the self-assurance, ebullience, and sociability of the manic, and the apparent strong self-confidence and sense of purpose of the paranoid, whose chronic suspiciousness would also make him especially able to sense his opponents' plans in time to forestall or circumvent them. The interpretation of this finding must be tempered by the recognition that the manics and paranoids probably had little competition if, as is likely, the other patients were primarily depressed, schizophrenic, or senile; the first two types tend to withdraw from social contacts, the last lacks initiative and vigor. Many political leaders show mild manic and paranoid traits which occasionally approach the pathological—Churchill, for example, whose energy was often stupendous, had frequent periods of lethargy and depression that he called "black dog";[2] Stalin's suspiciousness reached pathological proportions in his last years.

People with manic or paranoid tendencies are quick to anger, especially when opposed, but it is not clear to what extent this may affect their attitudes and behavior toward opponents, although the effect may well be greater than appears. A man can appear cool and collected while his anger is gently prodding him toward choosing harsher tactics and words, and is reducing his ability to listen to his adversary's view point or his willingness to entertain alternatives that might contribute to the latter's welfare.

I have suggested that in order to get and keep power, leaders must be concerned with maintaining their image and be willing to take risks. An interesting relationship between these two qualities was revealed by an elaborate psychological study whose subjects, hundreds of male and female undergraduates, were given a variety of tests that required risk-taking—games of chance, opportunities to bet on their skills, and the number of clues they required before hazarding a guess on the outcome of a situation. When their behavior was checked against a large number of personality variables as determined by other tests, the pertinent finding was the emergence of a relationship between anxiety, defensiveness (defined as concerned with maintaining one's image), and risk-taking. Among those who were high in both qualities and had a risk-taking bent, "to change decisions in the face of failure is to acknowledge that a risk-taking course is something less than wise. One must therefore pursue risk-taking all the more irrevocably." [3] Male subjects of this type expressed more satisfaction with their bets, when betting on their own skills, the less they won; failure caused them to increase rather than reduce their risk-taking. Conservative, anxious, and defensive subjects used failure to justify their continuing all the more rigidly in a conservative path, while those with little anxiety or defensiveness took more rational risks, expressed satisfaction or dissatisfaction appropriate to the outcome, and modified their risk-taking on the basis of the previous trial's outcome.

While most national leaders probably do not become unduly anxious or defensive in crisis situations, the disquieting implication of this study is that the exceptional ones who do have "test-anxiety" (although they may be adept at concealing it) would be apt to cling to an erroneous decision and to react to its bad consequences by becoming more reckless. The qualities which enable a person to gain power are not identical with those which enable him to exercise it wisely. The hallmark of a good leader is that he can make decisions that serve his group's best interests, even when the group opposes him. Some personal attributes that facilitate rise to leadership roles—love of adulation, personal ambition, a low suspicion threshold—may impair his judgment by leading him to reject valid criticisms or be overly swayed by the desire to be popular; they can be disastrous in times of crisis.

ASPECTS OF A LEADER'S ROLE AND POSITION
THAT MAY AFFECT HIS JUDGMENT IN CRISES

The behavior of leaders is affected not only by their personal traits but by features inherent in formal and informal aspects of their roles, the political organization and bureaucratic structures of the societies they lead, and their interaction with their constituencies. While each of these topics leads far beyond the confines of this book, certain of their aspects that bear directly on decision-making in times of crisis require brief mention.

Informal Aspects of the Leader's Role

As a leader rises he is forced to rely increasingly on others to filter and condense the information that comes to his attention, and to shield him from the innumerable pressures of his job. Because his words and acts can have such momentous consequences, he can relax only in the company of trusted intimates and thus he inevitably associates with and relies on those who are temperamentally congenial and see the world as he does. As his power increases, to these genuine friends are added others who wish to please him because their own power and position depend on his good will. Since a person's self-image is initially formed and thereafter affected by others' behavior toward him, a leader continually surrounded by agreement, deference, and praise is likely to acquire an exaggerated opinion of his own capabilities and judgment which can have subtle effects at a moment of crisis.[4]

The wisdom of any decision depends on the completeness and accuracy of the information on which it is based, and the information reaching a leader is subject to two sources of bias. Often without deliberate intent, his associates selectively emphasize what they think will please him, and he may avoid those who do not think as he does. This can be carried to extremes, as when President Wilson, using his illness as an excuse, refused to see Viscount Grey of England who had come to persuade him to make some concessions that might make entrance into the League of Nations acceptable to the Senate.

Since national leaders arrive at most decisions only after consulting with their advisors, it might be expected that this would improve the quality of the decisions and counteract those aspects of the leader's personality and built-in features of his position that could adversely affect his judgment. A group has access to more information than any one of its members, so information-weighing against an ill-advised decision would be more likely, and committee members would be reluctant to take extreme positions because of fearing to appear irresponsible or without good judgment. All extremists, as minorities, would be under pressure to conform to the majority consensus, and extreme views would tend to cancel each other. Unfortunately, this does not necessarily eliminate bias, for the quality of a group's decisions depends heavily on how their members are selected, their relations with each other, the context of their deliberations, and the ground rules under which they operate.[5]

It is impossible to explore this vast topic here, but one experiment concerning risk-taking in decision-making warrants a brief description because its findings raise doubts about the comforting assumption that group policy-making must decrease the probability of rash decisions. The subjects, male and female undergraduates in groups of six of the same sex, were given a series of dilemmas and asked to choose among ten courses of action graded according to the degree if risk involved. (For example, they were asked to advise a man with heart disease whose choices were severely curtailing his activities or submitting to an operation that would either cure or kill him.) Subjects made their choices individually, then each group of six was asked to discuss each dilemma and reach a unanimous decision; two to six weeks later they were again asked to indicate their individual choices. As compared with controls who made individual choices twice, a week apart and without any intervening discussion, the consensual decisions (both group and individually afterward) were significantly more risky.[6] A second study which confirmed these results, carried the analysis farther by showing that the "risky shift" depended solely on discussion—arrival at consensus was not necessary.[7]

Several factors might contribute to this finding, among them that risk-takers may be more active in discussion and that the affective bonds built up during discussion make it easier for each individual to "feel less than proportionally to blame when he entertains the possibility of failure of a risky decision." [8]

It is risky, of course, to draw conclusions about decisions concerning real, highly consequential alternatives made by policy-makers who are mature adults, well-acquainted with each other, from decisions about hypothetical dilemmas made by undergraduates who were strangers. But in both circumstances the participants make decisions about others' lives, not their own, and the researchers attribute the risky shift largely to the emotional bonds created by discussion which are strongly present in all ongoing policy-making groups.

Organizational Aspects of the Leader's Role

In addition to the informal pressures and constraints exerted on a national leader by his cronies and advisors, other pressures arise from the organization of the power structure of which he is a part and through which he must operate, his role's demands, and his constituents'.

All bureaucracies screen and condense the information that reaches the leader and supply the machinery through which his orders are executed. Since both functions are subject to many kinds of distortion and delay which multiply when more people are involved, the impediments thus introduced can assume crucial importance in times of crisis. In what may be a real-life example of the strategy of tying one's own hands to make the adversary back down, just before the outbreak of the First World War the Kaiser and the Tsar both asserted that they had lost control of their own military and that only the adversary's could prevent further escalation. The antagonist in any serious conflict is motivated to insist that he has no choice, as a means of transferring blame and guilt to the other, but the evidence in this case suggests that cumbersomeness and inertia of the machinery of mobilization was so great in both countries that, once set in motion, it could not be stopped without causing chaos.[9]

Other pressures and constraints lie in the requirements of a person's role which may force him into actions incompatible with his private convictions. To take a mundane example, I know a builder who must build segregated housing although he sincerely believes in integration, because in his city the alternative is to go out of business, thereby failing in his responsibilities to family, associates, and employees; he has resolved his dilemma by working hard for the passage of an open-occupancy law, so that he can act on his convictions without giving his competitors a crushing advantage. To ascend to higher spheres, Thomas Jefferson's purchase of Louisiana clearly violated the Constitution as he interpreted it. On the contemporary scene, the contradiction between Secretary McNamara's actions and certain of his public statements perhaps can be explained by the constraints of his role, which requires that he create the best possible military machine—an assignment he has carried out with unprecedented efficiency; yet there was no reason to doubt his sincerity when he said: "We still tend to conceive of national security almost solely as a vast, awesome arsenal of weaponry. Security is *not* military force—though it may involve it. . . . Security *is* development." [10]

A final set of determinants of national leaders' behavior and attitudes arise from their interaction with various audiences, at home and abroad. They may pay little attention to public opinion in reaching a decision during a crisis, but all political leaders try to mobilize popular support for their long-term policies. Present-day public opinion has influenced leaders' actions even in autocracies, and its power has been sharply enhanced by the mass media's explosive advances, especially television, and the increasing importance of a loyal population as an ingredient of national strength.

Since a popular leader must have been able for many years to express effectively his countrymen's aspirations, goals, and ideologies, he would have to be unusually cynical not to have committed himself to the views he has persistently espoused; moreover he cannot afford to be seen as less patriotic or less protective of the national interest than his rivals. Thus, although a national leader may have considerable power to change national images, he is more likely to be captivated by and to reinforce them.

Modern methods of mass communication have vastly increased the amount of interaction between a leader and his public, both domestic and foreign (the special characteristics of television and radio are also forcing changes in their communication techniques).[11] To a considerable extent in even the most democratic and pluralistic society a national leader can control the output of the mass media, enabling him to manipulate public opinion more successfully than in the past. But since public opinion looms so large in a leader's mind, how well a policy will "sell" is an important consideration in arriving at it. A national leader can learn almost continuously from public opinion polls how the public is reacting to his policies, and this may strengthen his concern—President Johnson, for example, seems to know at any moment precisely what percentage of the population in various regions supports him, suggesting that to some extent this information influences his policy choices. A modern leader's communication problems are complicated by the fact that he must try to harmonize the interests of many different, often conflicting groups, and the mass media assure that each group knows what he is saying to the others. In foreign affairs there is a further complication because his audience is the world.

In order to strengthen their position domestically, reassure themselves that they are right, and impress allies and enemies with the firmness of the nation's resolve, leaders try hard to mobilize popular support as tensions rise. Leaders and public combine in their interaction to discredit opposing voices, and dissenters' motives become increasingly suspect. For example, in December of 1965 a poll of Americans found that only one-fourth thought that individuals actively opposing United States policy in Vietnam were expressing honest disagreement with it, one-fifth had no opinion, and the remainder were evenly divided on the question's two other alternatives—that the dissenters were either carrying out communist plans or were mostly draft-dodgers.[12] It is only a short step from suspecting dissenters' motives to pressuring them overtly to fall into line. Leaders increasingly demand and get public expressions of support, and public rituals of allegiance often accompany the national anthem, the flag, and the like.

The other side of this coin is derogation of the enemy and expression of hostility and belligerence toward him in an effort to strengthen one's own resolve to intimidate him. This is reinforced by the enemy image: all his moves are hostile in intent while ours are defensive. Portrayal of the enemy in the harshest terms performs useful psychological functions domestically. It mobilizes not only aggressive but altruistic motives for the conflict, which can now be seen as the defense of hearth, home, and loved ones against a ruthless predator: "He started it!" frees both combatants' hands by relieving their guilt. All national leaders go to considerable lengths to convince themselves, or at least to convince their people, that the other party started hostilities. Even Hitler took the trouble to create an "incident" that made it appear to the Germans that the first overtly hostile act was Poland's.*

Nations might start wars in the past with openly aggressive aims bolstered by such self-justifications as the obligation to assume the white man's burden, to stamp out a heresy, or to wrest the territory of western United States from Mexico in the name of Manifest Destiny, but for a nation to admit today that its purpose in waging war is aggressive would be to commit an in-

---

* An eminent anthropologist believes that Americans find it especially necessary to convince themselves that the enemy made the first move: "For two years we have been engaged in 'National Defense'; unwilling to start anything . . . hog-tied by our own phrasing of life which forbade our starting a war. . . . And then Japan pushed the chip off [our shoulder] and we could fight; fight with a clear conscience, because we didn't start this fight. Japan did. . . . Axis propagandists have tried to make a good deal of the fact that we presented Japan with impossible terms . . . that we put the chip on our shoulder. And so we did. . . . It's an old American custom, and . . . has behind it that part of the American character which fights best when other people start pushing us around." [13]

excusable international *faux pas*. A nation now goes to war only for such "acceptable" reasons as defending itself or a friendly government against external aggression or aiding an insurgent movement battling a regime supported by another nation, a change in motivations perhaps partly attributable to constraints introduced by modern weaponry's genocidal potential.

Because a leader's audience in this age of mass communication includes the enemy as well as his own people, pronouncements that strengthen morale at home provoke the enemy to greater hostility. Leaders on each side assume that the former effect outweighs the latter, of course, but if both parties are viewed simultaneously, it is clear that their belligerent statements reinforce each other's unfavorable images, making reconciliation increasingly difficult—continual accusations of bad faith are not the best way to win someone's friendship. And the result is that in a strange way the militants on both sides are allies: the hawks reinforce the hawks; the doves, however, have not yet found a way to reinforce the doves.

An important feature of the conflict spiral is the interaction of hostile nations' leaders with each other, and with their constituencies and the adversary's public. In a well-advanced interaction process the reverberations between leaders and followers in each country, reinforced by the other's corresponding processes, as well as the general sluggishness of public opinion create obstacles to changing a belligerent policy, should the leaders wish to do so.[14]

A Psychological Motive of the Search for Allies

As an obvious means of increasing their relative powers, nations seek allies and attempt to detach them from actual or potential enemies. The search involves a psychological motivation that harks back to the discussion in Chapter 6 of the formation of the reality world which derives from interactions with others, whose opinions in certain realms are the only available criterion of validity. Thus, one way to shore up a threatened belief system is to try to win converts to it, a process strikingly illustrated by those messianic religions whose members have publicly committed themselves to a prophecy that the world would end at a certain time—a prophecy that, so far, has always proved wrong. Some of these, notably Jehovah's Witnesses, tried to win converts from their inception; others, like the Anabaptists in the sixteenth century and the Seventh Day Adventists in the nineteenth, only after the date of the prophesied disaster had passed, when, instead of disbanding, as might have been expected, they started to proselytize. A few years ago the process was observed by some social scientists when a minor cult developed in Michigan around a leader who prophesied that on a certain date there would be a worldwide upheaval accompanied by flooding of most of the United States; those who knew of this and accepted the prophet's leadership would be rescued by flying saucers. The cultists publicly announced this revelation (enabling the social scientists to become acquainted with them) and openly prepared themselves for their departure, but made very little effort to proselytize and in fact were evasive and secretive, turning away visitors and rebuffing the press. Their behavior changed abruptly after the prophecy was proven false: they developed a rationalization for the failure and tried strenuously to win converts, welcoming visitors, inviting newsmen and photographers, and telephoning press releases to the local papers and the major news services; they also made several tapes for radio broadcast and released "secret" tapes to anyone interested and to the network broadcasting stations. In sharp contrast to their previous behavior, they invited the public to a vigil. The researchers explain this change in behavior as an effort to maintain faith in the validity of their beliefs in the face of contradictory evidence by trying to get others to confirm them.[15]

It may not be too far-fetched to suggest that similar motives contribute to a leader's desire to mobilize not only domestic support but also foreign allies, especially when his policies are failing. The United States currently makes great play of the handful of small, weak, countries, largely dependent on its military and economic power, that it has succeeded in persuading, pressuring, or bribing into sending token troops to Vietnam. The moral support apparently gained from these allies by the American leaders and public is probably much more significant than their actual military contribution which is scarcely noticeable in comparison with the mammoth American investment.

DECISION-MAKING IN CRISIS:
THE OUTBREAK OF WORLD WAR I

Crises, one of whose essential features is unpredictability, have been defined as those times when a major threat to national goals has appeared, and decision time is short and advance planning inadequate. "It is the essence of crisis that the participants are not fully in control of events." [16] At such times emotional tensions would be expected to accentuate certain of the personal qualities of leaders that, I have speculated, many possess: they would be likely to be suspicious of their adversaries and underestimate their military capabilities and determination; in arriving at decisions, they would emphasize short-term rather than long-term gains and losses. Since government information-gathering and executive organizations are taxed to the utmost during crises, increased distortion and restriction of information reaching the leaders and lapses in execution of their decisions could be expected.

A crisis of recent history was precipitated by the assassination in June, 1914, of the Austrian Archduke Ferdinand at Sarajevo, and a pioneering quantitative empirical study of it that illustrates some of these points is worth pausing over. The guiding hypothesis was that national leaders' feelings and perceptions influence their decisions and thus the course of events; the data were thousands of perceptions, variously categorized, that had been extracted from all verbatim documents of the five major involved powers' key leaders. Indices of psychological tension traced a pattern over time almost identical with such "hard" indices as gold flow, security prices, and commodity futures,[17] and hostility levels were significantly correlated with those of mobilization of European armies.[18] Correlations of events permit no conclusion as to which is cart and which horse, but they do suggest that measures of psychological states can help predict "real life" events, whether or not they cause them.* The major results of the study can be summarized in terms of two related phenomena: information overload and rising emotional tension.

During late June and early July, 1914, the average frequency of daily messages from a nation's diplomats abroad was about four; by the end of July it had increased to over forty: "Old World bureaucracy was simply snowed under by the blizzard of information that descended upon it. The keenest and most orderly minds could no longer digest and assimilate the raw data that were being fed into them, and in every capital decisions tended to lag behind events, so that each new move on anyone's part was likely to be a false move, adding to the general confusion." [20] As their number increased, the messages became shorter and more stereotyped. With increasing pressure of time leaders turned more and more to extraordinary or improvised channels, and in the final week of the crisis heads of state communicated directly, by-passing their ambassadors twice as frequently as in the preceding month.

The clogging of information channels probably heightened the tendency to attend selectively to those communications that fitted the receiver's preconceptions. The Kaiser refused to heed the consistently accurate reports of his ambassador in London regarding British intentions, but accepted uncritically those of the German ambassador in St. Petersburg supporting what he wanted to hear—namely, that Russia was bluffing in her announced policy of supporting Serbia. This example also illustrates how field observers may send back information they think their chief wants: in his personal diary the German ambassador recorded crucial conversations with Russian officials that implied the opposite of his reports to the Kaiser,[21] the deceit appears to have been deliberate, although it is possible that the ambassa-

---

* In a study of Russian and Chinese perceptions and actions through three periods of crisis, the same researchers found that how national leaders *think* other states are behaving toward them during a crisis is the best predictor of their actions. During non-crisis periods other nations' actual behavior toward the perceiving state becomes the best predictor of its response.[19]

dor's own preconceptions caused him to misinterpret what he had been told.* Until Russia mobilized, German and Austrian decision-makers persistently underestimated the likelihood that she would come to Serbia's defense, a miscalculation perhaps reflecting the characteristic optimism of national leaders, in this case reinforced by biased evaluation of information.

The emotionally determined distortion of perception that may have been decisive in 1914 was that each nation saw itself primarily as offering friendship but receiving hostility from its political enemies. Moreover, ". . . each nation (through the nervous system of its key decision-makers) most strongly felt itself to be the victim of injury precisely at that time when its leaders were making policy decisions of the most crucial nature." [22]

Emotional tension affects various dimensions of perception: time perspective shortens and the range of perceived alternatives decreases, as illustrated by data from the analysis of the 1914 crisis. Of 160 statements in which time was perceived to be a factor in decision-making, only 8 revealed a concern for the distant future, all of them in the first four weeks after the assassination, none in the last week before the outbreak of war. The study also documents that decision-makers in each nation except Austria perceived fewer options open to themselves and their allies than to their enemies.

The spiral of rising tension finally reached a point at which, at least for the Kaiser, perceptions of inferior capability were not sufficient to deter him from plunging Germany into war. History is strewn with similar examples, but two statements made by national leaders adequately illustrate the point: in 1914 the Kaiser said, "Even if we are bled to death, England will at least lose India"; and in 1941 the Japanese War Minister declared, "Once in a while it is necessary for one to close one's eyes and jump from the stage of the Kiyomizu Temple." [23]

* Similar processes may account for the gross misinformation on which United States leaders based the decision to undertake the Bay of Pigs invasion. Possible sources of distortion include the CIA agents, their informers, and the Washington officials who evaluated their reports, all of whom presumably wanted to think that the invasion would arouse mass Cuban support.

The disquieting implication of this finding lies in the fact that the cornerstone of nuclear powers' deterrence policies is the assumption that the acts of the nation to be deterred will be guided by a rational calculus of probable costs and gains of different alternatives; the most important variable is assumed to be one's own capability compared to the enemy's. The evidence from these studies suggests that "perceptions of inferior capability, if perceptions of anxiety, fear, threat or injury are great enough, will fail to deter a nation from going to war." [24]

Crises occasionally do not run the malignant course of 1914. The best recent example is the Cuban missile crisis, on whose different ending the same research team that reported on 1914 has made some informal observations, pointing out that neither major power had tied its policies to a weaker hot-headed ally (as had Russia to Serbia and Germany to Austria in 1914)—both Khrushchev and Kennedy acted as if Castro did not exist. Probably more important (data are available only from the United States) was Kennedy's successful effort to make the information the United States both sent and received as unambiguous as possible. [25]

Until it was too late Russia did not make sufficiently clear her intention to support Serbia in 1914. President Kennedy saw to it that American plans for action were unequivocal if Russia did not withdraw the missiles, but he was careful to take no action until he had complete information, and then he started with the lowest level of violence necessary to achieve American aims—a blockade rather than, for example, an invasion of Cuba. He carefully avoided making any demand that Russia could not meet, and at every step took care not to humiliate Khrushchev. Both nations knew that the vital interests of the United States were at stake, while those of the Soviet Union were not, and no one knows whether the President's maneuvers would have sufficed to forestall disaster if Russia had felt equally committed.

Perhaps the main achievement of the study of the 1914 crisis was the development of research tools for measuring subjective, emotional influences on policy-making which are now being applied to research on other problems of international conflict. These tools also offer exciting possibilities for developing indices of national suspiciousness, hostility, and other pertinent attitudes that policy-makers might consult to help guide their moves. Just as Dow-Jones averages, freight car loadings, and the like help policy-makers to foresee economic depressions and take counter-measures in time, regular periodic determinations of national psychological states might help leaders to note when tension is getting dangerously high so that steps can be taken to reduce it in time to prevent war. ". . . Such research can enrich wisdom gained through experience, clarify the ambiguities of common sense, and provide more precise tools through which to assess the incredible complexities of international relations," [26] thus increasing the decision-maker's freedom of action and helping to reduce the likelihood of catastrophic misjudgments.

THE ENEMY IN WAR

The outbreak of war sharply intensifies all the psychological aspects of conflict by introducing a crucial new feature—the effort to defeat the adversary by inflicting pain and death on him. Enemies become direct and immediate dangers to each other rather than merely potential ones; each endures losses of life and property and terrorization of the survivors, and each is threatened with the loss of certain possessions it regards as vital or even with total destruction. Yielding to an enemy damages a nation's self-image as a strong, successful, growing organization, and threatens its ideological base. Thus, war engenders an enormous increase in emotional tension and mutual hatred leading to increased rigidity of action and thought and an intensification of psychological defenses against changing them —which helps to explain why wars once started are so hard to stop and why the escalator goes up more easily than down.[27]

Dehumanization of the Enemy in Wartime

This topic brings us back to a question broached in the discussion of biological bases of aggression. What frees *homo sapi-*

ens from the inhibition, apparently shared by all other vertebrates, against massive slaughter of his own kind? How can a loving American husband and father drop napalm on Vietnamese wives, mothers and children? Strongly inhibited from killing family members or fellow countrymen and sometimes willing to risk our lives to save the life of a fellow citizen who is a stranger, humans kill without end in war. Several factors already touched on undoubtedly make this possible, especially the very powerful force of obedience, which includes the ability to shift blame and guilt to the person who gives the order to kill—many Germans, for example, successfully exculpating themselves for the death camps by fastening the guilt on Hitler.

A different source of removal of restraints on killing is the "dehumanization" of the enemy.[28] Human symbolic powers and the conditions of modern war conspire to weaken the soldier's feeling that he is killing fellow humans, for the act of killing has become ever more massive and impersonal, and often the victims are unseen. Statistics, it is said, do not bleed—and it is this impersonal quality that permits killing more readily than before. Yet other dehumanizing factors must be involved because even when every death in war had to be personally inflicted, the amount of killing was often limited only by the inefficiency of weapons or fatigue of the killers. Dehumanizing factors not only make killing easier but they instigate it; they are intensifications of attitudes described earlier, one of which is the identification of each individual enemy with a hated, threatening abstraction. The enemy are not people but communists, fascists, imperialists, Christians, Moslems, or whatever, and in this sense they are seen as agents of the Devil.

Probably the most powerful inciter of hatred toward an enemy is the injury and pain he inflicts,* especially on civilians. War frees soldiers from peacetime's customary moral restraints, and rape and pillage have been features of all wars. In modern wars killing civilians has become increasingly prominent and has taken the additional form of mass destruction by shells or bombs—the ratio of Vietnamese civilians to soldiers killed by

* See Chapter 5, pp. 68f.

American weapons, for example, is said to be about ten to one. It is assumed that slaughtering civilians, terrorizing the population, and upsetting the soldiers through harming their families will weaken the enemy's morale. And especially in guerrilla wars many of the fighters are not uniformed, so combatants cannot be distinguished from noncombatants.

Killing civilians is still not generally accepted as legitimate by the side whose civilians are victimized, so it arouses stronger feelings than does killing their soldiers which is in accord with the rules of war. Although only a small portion of the population may actually be attacked, the rest identify with them and share the thirst for revenge. Attacks on civilians by each side's soldiers confirm the other's view of them as bestial and thus justify their own similar conduct.

The double moral standard comes into play with respect not only to who is killed but to how it is done. Conventions develop according to which some methods of killing are legitimate, while others, which appear eventually in every war and are analogous to fouls in games, are regarded as atrocities, a distinction that appears to be unrelated to the suffering caused by the different methods. A method of killing is often regarded as atrocious by one side but not the other—Americans are outraged by the National Liberation Front's disembowelings and beheadings, while they in turn refer to napalm and crop poisoning as "the most cruel and barbaric means of annihilating people." [29]

Each side uses psychological defenses to hide its own atrocious acts from awareness or to justify them, another illustration of shifting the burden of choice and of guilt to the enemy by claiming that one's own hands are tied—the enemy's barbarisms are attributed to his bestiality, while ours, if they are recognized as blameworthy at all, are viewed as regrettable necessities or as justified by the enemy's atrocities. In the First World War the German General von Hausen justified rounding up and shooting civilian hostages on the grounds that the Belgian government "approved perfidious street fighting contrary to international law," and General von Kluck went so far as to claim that Belgian government posters warning the citizens against hostile acts were actually "incitements to the civil population to fire on the enemy." [30] By playing up enemy atrocities, each side not only justifies its own cruelties and dehumanizes the enemy, it further arouses its own citizens' blood lust. This can reach such a pitch that a United States Senator could advocate "desolating" North Vietnam in reprisal for the threatened trial and execution of a few American flyers.

The ferocity of war is both made possible and enhanced by the denial of humanity to the enemy: he becomes a statistic, an abstraction, and a beast, and the perception of him as subhuman reinforces the conviction that, like an animal, he is impervious to reason and will respond only to punishment. This discourages searching for means of peacefully resolving the conflict.

SPECIAL PSYCHOLOGICAL FEATURES

OF INTERNAL WARS

The question arises now as to whether dehumanization of the enemy adequately accounts for the ferocity of civil wars and revolutions. Since the antagonists are members of the same society, it should be more difficult for them to dehumanize each other; but by the time organized violence breaks out, each side has seceded, in effect, from the society defended by the other, so that to this extent they are no longer subject to the inhibitions against killing their own kind. Combatants in fratricidal wars, moreover, mobilize special sources of bitterness springing from their initial membership in the same group. In revolutions both sides experience the frustrations of disappointed expectations: the underdogs feel that their legitimate demands have been spurned by those in power, who could have alleviated their misery but did not; and the elite are infuriated by the underdog's refusal to behave in the expected subservient fashion. In civil wars, where all classes may be involved on both sides, the mutual sense of betrayal is also strong—each group is shocked by the other's failure to give it the support for its own beliefs that it wanted and expected.[31]

Another factor in the destructiveness of internecine war is perhaps that people who know each other well can hurt each other more than strangers, just as family quarrels can be so bitter because everyone knows just what behavior will most hurt or infuriate the other.

The strain toward consistency may also be involved. If attacking a certain group creates conflicts with other beliefs—for example, that it is wrong to attack a compatriot—then one must find all the more reason to hate him in order to justify the action.

A final aggravating aspect of internal wars lies in their involvement with the issue of who will be master of the house, for members of each faction know that defeat means the end of their group's existence as an organized group. To the extent that group membership is a part of personal identity, defeat in civil war poses a worse psychological threat for the survivors than does defeat in international wars, from which defeated nations have a hope—though it is not always realized—of emerging with their social and political structures intact.

Since the victor over a foreign enemy usually wishes to preserve it as an organized entity with at least some of its authority structure intact, if only to negotiate and carry out the terms of surrender, the leaders of enemy nations can hope to maintain their positions even if their powers are reduced. After the First World War, much of the top German leadership retained considerable power despite a revolution, usually as "advisors" to the new leaders; the title of a popular postwar German novel epitomized the situation: *The Kaiser Went—The Generals Remained*. Even following Nazi Germany's unconditional surrender and the execution or imprisonment of the top leaders, the lower echelons of government continued to be filled by ex-Nazis.

Leaders of defeated factions in internal wars expect to be treated by the victors as renegades rather than honorable enemies, so they stand not only to lose their power but also to suffer disgrace, banishment, or death. Hence, in internal wars both leaders and followers believe they have more to lose by defeat than in foreign ones.

SOME PSYCHOLOGICAL ASPECTS OF
COMMITMENT

As military and civilian casualties mount, privation at home increases, and more and more resources are committed to the struggle, continuing the fight becomes a means of justifying past sacrifices. The predicament is somewhat like that of a gambler who keeps raising his bets to recoup his past losses—the sacrifices would be justified only if the goal for which they were made was really worthwhile, and the way to prove the goal worthwhile is to redouble efforts to gain it. The gambler is usually motivated in part by the need to show that his judgment or his faith in his luck that led him to incur his original losses is, after all, correct—the purpose of the effort now becomes to protect his self-image, and achieving the goal becomes a means to this end. In war the same process may lead to a shift in motivation: proving one's courage and determination by continuing to fight becomes an end in itself, more important than gaining the object of the fight, and the issue of who is tougher becomes overriding. A tragic example was the terrible and relentless struggle for Verdun in the First World War, which continued after its ". . . strategic significance . . . had long since passed out of sight; yet the battle had somehow achieved a demonic existence of its own, far beyond the control of generals of either nation. Honor had become involved to an extent which made disengagement impossible." [32]

Blind commitment is made possible by the fact that the prospect of defeat is for many people a worse alternative than death. Death is not a real alternative for most people—each of us, even the soldier in battle, has the illusion of personal immortality; and since no one who has ever experienced it has lived to tell the tale (modern medicine has created a handful of apparent exceptions, but the generalization still holds), no one really knows what it will be like. On the other hand, all humans have suffered the mortification of defeat, so it is a very real eventuality. The prospect of dying in defense of one's country or its ideals, moreover, enhances one's self-image. The soldier contemplating death in battle can identify himself with the heroes whose glorious reputations brighten all history; but surrender is linked to cowardice, a loathed human weakness.

Another psychological process that may help to explain why a war absorbs more and more of the combatants' emotions and energies has been given the mouthfilling designation "circular incremental magnification." [33] It ensues when a threat-defense-threat sequence develops so that each defense is overcome by a stronger threat; the successive breakdown of each newly improved defense generates a magnification of the sense of threat and the emotion it evokes. America's increasing commitment in Vietnam may reflect just such a process: several times the leaders have assumed that one more escalation would bring the National Liberation Front to terms, only to find that the response necessitated a still greater military commitment—a process that can be traced step by step from the initial increase of American military advisors from four thousand to twelve thousand, to the bombing of Hanoi.

In view of the degree of commitment, the size of the stakes, and the heightened emotional tension, it is not surprising that each combatant in war becomes increasingly wedded to his course of action, and that filtering and reinterpreting information to support these courses reaches monumental proportions.

Military leaders show extraordinary ability to reject information that would necessitate a change of their plans. Turning again to the first days of World War I, nothing could convince Marshal Joffre that the Germans were following the Schlieffen Plan and making their main thrust through Belgium, since to believe this would require that the French General Staff abandon their "Plan 17," which called for leaving two-thirds of the Belgian frontier undefended. The Schlieffen Plan had been betrayed to the French some ten years earlier, but they dismissed it as "a feint designed to draw the French army away from the area of real attack." [34] It required the Germans to use reserves as active troops, which they did, but the French discounted the information that they were doing so. All day on the third day of the war

"[Intelligence] collected information, interrogated prisoners, deciphered documents, and passed on its reports to [Operations]. All day [Operations] read the reports . . . and refused to believe them if they pointed to conclusions that would require the French to modify their plan of offensive." [35] And as late as the ninth day, when Germans were beginning to cross into Belgium, French Headquarters felt "confirmed in the impression that the principal German maneuver would not take place in Belgium." [36] One cannot help wondering what went on in General MacArthur's headquarters during the Korean War that enabled him to maintain his conviction that the Chinese would not cross the Yalu if he pushed through North Korea.

If a line of action based on a belief fails, it is still possible to maintain the rightness of the belief by blaming the failure on something else. The simplest device is to attribute the failure to faulty execution of the plans based on the belief. Thus, after the collapse of Plan 17, "Joffre, standing amid the tumbled debacle of all French hopes, with responsibility for the catastrophe resting finally upon him . . . remained magically unperturbed. By immediately casting the blame on the executors and absolving the planners, he was able to retain perfect and unblemished confidence in himself and France. . . ." [37]

As an armed conflict drags on, both sides sacrifice more blood and treasure and endure increasing hurt and humiliation. These experiences mobilize in each citizen psychological forces that progressively deepen his commitment to the conflict and intensify it, including determination to recoup the nation's losses and to defend its honor, and moral indignation at the enemy's atrocious conduct. War also mobilizes such motives as the need to prove masculinity and courage by willingness to kill, and the urge for revenge and primitive blood lust.

As a result conflicts tend to escalate, and each step up intensifies the forces toward further escalation. As Homer described Strife, the War God's sister: "Once she begins, she cannot stop. At first she seems a little thing, but before long, though her feet are still on the ground, she has struck high heaven with her head."

These considerations may help explain why psychologists cannot place much faith in the capacity of modern nations to limit wars. The combat escalator does not run smoothly—it pauses and lurches, and at any pause the combatants may be able to get off—and any war offers many psychological "thresholds," a geographical boundary like the Yalu River or the technological gap between high explosive and nuclear weapons, that facilitate the exercise of restraint by tacit agreement.[38] The major restraining force on combatants today is probably the mutual fear of nuclear weapons, but there are grave doubts that this restraint can hold through an indefinite series of limited wars. And it has to give way only once.

Although this analysis leads to a pessimistic prediction of a major, perhaps ultimate, disaster unless the institution of war is soon brought under control, the encouraging fact remains that many wars have remained limited and nations have been able to settle serious differences by negotiation, sometimes even without a preceding war.

10 · *Psychological Aspects of Disarmament and International Negotiations*

SOME YEARS AGO the UN General Assembly unanimously passed a resolution stating, "the question of complete disarmament is the most important one facing the world today." It is no news that progress toward this universally sought goal has been backward: far from being checked, the accelerating arms race is involving more and more countries; and the only favorable events have been the atmospheric nuclear test ban, which has perhaps slightly slowed research and development, and the United Nations resolution against sending armed satellites into space, which concerns future rather than existing arms. Nations, still committed to policies of self-help, still cling to their sovereignty and regard superior military power as the ultimate arbiter of international disputes. The halting of the arms race followed by disarmament is the most urgent and discouraging task confronting nations today.

To achieve lasting peace among nations requires substitution for armed might of peaceful ways of settling their disputes; and this depends in turn on the strengthening of methods for peaceful resolution of international conflicts and on developing more effective ones.

Such methods as negotiations between ambassadors, foreign ministers, heads of state, and national delegations are as old or older than nations themselves, and new ones have been emerging, particularly the continuing forum of the United Nations Assembly and Security Council, and the rudiments of an international judicial system in the World Court of International Justice.

To keep the topic within manageable limits, I shall consider mainly bilateral negotiating or bargaining between individuals or small groups, focusing on psychological obstacles to reaching agreement. Students of international relations and industrial bargaining have amassed a wealth of information that I have not been able to explore.[1] My material is taken from psychological sources and deals with empirical studies of international negotiations and with experiments that try to penetrate to general principles.

The main determinant of success or failure in negotiations is the nature of the issue itself. The more the negotiators desire an agreement on an issue and the greater the relative rewards for success and penalties for failure, the greater the chances that an agreement will be reached. Furthermore, it is easier to reach agreements where very high stakes are not involved and when gains and losses are immediate and obvious. It was considerably easier to negotiate an agreement for scientific cooperation in the Antarctic, for example, than it would be to negotiate one to halt the arms race—life and death were not at stake, and the potential rewards for agreeing were clear and immediate; but the latter's stakes are astronomically higher, and the gains from a disarmament agreement and the penalties for not agreeing are unclear and hard to place in time.

Psychologists are interested in the self-aggravating aspects of negotiations that are relatively independent of the substantive questions involved and that can impede or facilitate negotiations about any issue. The influence of these on the outcome is often only marginal, but they can influence the very definition of the issue to be negotiated and the participants' perceptions of the potential rewards and punishments for different outcomes.

The most pervasive psychological obstacle to successful negotiations is mutual mistrust: each side fears that the other will cheat him in arriving at and carrying out agreements. A former high State Department official stated the American attitude well: "For Moscow to propose what we can accept seems to us even more sinister and dangerous than for it to propose what we cannot accept. Our instinct is to cast about for grounds on which to discredit the proposal instead of seizing it and making the most of it. Being distrustful of the Greeks bearing gifts, we are afraid of being tricked." [2] The Russians, no doubt, feel the same way about us.

Mistrust is aggravated by and contributes to difficulties in communication based on other grounds—negotiators often cannot make clear their own positions or hear accurately those of their adversaries, especially when they come from different societies which differ in certain attitudes, values, and habitual ways of thinking. Negotiations can also be impeded by certain aspects of the dynamics of conflicting groups and by features of the negotiating process itself.

PSYCHOLOGICAL PROBLEMS OF
DISARMAMENT

It must be admitted that on this issue the mutual distrust of nations is justified. The troubles start with the paradox that each nation believes that successful negotiations are possible only if it is stronger, in effect taking the position that disarmament is eventually necessary, of course, but bitter experience has shown that the adversary cannot be trusted and understands only force; therefore, only by being strong can we hope to negotiate successfully with him. The analysis in Chapter 7 of Soviet and American mass media found that about two-thirds of statements in American magazines support the view that successful negotiations are likely to occur when America is stronger and that the percentage of similar statements in Russian journals was, unfortunately, virtually the same—that is, the very conditions regarded by one side as favorable for negotiations are regarded by the other as unfavorable.

Furthermore, because nations rely on arms for their security, none enters disarmament negotiations in good faith; their orientation is competitive rather than cooperative, and they bring to such negotiations the attitudes that led to the arms race initially. Each strives for an agreement that will increase its relative advantage at the adversary's expense rather than one that will lead to the greatest possible degree of mutual disarmament; and each wants to reserve the right to accumulate those weapons it believes to be most essential to its security and power. Hence, such negotiations in good faith as there are tend to be about relinquishing weapons that do not really matter, like obsolete bombers, and "disarmament turns out to be but one of the forms the armaments race can take." [3]

Negotiations will become genuinely cooperative only when nations accept the truth of President Kennedy's September, 1961, statement to the United Nations that "The risks inherent in disarmament pale in comparison to the risks inherent in an unlimited arms race." [4] If nations really believed this, they would be willing, in order to reach disarmament agreements, to run risks comparable to those run in pursuit of illusory security through arms, because disarmament negotiations can succeed only to the extent that participants are convinced that the risk of no agreement outweighs the risk of being cheated by the adversary.

Both risks are familiar—the latter is as old as human perfidy, the former simply means continuing an arms race which each side hopes to win—but the advent of modern weaponry has drastically altered the first risk. Humanity has never before experienced an uncontrolled nuclear, chemical, and biological arms race, and the psychological obstacle to success in disarmament negotiations seems to be the underestimation of this new danger as compared with the familiar one of being cheated, which as everyone knows is a highly unpleasant, embarrassing, and sometimes dangerous experience. The arms race presents an enormous risk in the long run, one involving all humanity, but since the risk that an adversary might gain a small temporary advantage by cheating on an agreement is far more potent in determining negotiating behavior, no agreements are reached. The dilemma, although not absolute, is compounded by a built-in property of negotiations: if one party knows that the other would rather risk a disadvantageous agreement than no agreement, he has a big bargaining advantage. Each must thus pretend that he prefers no agreement to a disadvantageous one, a situation in which it would be unreasonable to hope for rapid progress. Perhaps it is too much to hope for any at all.

Logically, disarming can be achieved by agreement or by unilateral action. But the mutual distrust of nations, especially the communist and non-communist, creates grave obstacles to disarmament by agreement; and no nation would dare initiate unilateral disarmament, for in the present state of international anarchy, it fears increased vulnerability if others do not follow suit.

Despite all discouragements, it is certain that nations will keep trying to solve the dilemma, because, as Vietnam indicates, the type of issue dividing nations today cannot be resolved by force of arms; arms budgets also block progress toward all nations' social and economic goals; and as indicated in Chapter 1, modern weapons become increasingly dangerous to their possessors beyond a certain point. Military experts keep proposing schemes for arms control or disarmament or a combination of the two, and disarmament conferences continue to meet. And these activities are important, although they are still unreal because nations do not yet accord high priority to disarmament, especially when it seems to conflict with their national interests or security. Proposals keep the problem in the forefront of attention, and the mere process of negotiating clears up extraneous obstacles, maintains communication, and occasionally results in an agreement like the test ban that may even slow the arms race a trifle. If it accomplishes nothing else, negotiating and carrying out such an agreement sows a few seeds of mutual trust that may germinate at some later time, and methods developed to meet and overcome the problems of making and keeping such an agreement facilitate arriving at the next one. The establishment of the United States Arms Control and Disarmament Agency was encouraging as an official recognition that these were desirable goals.

Two types of activity might reduce mutual mistrust to the point where disarmament negotiations have some chance of success: inspection for concealed armaments and unilateral tension-reducing acts.

Problems of Inspection

If reliable methods of inspection for hidden arms could be devised, so that nations were reasonably sure the others were not cheating, prospects for agreements on arms control and disarmament would be enhanced.* Since Russia and the United States have actually been involuntarily submitting to rather extensive inspection by observation satellites for some time, they must have pinpointed each other's major military installations, and this may have reduced the area of suspicion, thus improving chances for formal agreements. They cannot distinguish munitions factories from other types, of course, or detect stores of chemical, biological or nuclear weapons.

All inspection agreements must rest on the assumptions that nations genuinely want to abide by them and prove to others that they are doing so, and that the main source of hesitancy is the fear that others will cheat. Inspection schemes have all concentrated on the detection of violations, but if inspection is seen as a means of promoting trust, its ability to enable each country to prove that it is not cheating would be as important as its

---

* An ingenious suggestion for initiating disarmament, one that has been worked out in some detail, is "War Safety Control": nations would maintain their present arsenals but would devote present arms expenditures to perfecting worldwide electronic methods of detecting other nations' clandestine preparations for war; simultaneously, they would institute international institutions for nipping such activities in the bud. Only after all nations had achieved security by these means would disarmament be possible, but it should then proceed rapidly.[5]

ability to detect cheating. The crucial aspect—the main safe-guard against a sudden flare-up of mutual suspicion that might precipitate a nuclear exchange—is the provision of a method by which a wrongly suspected nation could establish its innocence.

Inspection can increase as well as reduce tension—it is an incontrovertible fact that any inspection is a kind of spying and that mistrust is implied in a demand to inspect. The description of a camp for delinquent boys, who displayed many of the be-haviors characteristic of nations, points out that the counselors' inspection for concealed weapons was resented by the innocent as well as the guilty.[6] If inspection's main purpose were to es-tablish innocence rather than detect guilt, its irritating aspect would be sharply reduced.

Inspection agreements would have to provide for continual adjudication of questions that arise in the course of carrying them out. Such provisions might be their most important feature because they would keep the parties in continuing contact, dis-pel unwarranted suspicion, and build up habits of resolving dis-agreements.

To get any inspection scheme into operation, participants would have to accept the fact that, human ingenuity what it is, any scheme involves some risk and no inspection scheme is ab-solute proof against cheating. With arms levels what they are today, however, it would take a lot of cheating to yield worth-while advantages—one or two clandestine underground explo-sions (assuming extension of the test ban to include under-ground tests), for example, could not yield enough technological gain to be worth the risk that their discovery would wreck the inspection agreement. As disarmament progressed inspection would have to be increasingly rigorous, for with conventional weapons the lower the level of armaments, the more secure na-tions could feel; but with nuclear weapons the lower the general level, the greater the advantage of a slight preponderance. The country that had successfully concealed a few nuclear weapons while the rest of the world had totally disarmed could blackmail all the rest. This discouraging thought can be countered, how-ever, by the encouraging one that disarmament can progress only as fast as international confidence grows, and that with increasing confidence would come increasing acceptance of inspection and familiarity with its procedures; thus total disarmament and inspection would probably become possible simultaneously.

Since the main danger of violations would come from clandestine disaffected groups within each country, the best place to start developing and testing inspection methods would be at home. Inspection games similar to war games could be devised in which one group would try to cheat and another to expose it; through such activities each nation would develop methods of inspection in which it had confidence, thereby increasing its willingness to use them and its ability to persuade other nations of their effectiveness.

Because weapons' caches can be so easily concealed and even secretly manufactured, especially chemical and biological ones, inspection for weapons, however elaborate, will probably never be able to afford adequate assurance against cheating. But there would also be clues in arms budgets, personnel and production records, and even the mass media to reveal, however indirectly, that weapons were being manufactured and stored on an appreciable scale.[7] And periodic systematic analysis of such records would, as an adjunct to direct inspection, increase its effectiveness. Governments would have to agree to make them available to each other, but this presents no greater obstacle than reaching agreement on any type of inspection. The facts that no weapon can be manufactured without many people knowing about it and that weapons are useless unless someone knows where they are and there is an organization trained to use them have led behavioral scientists to propose a variety of schemes for inspecting people rather than weapons.[8, 9] Without an occasional on-the-spot check it would be impossible to be sure whether suspected violation of any scheme had in fact occurred, but knowledge inspection would greatly reduce the number needed.

One proposal, "inspection by the people," which would require laws in every country encouraging the populace to inform an international inspectorate of any known cheating, has been

worked out in considerable detail, including methods of protecting informers and insuring free communication between the inspectorate and the citizens of the countries involved.[10] In public
opinion polls in the United States, Western Europe, India, and
Japan 70 to 90 per cent of respondents have indicated that they
approve of such an inspection organization and that they themselves
would report attempts to make forbidden weapons to a
worldwide inspection agency.[11] Whether people would actually
behave as they say they would is uncertain, but the polls at least
suggest that the possibility of inspection by the people is not as
fantastic as might appear at first glance. A leading atomic scientist
who had the opportunity to present this proposal to Premier
Khrushchev reported that he "got the point, got it fully and his
answer was very gratifying." [12] Interest in it seems to have
lapsed, but having received this much recognition, it should be
easily revivable at an appropriate time.

The second approach to knowledge inspection is through direct interrogation of people who might know of violations.
A scientist whose opinion must be respected believes that modern detection techniques using such physiological indices as
changes in brain-wave patterns could be raised to a level of over
90-per-cent certainty; if so, this approach holds out substantial
hope for checking the veracity of an official's public statements
or statements to an adversary in negotiations.[13] He would have
to submit to the tests, of course, but since this would be part of
the overall agreement, refusal to be tested would be a virtual
admission of lying. Furthermore, a leader who suspected that his
nation was about to be falsely accused could volunteer to undergo the examinations.

Unilateral Moves to Reduce Mutual Mistrust

Inspection schemes would come into force only after negotiations had yielded agreements to disarm, but there is still the
problem of how to reduce mutual mistrust to the point at which
negotiations—confrontations bristling with mutual fears—have
some chance of succeeding.

Because of their interdependence and the workings of the self-fulfilling prophecy, the range of alternatives for each modern nation is heavily restricted by the others' actions. Since each has some freedom of choice, however, and the more powerful the nation, the greater its freedom, nations might be able to act unilaterally to reverse the tension-armaments spiral. One psychologist has detailed this in a program termed Graduated Reciprocation in Tension Reductions, or GRIT.[14] One of the greatest hurdles for the nation taking the lead is that its actions would have to be calculated to diminish the apparent threat it poses to other nations but without frightening itself. Fortunately, the effect of a nation's actions on the international tension level is somewhat independent of their military significance: the Berlin Wall increased East-West tensions without affecting the balance of military power in the least.

Another example was the American insistence that the second chairman of the International Atomic Energy Commission be a Swede, although the Soviet Union, as the second largest producer of atomic energy, was the more appropriate choice. Although victory in this type of meaningless Cold War battle may gain a bit of prestige, it has no military meaning and serves only to keep the tension high.

On the other hand, if a major nation publicized detailed plans for converting its armaments industry to the manufacture of other products when a disarmament agreement was reached, the confidence of other nations in the sincerity of its desire to disarm would be increased. Such a unilateral step might improve the international atmosphere without incurring any risk at all.

Any conciliatory move by one nation would probably be regarded initially by the other as a ruse to get it to drop its guard. To have any hope of eliciting a reciprocal move, therefore, the initiating nation would have to take a big enough disarmament step to clearly weaken itself and persist in it despite a suspicious or hostile reception. But in the context of the universal reliance on force, such an act would tend to be viewed as surrender by both the sides, demoralizing the one that did it and perhaps tempting the adversary to attack while it saw an advantage. Since it would also be likely to be interpreted as a sign of weakness, it would have to be done purely voluntarily. The removal of United States missile bases from Turkey may fall into this category; but this was not done until well after the Cuban missile crisis in order to reduce the suspicion (actually unfounded) that it was a *quid pro quo* for Russia's removing the missiles from Cuba.

An inconclusive but encouraging experiment with reciprocal unilateral initiatives—what Premier Khrushchev termed the policy of mutual example—began with President Kennedy's conciliatory speech at American University in June of 1962 in which he announced America's unilateral halting of atmospheric tests; widely publicized in Russia by newspapers and radio, it was soon followed by Khrushchev's announcement that Russia was halting production of bombers. At the United Nations other conciliatory gestures by both followed, and by August a ban on testing nuclear weapons in the atmosphere or outer space had been successfully negotiated.

Strangely enough, the Cuban missile crisis of October, 1962, interrupted conciliatory gestures only temporarily, and by giving leaders of both the United States and the Soviet Union a close view of the nuclear abyss into which mutual intransigency threatened to plunge their countries, it probably actually strengthened their incentives to find ways of reducing tension. In any case, subsequent agreements included the American wheat sale to Russia and the United Nations resolution against orbiting nuclear weapons. The initial steps were greeted with considerable ambivalence, as expected, but the decline of mutual distrust seemed to accelerate with time, and even the Vietnam war does not seem to have brought American-Soviet tensions back up to their pre-1963 pitch. The experience is inconclusive, however, for it did not lead to any major slowing of the arms race. Both countries' actions were essentially psychological gestures that had no significant effect on their actual relative power. Possibly a policy of "mutual example" cannot do more than start the ball rolling and its main effect is only to reduce the mutual fear and distrust of the citizenry of hostile nations, thereby giving the leaders more freedom of action.[15] Perhaps it can only be hoped that the limited success of this policy in 1963 will encourage national leaders to try it again.

PSYCHOLOGICAL ASPECTS OF NEGOTIATIONS

Reliable, non-provocative inspection methods and unilateral tension-reducing moves can pave the way for negotiations and increase the chances for their success, but in the last analysis international conflicts will have to be resolved at the conference table. The psychological factors that affect other features of international relations also intrude into negotiations, among them the negotiators' personal qualities, differences in the use of words, and culturally determined ways of thinking and of seeking agreements.

What has already been said about the role of the leaders' personal qualities and states of health also applies to negotiators: "Nobody who has not actually watched statesmen dealing with each other can have any real idea of the immense part played in human affairs by such unavowable and often unrecognisable causes as lassitude, affability, personal affection or dislike, misunderstanding, deafness or incomplete command of a foreign language, vanity, social engagements, interruptions and momentary health." [16]

The skillful negotiator, like the skillful poker player, tries to learn all he can about his adversary's strengths and weak points, and how he can best be influenced. While this aspect of the art of negotiation could never be systematized, it could perhaps be developed more systematically than it has been. For example, negotiators' personal attributes might be taken into account in selecting them for particular jobs, as Francis Bacon long ago suggested: "Use . . . such persons as affect the business wherein they are employed, . . . and such as are fit for the matter, as bold men for expostulation, fair-spoken men for persuasion, crafty men for enquiry and observation." [17] A risk-taker might be best in one type of negotiation, a conservative in another, an authoritarian person for dealing with representatives of an authoritarian culture, a democratic one to confront a democracy's delegates.

Moreover, negotiators might benefit from a systematic knowledge of the effects of mental illness or deterioration on behavior of those with whom they are dealing,[18] including how the delegate's own society regards deviance and illness. It would be important to know, for example, how much power subordinates have to make decisions for a delegate who is not functioning up to par.

The status of the negotiators also makes a difference. Chiefs of state can reach binding decisions directly, but since they symbolize their countries, they must also be more concerned than lesser officials with face-saving.

The medium of negotiations is language, and shades of meaning can occasionally make a big difference; imprecise translations of a word, evoking different connotations in the other language, can sometimes have important consequences. Though not uttered in the context of negotiations, Khrushchev's famous "we will bury you" is a case in point.[19]

Culturally Determined Biases of Negotiators

The greatest obstacles to international negotiations are probably the preconceptions, expectations, and traditional ways of conducting negotiations brought by the delegates to the conference table. Without ever coming into focus, they form part of the background pervading and influencing everything that transpires, but bringing them to awareness greatly increases the chances of overcoming or circumventing the obstacles they create.

An analysis of the first 116 sessions of the eighteen-nation disarmament conference suggests what some of the Russians' background assumptions might be.[20] (Since the study was done by Americans, it was easier for them to see Russian preconceptions than American ones.) Their greatest concern seems to have been with preserving their national sovereignty, and they regarded most disarmament proposals by others as covert efforts to encroach upon it. They were also deeply concerned that the secrecy of their territory might be violated, a fear understandable in a militarily weaker nation, much of whose security rests on keeping the opponent guessing as to the actual extent and location of its weapons. Less central preoccupations seem to have been with German "revanchism" and with the conviction that the purpose of American bases on foreign soil was purely aggressive, although Americans, of course, saw their function as defensive.

The fear of being taken advantage of seemed related to their propensity to reject any suggestion if it came from the other side —even such trivial ones as when a certain matter should be taken up: if the Americans suggested one day of the week, the Russians would suggest another. Similarly, they sometimes signified acceptance of an American proposal by introducing it as their own after having previously rejected it; but since they also regarded an offer to compromise as an admission of weakness, their response would be to push all the harder for their proposal. They preferred to reach agreement through barter—trading a concession in one area for a simultaneous concession in another. The researchers believe that the occasional introduction of extraneous issues represented covert invitations to such activities.

Behind all the obstacles to agreement on specific issues or modes of procedure was a difference in American and Russian methods of tackling problems: the Russians are universalistic and deductive—they want to deduce the specific case from the general principle; but Americans are pragmatic and inductive— they prefer to decide on one step after they see how the previous one has worked. Appeals to reason or principle work best with Russians; appeals to fact and concrete details carry most weight with Americans. These traits are reflected even in the language used to characterize negotiating proposals: the Russians use words like "correct" and "incorrect," the Americans "acceptable" and "unacceptable"; the Russians look for the "right" solution, the Americans the "preferred" one.[21]

American and Russian disarmament proposals have long reflected this difference in approach: the Americans proposed proceeding step by step, checking how well each had worked before moving on to the next; the Russians insisted that the Americans commit themselves in advance to every step toward total and complete disarmament. Perhaps the Americans feared to accept the general principle in advance because they could not foresee all its consequences, some of which might prove to give the Russians an advantage. The Russians, on the other hand, might have feared that unless the Americans committed themselves to the whole process, they might refuse to go on if any step turned out to give the Russians an edge.

From the standpoint of the general structure of bargaining situations, the Russians may be right in some circumstances and the Americans in others. An experiment that seems to support the Russian view involved pairs of students asked to reach an agreement that included five issues. The conditions resembled real-life negotiations in one important respect: each negotiator had a different ordering of the importance of the issues, but neither knew nor could find out directly what his adversary's priorities were. Each subject repeated the procedure five times with a different adversary and different priorities. As negotiators became more experienced, they became less inclined to propose reaching agreement on one issue at a time and more inclined to prefer a general exploration followed by offer of a package deal (the percentage of those whose first offer was a package deal of all five items rose from 23 on the first trial to 77 on the sixth). Apparently they feared that agreements on single issues might narrow available alternatives prematurely, reducing the chances for ultimate agreement—a supposition borne out by the fact that five of the six pairs who failed to reach agreement on all five issues in the first session had reached piecemeal agreements.[22] These results support the contention of many statesmen that it would be easier to reach an agreement for general and complete disarmament as a package than to attempt to negotiate one item at a time.

On the other hand, a persuasive case can be made for fractionating conflicts as a means of reducing tension. This would include, when possible, defining the conflict as between small rather than large units, between small substantive issues rather than large ones, between specific applications of a principle rather than the principle itself, and as one whose solution establishes small precedents rather than large ones.[23,24] Mediators in industrial bargaining often try to get the parties to agree immediately on small, peripheral issues in order to create an atmosphere that facilitates agreement on the major ones. But this may work only when each side feels that it can rely on the mediator to prevent the other from exploiting the initial agreements to its own advantage, and in the absence of enforceable rules to this effect, it may be less risky to avoid freezing any aspect of the negotiations until the whole bargaining process is complete.

To return to Soviet-American negotiations, the tensions and misunderstandings created by culturally determined differences in preconceptions are well illustrated by the vicissitudes of the Russian-American student exchange programs. The Russians saw the program as an agreement between governments, which make decisions and speak for their citizens; the American government saw itself as the Agency of the Inter-Universities Committee on Travel Grants, which represented individual students who wished to study in Russia. The Soviet ministry expected that the American universities would accept its candidates without question and that it would supervise the American students' study programs. When the American committee requested more data to determine where the Russian students could best be placed and then rejected a few as insufficiently qualified, the Soviets took this as both a politically inspired capricious rejection of official judgments and a derogation of Soviet academic degrees. On the other hand, Americans raised in the tradition of free scholarship were resentful when they found that they were expected to accept programs given them by the Societ educational authorities and that they would not be permitted to study certain subjects ideologically distasteful to the Russians: ". . . each side felt the other was sabotaging the agreement and each was trying quite vigorously to impose its standards on the other. . . . There could be no doubt of the sincere efforts of each side to make the program work, to be maximally accomodating to the other, and there could be no doubt . . . each side believed the other to be deliberately obstructionistic. . . ." [25]

The exchange program has managed to limp along despite such misunderstandings, however, and perhaps the experience gained in circumventing them will make new agreements easier to arrange.

SOME BENEFICIAL PSYCHOLOGICAL FEATURES OF THE UNITED NATIONS

The only way to conduct international affairs on a continuing basis used to be through ambassadors and foreign offices. Day-to-day negotiations were bilateral; and opportunities for multilateral negotiations were afforded by occasional congresses, peace conferences, and the like, but these were convened for special purposes and disbanded when their aim was achieved. The creation of the League of Nations—a permanent institutionalized forum where representatives of various nations could meet continuously—introduced new opportunities for the peaceful resolution of international conflicts. Today, behind the furor, fireworks, and deadlocks of the United Nations General Assembly and Security Council, new forces are quietly and continually at work which have been beneficial already and will undoubtedly affect international relations for the good in the long run.

From a psychological standpoint, the United Nations' major contribution is the provision for delegates from all nations of opportunities for continuing contact, both formal and informal, around a common agenda on neutral ground. Indeed, for many of the small new nations it is the only opportunity for such contact. Responses to a questionnaire by seventy-five randomly selected members of national missions showed that 86 per cent had more contact with diplomats from other countries than they would on a post in a national capital; 82 per cent found these contacts to be less formal, and two-thirds found it easier to exchange "off the record" information; most significant of all, 90 per cent had more contact with delegates from unfriendly countries. Since these contacts can be private at the UN, some governments actually instruct their delegates to make them, while forbidding their representatives in national capitals to do so.[26]

Informal face-to-face contacts, with opportunities to ask questions, not only help to correct distortions based on national stereotypes but also make it possible to offer proposals without commitment. The first move toward settling the Berlin blockade "was a carefully casual statement from Moscow, picked up in a carefully casual conversation by two United States representatives at the United Nations." [27]

By formally appealing to the UN as a forum, nations can place their national prestige "on deposit" in a crisis, thus gaining time to consider how best to protect their interests without having to choose immediately whether to act violently or retreat. Continuing contact also permits continual shifts of alliances and coalitions—nations allied on one issue may be opposed on another. Most find themselves in overlapping groups, while some, like Iran, form "linking pins" by belonging to the Western security system but sharing the economic aspirations of noncommitted Asian nations. Interlocking group memberships are likely to help solidify international society as they do smaller social units.

The fact that delegates must fill multiple roles creates pressures toward fairness in dealing with each other. The member of a national delegation who simultaneously must defend his nation's interests in one committee and act as chairman of another, for example, is motivated to be impartial in the latter role by the knowledge that a committee member may someday be chairman of one in which he is a member.

Finally the Secretariat is a strong influence for the improvement of international negotiations. A man cannot serve two nations without being a traitor to one, but he can perform an international function while still remaining a loyal citizen of his own country; when he works as an international civil servant, he develops habits of thought and action that weaken nationalistic ones. Moreover, as a source of information for all nations the Secretariat facilitates agreement on facts, and counteracts biased information supplied by national governments. It is also a reservoir of past practices and norms that help to improve the UN's functioning.[28]

In at least three ways the UN is promoting world peace, continuously, unspectacularly, and without regard to the waxing and waning of international crises. It is breaking down national stereotypes by acting as a permanent meeting place, where delegates can work together in various roles on a variety of issues, sometimes on the same side, sometimes opposed—it is hard to maintain simple national images when the "good guys" aren't always good and the "bad guys" bad. The UN also acts as a training ground for international cooperation, "a laboratory where a worldwide intergovernmental community has developed its own techniques for intergovernmental relations" [29]—and since only a small number of the delegates are permanent, every nation is gradually building a group of officials who have had some training in functioning as members of an international organization concerned with promoting universal welfare. Finally, while the UN's open forum aspect introduces obstacles into the negotiations of some issues—for example, it makes difficult the introduction of apparently extraneous issues for bargaining purposes—it is also slowly creating a world public opinion, which acts as a constraining force on all nations through developing international norms as to what is acceptable behavior: "The continual pressure of the Charter upon debate in the presence of a world Community is a powerful political fact not to be disregarded. Opinion is also power and what people think about conduct has a lot to do with the kind of conduct they will support or oppose." [30]

EXPERIMENTAL STUDIES OF NEGOTIATION AND BARGAINING

In addition to the empirical studies and observations that have contributed to the understanding of international negotiations, there is a growing body of experiments that cast light on some aspects of the process. Experimental studies fall into three broad groups—inter-nation simulation, the dynamics of groups in conflict, and mixed motive or "prisoners' dilemma" games.

Inter-nation simulation will receive only a brief mention here because it is so complex in conceptualization and technique that I can neither describe nor evaluate it adequately. It is a highly ingenious effort to duplicate in the laboratory the processes of international negotiation. A miniature world of fictitious nations is created in which individuals take the roles of key national decision-makers; they are each given a brief historical orientation as to the nature of the "world" in which they are to operate, as well as certain information about their "nation's" capabilities and resources and the degree of domestic freedom in reaching decisions it permits them. The decision-makers' task is to allocate their national resources to further their national interests best. Computers record and analyze the military, economic, and political consequences of their decisions in domestic and international spheres. The pertinence of inter-nation simulation to international affairs has been tested by giving the players disguised data from historical crises and observing how closely the unfolding of the simulated conflict corresponded to the historical course of events. The findings have been sufficiently encouraging to justify use of the method to test a variety of hypotheses about international behavior.[31, 32]

To emphasize the need for caution in generalizing about international negotiations from experimental situations, some of their major differences should be mentioned. Although some experiments on group conflict and bargaining have used mature adults, their participants are usually college students, and none are diplomats. The stakes of the international game are incomparably greater than those in experiments which are usually points or small sums of money. Since the "players" in international negotiations represent complex groups, often containing subgroups whose interests conflict, rather than only themselves or small, unified teams, each international negotiator must consider multiple audiences—the subgroups at home, the subgroups in the adversary's camp whose differences he may be able to exploit, his allies, his adversary's allies, and the uncommitted nations.

None of these considerations plagues the experimental negotiator. The rules of the experimental game are the same for all players, and all know them. On the international scene, the rules are among the central issues at stake and may have to be formulated as the negotiations proceed. Because the main job may be to get the adversary to accept and abide by a certain set of rules, wrangles over minor procedural points may involve deeper issues than are immediately apparent.

Finally, international problems have no perfect solution; there are many possible solutions, and the contestants come to the bargaining table with different preferences whose rank orderings are only imperfectly known to one another; as the result of past experiences each may have a different perception of the possible solutions. These last points are gradually being included in experimental designs, but no major results have been reported. [33, 34]

Yet despite their drastic oversimplification of international bargaining, the findings of some experiments so closely parallel what actually occurs that they suggest that these approaches may eventually make significant new contributions to the understanding of international negotiations.

Group Dynamics in Conflict Situations

Recently there have sprung up throughout the country training laboratories in group development in which those who must work with groups and want to learn how to do it better get together for several days or weeks to increase their understanding and skills; they come primarily from industry, the churches, teaching, and the helping professions. Isolated from their usual associates and freed from job obligations in an environment devoted entirely to the formation and study of small groups, they rapidly form groups whose properties are the same as those in which they normally work.

Training laboratories afford an ideal setting for experiments in group dynamics. One basic experimental design for studying group conflict, used repeatedly with systematic variations, has yielded the findings to be reported.[35] During the first three days arbitrarily formed groups with seven to twelve members meet in five or six two-hour sessions to study, on themselves, the process of group formation; at the end of this time they have become real groups with a sense of identity, cohesiveness, and a rudimentary group structure. Each group is then given a familiar type of problem—one concerning the operation of a business firm or the handling of a deviant student in college—and told to prepare and type up a solution in three hours. In any one experiment, all groups receive the same problem.

Each group's solution is distributed to the other group or groups involved in the experiment who are asked to familiarize themselves with the others' solutions, by studying them separately or listening to discussions among the captains elected by each group. When the groups signify that they understand each other's solution, the captains meet in the presence of their groups to try to agree on the better solution. Members of each group may communicate privately with their captains, but they cannot enter the discussion.

The basic pattern resembles international negotiations in that negotiators are representatives of groups that already have their own proposed solutions to the problem; but experimental negotiators cannot modify their groups' solutions, and a neutral individual or small panel makes the final decision if the negotiators cannot agree.

It should be mentioned in passing that the team leaders are usually their groups' more independent, nonconforming members,[36] as if the members sense that this type of person would be less likely to yield to the opponent's pressure; but in the conflict situation their own self-esteem becomes identified with their group's proposal, and they identify strongly with its position.

The central finding of these studies among several that seem relevant to international negotiations was that the negotiations almost always ended in deadlock: in one series, in only two of sixty-two confrontations did the captain of one team finally capitulate (by contrast, the uncommitted judges easily picked the better solution every time). This unhappy outcome arose, of course, from each group's deep commitment to its own solution, with the result that whenever a team captain showed signs of yielding, his fellow group members demanded that he stand firm. The two captains who gave in were severely criticized by their teammates.[37] The team captains showed a similar rigidity even when negotiating in private, probably because they knew they would have to face their teammates afterwards—the "traitor trap" [38] is obviously very powerful.

Commitment to their own solutions distorted the group members' perceptions, and one striking feature, a cautionary one for all negotiators, was that despite the group members' subjective convictions that they fully understood their rivals' proposals, they actually did not. The clearest demonstration of this involved a modification of the experiment in which three groups were asked to study and then defend to each other the solutions created by earlier groups. (This takes into account that a group spends much more time preparing its proposal than studying its rival's, which could have accounted for the results.) The same solutions were also given to groups told simply to evaluate their merits—that is, no element of competition was introduced. The competing groups then met in pairs and their captains questioned each other, ostensibly to clarify their understanding of each others' proposals, but actually to belittle the other group's proposal and show its inferiority to that of his own.

When the members of both groups had stated that they fully understood their rival's proposal, each participant was given a list of forty statements—ten contained in both groups' proposals, ten contained in neither, and ten each in the proposal of a member's own group but not in the other's—and asked simply to classify them in their appropriate categories.

The findings are quite striking: all of 20 groups and 165 out of 195 group members correctly identified more items from their group's position than from their competitor's;[39] they identified items from both groups' proposals as exclusively in their own group's much more often than as absent from both or exclusively in the opponent's.[40] The same selective recognition was found when groups studied each others' solutions privately for two hours and then signified that they understood them perfectly.[41] Needless to say, the control groups who simply studied the proposals without a competitive "set," showed no such distortions.

That this type of selective attention exists in real life is shown by a summary prepared by management in the course of some negotiations with a union which listed 62 items of disagreement but failed to mention the 182 areas of agreement.[42]

In addition to an inability to hear what the adversary was saying or correctly identify its source, there was an overvaluation of the solution of one's own group. In one experiment in which groups were asked to compare their own solution to the adversary's, forty-six of forty-eight possible comparisons favored their own solution, and the remaining two were tied.[43] When group teams were used, the same overvaluation extended to the members of one's own group and allied groups; it increased during the negotiations until the judge's decision,[44] at which point, predictably, the victors' morale continued high but the losing group's plummeted, as did its estimate of its allies. (Its own morale recovered somewhat by the next day, though not to its original height, but its estimate of its allies did not.) Both groups agreed before his decision that the judge was intelligent, unprejudiced, and capable; after it, the victors were confirmed in their good opinion, while the losers blamed their defeat on his failure to understand their proposal.[45] It should be added that the defeated group's effort to preserve self-esteem by shifting blame to their allies and the judge could not be maintained, and they eventually splintered as the members began to blame each other.

If artificially composed groups dealing with hypothetical problems repeatedly developed this much distortion and rigidity when in conflict, it is a wonder that international negotiations over vital issues are ever successful.

"Prisoners' Dilemma"

Whether the international power struggle is waged by warlike or peaceful means, it remains a mixed-motive game in which the participants have some common and some opposed interests. "Chicken," examined in connection with the arms race, is a drastic form of this game. Another version, "Prisoners' Dilemma" may help to clarify some psychological problems of negotiation.

Mixed-motive games will henceforth be called variable-sum games, to indicate that the sums of gains and losses vary with different outcomes, in contrast to most games, in which the victor's gains always balance the loser's losses so that their sum is zero.

In a variable-sum game the best solution would be that in which all players' sum is greatest, the worst the one in which all players' sum is least. The central feature of these games for our purposes is that the best outcome for both players can be obtained only if each takes the other's interests as well as his own into account; if each considers only his own interests, both wind up with an outcome that neither prefers.[46]

Consider the story of the prisoners' dilemma: a district attorney holds two suspects whom he does not have enough evidence to convict. So he goes to each and says that if he confesses and his partner does not, he will get off with a one-year sentence for turning state's evidence, but if he refuses to confess and his partner confesses, he will get the maximum penalty of ten years for his stubbornness; if both confess, each will get a five-year sentence, but if neither confesses, they will be convicted on a lesser charge and each will get two years. Each prisoner thinks to himself: "If I do not confess, I stand to get a two-year sentence (if I can trust my partner also not to confess) or a ten-year sentence if he confesses; but if I confess, the worst that can happen to me is a five-year sentence (if my partner confesses) and I may get off with one year if he does not; so it is to my advantage to confess, especially since my partner is going through the same calculation and will therefore probably confess." Both confess and get five years, whereas if they had trusted each other, they would have been given only two.

Nations would face an analogous problem with a test ban agreement that lacked a foolproof inspection system, so that cheating would be possible. Let us assume that two nations, Neptunia and Plutonia, have signed such an agreement: " 'If Plutonia does not cheat,' the Neptunian strategist reasons, 'then clearly it is in Neptunia's interest to cheat; for then we shall be ahead of Plutonia in our research on nuclear weapons. If, on the other hand, Plutonia does cheat, this is all the more reason why we should also cheat; for otherwise we let them get ahead. Consequently, regardless of whether Plutonia cheats or not, it is in our interest to cheat. We must therefore cheat in order to serve our national interest.'

"The Plutonian strategist, being in exactly the same position, reasons in exactly the same way and comes to the same conclusion. Consequently, both countries cheat and in doing so are both worse off than if they had not cheated, since otherwise there was no point to the agreement (which presumably conferred benefits on both countries)." [47]

The issue at stake in such games determines the size of the "payoffs" for the various possible outcomes, thereby influencing the relative strength of the players' motives to cooperate or defect. Regardless of the issue, however, the best outcome for both players will be reached if they trust each other. In Prisoners' Dilemma even the best outcome involves some loss for both, but in disarmament negotiations the cooperative solution would yield great rewards for all parties concerned.

The crucial feature of Prisoners' Dilemma is that it requires mutual trust while strongly tempting the players to try to double-cross each other: to reach the best outcome for both, each must trust the other in the very real sense of giving the other an opportunity to hurt him if he so chooses, but the game puts a premium on successful deceit. The best strategy for each contestant would be to convince his opponent that he will cooperate—so that the opponent will make a cooperative choice—and then defect. In the examples, Prisoner A would fare best if he could convince B that he (A) would never confess so that B would not do so; A could then confess and get a very light sentence at B's expense. In the international version, Plutonia would gain the greatest advantage if it could convince Neptunia that it would not cheat (so that Neptunia would not) and then cheat. Each contestant is torn between the contradictory goals of winning the other's trust and cheating him, and between his desire to trust the opponent and his fear of betrayal.

Prisoners' Dilemma lends itself readily to experimental ma-

nipulations—the payoffs can be quantified and the game computerized so that a lot of data can easily be obtained and analyzed.
The game's dimensions can all be systematically varied—the
payoff schedules, the number of trials permitted, the amount and
type of communication permitted the players between and during trials, the extent to which players can "threaten" each
other, as well as the players' personal qualities and relations to
each other. Prisoners' Dilemma is a happy hunting ground for
experimentally-minded social psychologists, and they have been
eagerly exploiting it.

Unfortunately, as seems inevitable in a new field, the first
crop of results are for the most part trivial or obvious, and their
interpretation proves to be more difficult than the researchers
had been led to expect. Subjects may be responding to motives
arising from the context of the experiment of which the experimenter is not aware and which he cannot control. The "game"
they are actually playing may not be the one the experimenter
had in mind—they may be trying to do what they think he
wants, for example, rather than defeat the opponent. While the
conditions of these games are remote from those of international
negotiations, some relevant sample findings are still worth presenting as examples of the promise held by experiments with
prisoners' dilemma games. One group of findings concerns the
role of communication in establishing mutual trust; the other the
effect of introducing threats.

COMMUNICATION AND TRUST. An experiment explored
the relationship between trust, trustworthiness, and amount of
communication between the players.[48] Each player could choose
one of two alternatives, and the payoffs were arranged to tempt
each to make the non-cooperative choice, leading to lower payoffs for both than if they had cooperated; to enhance this temptation, each was told to try to win as much as possible for himself without regard to how his opponent fared. The second
player was actually an accomplice who made a cooperative
choice on the first trial (there were five) and then followed the
subject, cooperating or defecting depending on what he had
done on the previous trial.

Subjects were divided into several groups, and the amount of communication between them was systematically varied—some neither sent nor received written communications before each trial, some only received them, some only sent them, none did both. The communications contained four levels of information: intentions, expectations as to how the other should respond, what the penalty for defecting would be, and how the other could absolve himself in the next trial if he defected. Of the many measures made, the most interesting for our purposes were perceived trust and trustworthiness—"trust" was defined as the subject's expectation that his opponent would cooperate, as determined by his answer to a question to this effect before each trial, "trustworthiness" as making a cooperative choice. Both were greater, the more complete the communication sent or received: 80 per cent of those who sent or received notes containing all four items of information expressed trust and made cooperative choices as compared to only 11 per cent of those not allowed to communicate at all;* of those who sent or received incomplete communications, the percentage who trusted and cooperated ranged between 30 and 60. This finding lends experimental support to two features of the GRIT proposal: nations should clearly announce their intentions in advance and invite the adversary to cooperate.

Of subsidiary interest is the finding that only 20 per cent of the subjects were double-crossers who defected after perceiving that the opponent trusted them, and only a quarter of these had sent a message indicating that they were going to cooperate—committing themselves apparently helped to keep them trustworthy.

COMMUNICATION AND THREAT. All negotiations include threats in some form, expressed or implied, and these often consist merely of one party's threat to prevent the other from achieving certain ends it desires, a type of threat that lends itself well to experimental study, since it is mild enough to be readily reproduced in the laboratory. The prototype for most such stud-

---

* Compare the finding (Chapter 7, p. 125) that communication diminishes dislike.

ies is a variable-sum game in which players pretend to operate rival trucking firms, and their earnings depend on being first to get their own trucks to a destination on a short road over which only one can pass at a time; either could use a longer road, which permits him to reach his goal independently of the other player's actions but which costs him money because of the time lost. In some variations one or both players control a gate that could deny the other's access to the short road—and this is the threat.[49] The players have a common interest in working out an arrangement for taking turns on the short road, since this would yield the highest total gain for both, but their interests conflict because the one who uses it first or more often (depending on the variation of the game being studied) profits more.

Three different instructions were used: cooperative—try to win as much for yourself as possible, but you want your opponent to come out ahead also; individualistic—try to do the best for yourself regardless of what happens to him; and competitive —try to come out as far ahead of him as you can. Since variations in instructions, kinds of communication permitted, the status or power of the players relative to each other, feelings of like or dislike, and schedules of costs and payoffs all have been found to affect players' choices, no general conclusions can safely be drawn from the findings. A few on the effects of communication and threat may be cited, however, as examples of the type of question that can be explored with this technique.

The more competitive the players' orientation, the less likely they were to avail themselves of opportunities to communicate.* Communication helped improve both participants' outcomes only when they were required to communicate a fair proposal before each trial, one they would accept if it were offered them by the adversary. If their first trials had ended in deadlock and mutual loss, the tutoring was unnecessary—experience was, as usual, a good teacher.

With respect to the capacity to threaten, a repeated finding was that when both participants had control of a gate—when

* Cf. Chapter 7, pp. 125–26, on the tendency to break off communication with an enemy.

both had weapons, as it were—they did worse than when neither had a gate.

Apparently, when a player uses a gate, he implies by this use of threat that he feels himself in some sense superior to his opponent—perhaps more courageous, perhaps of higher status—so that it is his opponent's duty to defer to him. To allow oneself to be intimidated would therefore implicitly grant the other's right to demand submission—a humiliating posture—and the most effective way of rectifying this blow to self-esteem is to intimidate the threatener.[50] These psychological motivations may contribute to the examples in Chapter 8 of counter-threat on the international scene.

The results in a modification of the trucking game, in which each subject could signal his intentions before each trial and also indicate what he thought the other would do, were shown to be strongly affected by whether the player intended to cooperate, to strive for precisely half the winnings, or to dominate. Cooperative pairs did much better than competitive pairs —hardly a startling finding—but in pairs in which one started with a cooperative and the other with a competitive attitude, both players fared badly in the long run. The cooperative partner's behavior apparently encouraged the competitive one to keep on pushing, until the former got angry and started to fight back, by which time it was too late. If the initially cooperative player immediately made a counter-threat, the players were much more likely to arrive at a cooperative agreement eventually.[51] The moral seems to be, Don't let your opponent think he can take advantage of you,* a finding that casts doubt on the effectiveness of turning the other cheek. To test this strategy further, the experimenters led subjects to think that their opponent refused to budge from a conciliatory strategy, even to the extent

---

* This can also be viewed as an example of the effect of disappointed expectations, like the finding that a friendly note following a hostile one elicits more friendliness than after a friendly one (Chapter 5, p. 76). There are many real-life analogies—for example, the interrogation technique of suddenly showing consideration for a prisoner after treating him roughly, or the negotiating maneuver of unexpectedly making a concession after being adamant.

of accepting an electric shock each time his adversary blocked him. Since the "pacifist" was simulated by a computer, one cannot be sure how convincing he was, but a pacifist strategy did not in itself cause any player to change from a dominating to a cooperative strategy. In some runs, the "pacifist" explained the reason for his behavior, stressing his conciliatory intent, making fair demands, and emphasizing his refusal to use the shock and his intention to force the other to shock him if he were going to continue to be unfair. A small crumb of comfort for pacifists is that of the subjects who changed from dominating to cooperating, all were in the group receiving this communication—unfortunately, however, it reinforced other subjects in their dominating strategy because they saw the pacifist's tactics as efforts to trick them or make them feel guilty.[52]

As far as they go, these experiments confirm the general experience that the more bargainers communicate their intentions and expectations, the better (provided, of course, that the communications are genuinely intended to achieve the best outcome for both parties), and that threats are apt to impede negotiations. The best results for both parties were obtained when neither used threats, but if one player did make a threat, a prompt, firm counter-threat was more likely than a conciliatory initial response to facilitate an ultimately successful outcome. At least in one experimental situation, pacifist strategies do not work.

IMPLICATIONS FOR INTERNATIONAL
NEGOTIATIONS

Empirical and experimental studies of negotiations confirm the obvious fact that regardless of the issues, a successful outcome is impeded by the absence of mutual trust and lack of full and accurate communication. Their contribution lies in highlighting specific sources of difficulty that should concern all negotiators, and they also offer certain leads as to how negotiations could be improved.

In almost all international negotiations it is reasonable to assume some potential basis for mutual trust—even in war there are often tacit bargains between the combatants. The Prisoner's Dilemma depends on trust to the extent that both players must trust the person who sets the rules: if the prisoners did not trust the district attorney, there would be no dilemma, and each would simply refuse to confess and would take his chances. One important way of improving the chances for the successful outcome of negotiations, regardless of substantive issues, would thus be to pinpoint and combat sources of mutual mistrust. Participants in all negotiations could well make special efforts to get into the open the psychological sources of mutual misunderstanding and mistrust that operate out of awareness, including conflicting habits of thought and ways of proceeding, and above all, the universal difficulty in really hearing what the other fellow is saying—Adlai Stevenson's quip, "I sometimes think that what America needs more than anything else is a hearing aid," [53] applies to all countries. If only it were enforceable, a splendid ground rule for all negotiations would be that there would be no bargaining until the parties could express each other's positions to their mutual satisfaction.[54] Unfortunately, as demonstrated by the experiments on understanding the adversary's position, this is much more difficult than it seems, and I urge the reader to try it in his next disagreement with a friend or colleague—it is amazing how one's own thoughts keep intruding. Even if it is unattainable, however, merely striving for this goal would improve the atmosphere of all negotiations. As all psychotherapists know, the best way to get someone's favorable attention is to listen to him, not talk to him. To feel that a person is trying his best to understand you, especially someone you believe to be hostile or indifferent, creates a very favorable impression of his good sense, intelligence, and good will, and you are then in a much more receptive frame of mind for his ideas.[55]

From the organizational standpoint, the goal would be to set up conditions that foster in the negotiators a cooperative rather than a competitive stance. The aim would be to reduce the barriers between the groups by making each feel, at every step of the way, that they are working on a joint enterprise. Instead of negotiators being selected by each group separately, for example, they could be chosen jointly from a panel of names put up by each; this "criss-cross" panel would weaken the "traitor trap," because the negotiators would consider themselves representatives of both groups, who would have implicitly committed themselves in advance to accept the outcome of the bargaining.[56] This procedure is hardly feasible at the moment in international political negotiations, but it could perhaps be used to improve cultural, economic, and scientific negotiations.

At every step of the way it might also be possible to involve both groups in selecting problems to be discussed and devising alternative solutions, thereby taking advantage of people's greater readiness to accept innovations when they feel they have participated in their planning.[57] An experiment testing the feasibility of such a procedure contrasted fixed with fluid negotiations: using the general group-conflict experimental plan, each of the competing groups first developed a set of alternative solutions to the problem rather than a single one. Group representatives in fixed negotiations were told to try to get their group's alternatives adopted, while in the fluid ones they were instructed to work with the other group's representatives to develop the best single ranking of both sets; according to independent judges, the list of alternatives arrived at jointly contained the best from each group, and included some new, creative ones not in either group's original list.[58] That such procedures are of more than theoretical importance is suggested by the finding that they improve outcomes of management-labor negotiations.

Perhaps the place to start would be in schools of international relations, political science, and law, where budding diplomats could participate in the kinds of experiments reviewed here. There would be powerful learning experiences in discovering at first hand that you really have not understood your adversary's proposal, despite your conviction that you have, or that group pressures hamstring you in reaching an agreement, or how differences in amount and type of communication can affect mutual trust.

An important lesson to be learned from this review is that

major psychological obstacles to successful international negotiations lie in the negotiating parties' attitudes. Procedural improvements can be of some help, but real progress depends on convincing nations that they have become genuinely interdependent. International negotiations, especially those involving armaments, have become prisoners' dilemmas in which all nations have more to gain by cooperating than by competing, and in which, in fact, persistence in competitive attitudes can bring all to disaster.

Day by day the advances in science, mass communication, and mass transportation are increasing this interdependence. The psychological problem is how to make all people aware that whether they like it or not, the earth is becoming a single community.

11 · Toward a World Community

THE METHODS just described may reduce international tensions somewhat and improve prospects for successful negotiations about specific issues, but substantial progress toward the elimination of war will require two far-reaching changes in traditional attitudes and patterns of behavior: a sharp downgrading of resort to violence as a way to resolve international conflict; and replacement of the anarchic international system of sovereign nation-states by a more organized one containing, among other features, supranational institutions for conflict resolution, operating under world law and empowered to enforce their decisions. These two aims are closely related, but for convenience we shall consider the problem of developing a world community in this chapter and the downgrading of violence in the next.

INTERNATIONAL INTERDEPENDENCE AND
WORLD GOVERNMENT

Humans must form communities in order to survive and prosper, but they could not do so unless concern for the good of the community or group were at least as strong as the drive toward self-aggrandizement. Psychologically, the two drives may be linked by the fact that part of an individual's sense of identity is formed by the groups to which he belongs. Everyone belongs to many overlapping groups, and when they conflict, the welfare of the one with which he most strongly identifies his own sense of well-being takes precedence.

Concern for the common good extends to people with whom relationships are rewarding—those, for example, with whom we play or work, who help us or whom we help—as well as to those with similar ideologies, a common language, similar social customs, and the like; groups are also partly defined by territorial boundaries, kinship patterns, and other qualities. But beneath all of these, group members are psychologically bound by a sense of interdependence, a recognition that they share a common fate. Negatively, this means they recognize that cooperation is necessary to survival, that, in Benjamin Franklin's words, "We must all hang together, or assuredly we shall all hang separately"; positively, it implies a recognition that the promotion of each member's welfare depends on the others. This dependence can include competition with certain restraints that protect the loser from excessive damage, but it consists mainly of various types of cooperative activity in a framework of institutions and rules.

During the last few centuries the nation-state has emerged in the Western world as the most suitable political structure for protecting its members and promoting their welfare, aims best accomplished on the whole by each nation's trying to promote its own interests as much as possible without regard to other nations' interests. But this is becoming increasingly unworkable, because national boundaries are losing their significance: nuclear fallout circles the globe, regardless of its origin; such scientific schemes as melting the polar ice cap, thereby raising the level of the northern oceans several feet, would obviously affect all maritime nations' coastal cities; observation satellites have opened all nations to military inspection, and delivery systems can send intercontinental missiles thousands of miles; and because of their increasing economic interdependence, no nation can thrive unless many others do.

In the future probably no nation will be able to guarantee its citizens' safety or unilaterally advance its national interests. The freedom of action of even the most powerful is already sharply curtailed—it is scarcely an exaggeration to say that America's foreign policy is made as much in Peking and Moscow as in Foggy Bottom—and the people of all nations will soon share a common fate.

From the psychological standpoint, the task is to find ways to use those forces that are making the nation-state obsolete— communication, transportation, and technological advances—to diminish distrust and fear among members of different nations and foster their sense of belonging to a world community. This would facilitate the expansion and modification of existing international organizations and the invention of new ones. While the relative merits of various proposals for achieving these ends depend on political, legal, and economic considerations that lie beyond the scope of this inquiry, a few psychologically oriented comments may be in order.

Many people believe that the way to start is by strengthening the United Nations' peace-keeping activities, and plans for world governments stress their peace-keeping functions. Peace-keeping seems especially attractive to nations like the United States which would gain most by maintaining the status quo, but while peace-keeping would be an essential function of any world government, this obviously would not be sufficient in itself to gain the allegiance of most of the peoples of the world, especially those who wish to challenge the current hegemony of the United States. No domestic government consisting only of a police force and judiciary and having only punitive powers could long survive; to win their citizens' allegiance, governments must perform positive services, and maintaining order is only one. In fact, to give a world government only peace-keeping powers initially might impede its development by making it so unpopular that nations would resist giving it other functions.[1] Such allegiance as the United Nations commands among the developing nations, for example, probably derives mainly from its health and economic development programs and not from its peace-keeping struggles, whose value is by no means negligible but whose success has hardly been spectacular enough to account for the organization's vitality.

On two recent occasions I have had the opportunity to listen in for some days on informal conversations between junior diplomats from the smaller nations. When their attention turned to the United Nations, as it often did, they did not speak of the headline-catching political battles in the General Assembly and Security Council, but rather of the day-to-day activities of the International Labor Office, the World Health Organization, and the Economic and Social Council—in their eyes it is these that make the United Nations valuable.

Looked at the other way, every community has some sort of government, and governmental functions in turn strengthen the community, but these grow out of community needs. The thirteen American colonies formed a federation only with great reluctance, and each increase of federal power has been vigorously opposed; yet the federal government has continued to grow as new institutions were necessary to prevent chaos in communication, transportation, commerce, labor relations, and many other fields. Similarly, a world government's functions will be determined less by itself than by world needs that cannot be satisfied except through it.

One powerful force for group formation is the existence of a common enemy. As scientists become increasingly convinced that the universe contains innumerable other societies of intelligent beings, the fantasy of a possible invasion by one of them takes on renewed life. Such an event would probably bring about overnight the unity of mankind, but even definite proof that we were under surveillance from another planet—and not all sightings of unidentified flying objects have been adequately explained—might give world government a powerful boost.

But a common enemy, which is not the only basis for group formation, is also a poor one, since groupings formed to fight a common foe fall apart once the enemy ceases to be a threat.

Other types of interdependence offer better inducements with more enduring effects. As such technological advances as communications satellites and international mass transportation create an ever increasing number of activities requiring international cooperation, all nations' self-interests will demand their increasing investment in a world government. Behavioral scientists have made some observations on how these new potentialities could be used more effectively to promote the sense of world community, and to these we now turn.

THE ROLE OF INTERNATIONAL MASS COMMUNICATIONS IN PROMOTING WORLD COMMUNITY

Among the most spectacular of the many current technological revolutions is that in the visual-auditory media of mass communication. Television, radio, and the movies are revolutionizing all aspects of life, and experts envisage a day when the home electronic communications set will not only provide radio and television, but will perform such varied services as printing a facsimile newspaper, shopping, and banking.

International television and radio now enable statesmen sitting in their own capitals to confer at a moment's notice, and they bring the far corners of the world into everyone's living room. Transistor radios and television sets are spreading rapidly throughout the world: the leaders of underdeveloped nations use them to unify their countries, educate the people, and maintain political control—Castro, for example, can frequently be seen on television in almost every Cuban village; and 93 per cent of American homes have television sets—considerably more than have telephones.

Television and radio have several advantages over print as means of communication: they reach illiterates, thereby overcoming one huge obstacle to mass education; and on the whole their immediacy gives them greater emotional impact since emotions are contagious, and witnessing someone else's grief, joy, fear, or anger can arouse the same feeling in oneself. Great writers, of course, arouse strong emotions through the printed word, but more emotion can result from hearing a poem or novel read aloud with feeling, or from seeing a play. And it takes considerable literary skill to elicit emotion, while a shriek suffices on radio, and television heightens the impact by adding the agonized face.

Telecommunication's emotional component increases prospects for promoting the sense of world community in two ways. First, it increases the persuasiveness of messages. Since information as such is not very compelling, especially if it conflicts with existing attitudes, the information necessary to change attitudes must be presented in a context that elicits an emotional response. Second, a shared emotional experience helps create a sense of solidarity. President Kennedy's funeral is a case in point: millions of Americans shared the emotions it aroused, and many felt a strengthened sense of brotherhood with their fellows, just as a family is drawn together at the funeral of one of its members. International communications satellites are rapidly making it possible to reach not only one nation but the entire world simultaneously, thereby creating new prospects for fostering a sense of the brotherhood of man.

International radio and television are, of course, only tools, and as such they can be used to fan hatreds and create distorted images just as effectively as to promote good will and understanding. Furthermore, by making the poor aware of what the rich are enjoying and by showing the citizens of poor nations the life in rich ones, they also contribute powerfully to domestic and international unrest by intensifying the sense of relative deprivation, as described in Chapter 6. But regardless of the intent of those who control them, international telecommunications will promote the sense of world community. They are bound to create pressure toward larger and larger language blocs which in itself will reduce international barriers. It will be a long time before there is agreement on a universal language, because none of the extant ones are acceptable to all nations, while invented ones do not offer sufficient incentive to learn them—few people will go to the trouble of learning a language simply to enjoy the opportunity to communicate with others who speak it. But it would be a great improvement if everyone knew one of the world's four or five major languages; and this is within the realm of possibility since many people have learned them because they were spoken by a ruling group or by traders. For generations the English led the field in both respects—they had the most populous empire and the most extensive world trade—and so English will probably remain the most widely spoken tongue. Many newly independent nations, like India and several in Africa, consist of groups that lack a common tongue, and many have no written language of any sort. The only language nearly all their inhabitants know is that of their former rulers, so it is not surprising that several African nations formerly under British rule have decided to make English their primary language.

Civil wars and revolutions are no less bitter because partisans of both sides speak the same tongue, but the existence of a shared language has the potential to destroy those barriers to mutual understanding created by sheer inability to communicate.

International mass-communication media will also promote international understanding, despite the program-makers, simply by supplying an increasing volume of information about each nation. The more complete the information people have about each other, the harder it is in general to maintain mutual hatred based on partial or distorted views; and given free access to information about another group, normal curiosity will impel people to try to learn more.

International supervision of the transmission of all international programs by communications satellites would be the best insurance against their misuse, and each nation would be able to put its best foot forward and to prevent other nations from defaming it. People would begin to see each other at work and play rather than only as participants in such formal or staged activities as political rallies or military parades, and new similarities and bases for mutual understanding, presently hidden by stereotypes, would be visible.

Emerging World Public Opinion as a Force for Peace

International mass communication is creating a world public opinion, which all nations' policy-makers will increasingly have to take into account. Existing rudimentary world opinion already exerts some restraint on the use of violence by the Great Powers. The United States, for example, could blow Cuba off the map and is certainly not well disposed to Castro, but it has been deterred from destroying his regime by force primarily by the adverse effects of such a move on its relations with the other Latin American nations. And I cannot but wonder whether this new concern isn't reflected in the strong emotional reaction of American leaders at the thought of a war crimes trial of American fliers in North Vietnam. The quiet execution of some twelve fliers created no uproar, but American leaders were apparently upset by the prospect of a public trial in which American soldiers' actions would be displayed before the world as crimes.

Having to keep in mind the multiple audiences of the world public puts a great premium on ambiguity of expression and may sometimes act as a disadvantageous constraint on policy-making. But the constraint will probably work against warlike policies more often than not. The potentialities of a mobilized world public opinion suggest that there may be great merit in the imaginative proposal for a "Court of International Delinquency." [2] Such a court would be empowered to try individual national leaders for offenses against mankind's peace and security, as defined by the UN International Law Commission, and if a leader refused an invitation to appear, he could be tried *in absentia,* if necessary without his government's consent. The court would have no power to impose sanctions on states, thus circumventing one of the main current obstacles to an effective World Court; and since it could not punish those found guilty by imprisonment or fines, there would be no problem of trying to enforce its decisions if a nation backed the accused leader. It could, however, hold the offender up to public disgrace and also recommend that other nations treat him as *persona non grata* by refusing to recognize his credentials of office, grant him a visa, and the like. In an extreme case this would amount to banishment from the world community: the convicted leader would be a prisoner within the borders of his own nation. A leader held up to international obloquy would also have trouble maintaining his position at home—even today national leaders work hard to appear in a good light, not only before their own countrymen but before the rest of the world. The sanctions at the disposal of such a court might thus be considerably more powerful than is immediately apparent.

Dissemination of Information to Reduce International Misunderstandings

We have been considering probable future developments foreshadowed by the revolutionary advances in electronic communications media. But the United States, for example, could be using these media considerably more effectively right now to improve understanding of its way of life and its foreign policy, and to reduce international tensions.

The simplest immediate measure would be simply to refrain from broadcasting programs that are damaging. Although not electronically transmitted, American motion pictures shown abroad convey a picture of American life that, without much exaggeration, could be called defamatory. A Russian delegate to an international conference described the impression they create of Americans: "You are made to seem very vulgar and materialistic. . . . Everyone in the movies seems to be stealing from the next fellow—either his money or his job or his wife. And everybody seems to be only a straw away from punching the next man in the face." [3]

With respect to positive programs, it is probably useful to distinguish three types of audience: the communist nations, the technologically undeveloped nations, and the Western European nations.

It is unlikely that the United States can change the communist nations' ideological orientation through any messages transmitted by mass communication, because such a change almost always requires a massive social upheaval led by magnetic personalities representing the new view—conditions that have been met by all major ideological revolutions, most recently the American, the French, and the Russian. Thus, it is unrealistic to hope to influence through mass communications the ideologies of nations with a strong sense of purpose and with rising living and educational standards; I can think of neither an incentive nor a leader the United States could offer the Soviet Union or its satellites, for example, that would be strong enough to cause their citizens to abandon their world-view in favor of the American one.

A realistic aim would be to use mass communications to reduce their fear of the United States, without encouraging them to believe that its will to maintain its own way of life was weakening. The means of doing this would probably be virtually the same as those used to increase the sense of world community, and the most important would be to stress the common features of "Communism" and "Free Enterprise" that have been largely lost sight of because the differences are so threatening and so much more obvious. These philosophies disagree mainly on the relative priorities assigned to individual self-development and group welfare, or rather on how they view the relationship between the two. The American orientation puts the individual first, but reminds him that he cannot maximize his own welfare without including his group's; the communist orientation believes that the individual can fulfill himself only by placing concern for the collective welfare first.

This difference in world-views certainly leads to sharp disagreement about the type of social, political, and economic organization that will best promote individual and group welfare; but while it is serious enough to threaten the world with a blood bath, both envisage the same ultimate goal and behind both are certain shared postulates about human nature. Both have great faith in the power of human intelligence and place a high value on increasing the well-being of all mankind. Both are optimistic about man, believing rightly or wrongly that people are basically good and that hatred and destructive behavior result from faulty education and a frustrating environment, and that proper educational methods and favorable environments will therefore produce peaceful and happy people.

Finally, in the great hope that both place in the power of science to mold the environment to man's desires there may lie a vast potential for achieving a world without war. For this hope leads believers in both world-views to deplore the arms race, if only because it diverts scientific energies and resources from constructive to destructive ends and delays the fulfillment of the promise science holds out for a prosperous and healthy world. And since the ideology and language of science are universal, it draws men together.

With respect to countries that more or less share the philosophy of the United States, international mass-communications media could be used more effectively to correct their distorted view of the American way of life, much of which is created by the American movies shown abroad. But other distortion is at a conceptual level, as strikingly illustrated by a public opinion study whose respondents in four Western European countries and the United States were simply asked to rate their own country and the United States and a ten-point scale (zero = completely capitalistic, ten = completely socialistic)[4]; they were also asked to indicate on the same scale the type of society they wanted for themselves. About two-thirds of the Europeans but no Americans scored the United States as completely capitalistic; most Americans scored their own society in the middle range (between 4 and 6), and this, interestingly enough, is where most Europeans scored the type of society they wanted—they wanted what Americans thought they already had.

This "international misunderstanding" apparently arises from different meanings of "capitalistic" and "socialistic." To Europeans "capitalism" means exploitation of the poor by the rich with no concern for social welfare, and thus has negative connotations. To Americans "socialism" means public ownership of the means of production; but to Europeans it means primarily concern for the general welfare, and so they overwhelmingly approve it, although they too generally oppose communism. American concern for the general welfare is actually great, as attested to by its social welfare legislation, of which Medicare is the latest example.

These considerations suggest two practical implications for America's use of international communications: it should resist communist nations' attempts to define the struggle as between socialism and capitalism—more accurately, it is between totalitarianism and constitutional democracy, or between conflicting national goals; and there should be greater stress on social welfare programs and less on American affluence.

As to the third international audience, the technologically undeveloped nations without strong ideological commitments are influenced most by the nation that can do the most for them. The influence of tangible aid is much more powerful than any messages transmitted by newspapers, radio, and, to a lesser extent, television. Today these reach only a small proportion of the population of these countries, mainly in the cities, but it is probably the most influential segment, and access to the mass media is spreading rapidly.[5] Insofar as they do play a part, they are effective to the extent that they convincingly convey the idea that the American way of life has more to offer than communism. Merely parading affluence probably generates more resentment than good will, but example is a powerful persuader— the communist countries' rapid economic advance, for example, has been their best propaganda weapon—and the greater the success of the United States in solving its internal problems, especially racial ones, the more successful its propaganda will be.

Advantages of Listening and Being Overheard

Because international mass-communications media have greatly increased opportunities to receive as well as to send messages, another area for exploitation has been opened. One of the best ways to win someone's favorable attention is to be willing to listen to him. Thus, the mere willingness to rebroadcast other countries' programs to one's own citizens can help reduce suspicion and ill will—the rebroadcasting in Russia of President Kennedy's American University speech, for example, helped promote the ensuing thaw.

The expansion of international communications also allows for international eavesdropping. A worldwide audience overhears public discussions, demonstrations, and Senate committee hearings about the war in Vietnam, for example, a display with the obvious disadvantages of casting doubt on the unity and firmness of American support of official policies, and perhaps of encouraging the enemy to persist in the hope that the United States will eventually give in. Yet the net effect may be more helpful than harmful, since no nations are really monolithic, and anything that dispels this impression promotes a more realistic appraisal of international affairs; more important, however, the sincerity of those who oppose government policy cannot be questioned. The convincing demonstration that important segments of the public are trying to understand the adversary's point of view and are constantly searching for ways out of the predicament in which both sides are trapped gives credence to the policy-makers' conciliatory statements. Without this supportive evidence, they would be dismissed out of hand by everyone, not merely the Chinese and North Vietnamese.

The opportunity to be overheard may also have advantages when the time comes for actual negotiations. Sometimes the first step toward reaching a frightened and suspicious patient is to let him overhear the psychiatrist talking to someone else about him, thus permitting him to listen without appearing to do so but not putting him under the pressure to respond of a direct approach; when he feels ready, he then joins the conversation with relative ease. Similarly, it is just possible that a nation can pave the way for direct discussions with nations that fear and distrust it by allowing them to listen in on its internal discussion about them.

On many counts, then, the new international mass-communications facilities could accomplish much toward eliminating war, if properly used. By increasing peoples' acquaintance with each other, mutual hostility, would, on balance, be decreased. A hostile stereotype is easily maintained in the absence of full information; but the more people know about each other, especially if distortions are not permitted by those who control the sources of knowledge, the more the realization of their common humanity is bound to emerge. Moreover, international television and radio are creating a powerful new force—world public opinion—which could be mobilized against any international troublemakers much more effectively than before the advent of communications satellites and the like.

For all their impact, however, mass communications, as indirect forms of contact, have less potential for improving international attitudes than personal interchanges and contacts, for these, too, have become possible on a vastly greater scale than ever before.

INTERNATIONAL PERSONAL CONTACTS

Within less than a hundred hours after the assassination of President Kennedy, national leaders had come to Washington from the ends of the earth, attended the funeral, met the new President, and returned to their homes—illustrating dramatically how the globe has shrunk. The rapid expansion of relatively cheap mass air transportation and nations' growing military and economic interdependence have led to ever increasing numbers of face-to-face meetings of people from different cultures, under a great variety of circumstances. Travelers include millions of tourists, hundreds of thousands of troops (chiefly American), students, members of all sorts of technical assistance missions, performing artists, and immigrants. While contact as such does not necessarily create good will, the favorable experiences it yields can help to disclose and correct mutual distortions, and diminish mutual antipathy. But it can also confirm the reality of certain areas of conflict and unearth hitherto unsuspected ones, create opportunities for unintended insults resulting from ignorance of social forms, inappropriate choice of words, and the like as considered in Chapter 6, and finally, it can heighten mutual misperceptions because of the tendency to filter incoming experiences in accordance with one's preconceptions. If groups have been trained to hate each other,[6] intimacy and prolongation of contact will, if anything, increase mutual dislike (as in the example in Chapter 8 of the Hindus and Moslems), the same phenomenon that characterizes some American racially mixed neighborhoods.

Age and Impressionability

Using as subjects students who come to the United States to study and stay for at least a few months, psychologists have been observing international personal contacts with a view to learning how to use them more successfully to promote the sense of world community.

Although their personal characteristics undoubtedly affect visitors' receptivity to impressions from the host country, only age has received systematic attention. Among adults, whose identities and roles are relatively fixed, intensified allegiance to home reference groups often results from visits to foreign lands. The most-traveled American businessmen, for example, most uniformly represent the standard business view—that of the Republican Party.[7] Youngsters, however, are more impressionable and their identities are not yet fully formed, so they are particularly receptive, provided the experience of meeting foreigners occurs in a setting that counteracts anxiety. Furthermore, it is easy for them to form new reference groups from among their age mates and teachers, hence the success in promoting international-mindedness in their participants of programs like the Children's International Summer Villages[8] and the Experiment in International Living.[9] In the former, eleven-year-olds from several nations attend camp together for a month, either in the United States or another country from which some of the members come; in the latter, late adolescents and young adults live for a month as members of families in other lands and then travel for a month in a group including the youths from their host families.

Personal Contacts and the Promotion of Good Will

To produce more than fleeting changes of attitude, visits should be long and with as numerous and varied experiences as possible with people in the host country. And they should be rewarding for both hosts and guests.

Short visits are also valuable. The exchanges of performing artists, for example, help to improve international good feeling, and when an American pianist or singer wins a prize at a Russian festival or a Russian ballet receives an enthusiastic American reception, people in both countries are pleased. But since such impressions are only superficial, their favorable effect is easily swept away when tensions arising from other sources increase. Both hosts and visitors may see each other in a short visit as representatives of their countries, and thus be unable to make necessary differentiations. Actually, travelers usually represent only one segment of their society, and may also not behave as they would at home—students, for example, are generally of a considerably higher class than immigrants, and travelers, freed from the watchful eyes of their own reference groups, are apt to behave with less restraint.

Members of host countries readily accept a traveler's behavior as representative of his compatriots' because they know less about the visitor's nation than about his sex or occupation. One American observer cites the example of a small Japanese schoolteacher who ate very little for lunch. Her behavior did not change his notions about the eating habits of small women or schoolteachers because these were anchored in a mass of prior information about both, but since he had no prior notion about Japanese eating habits, he concluded that Japanese are small eaters.[10]

Unless visitors deliberately isolate themselves from their surroundings during long visits, they are almost certain to have varied contacts. But it may be worthwhile during a short stay if the hosts make special efforts to give the visitor a variety of experiences, especially informal ones, as antidotes to stereotyping. Visiting dignitaries who are guests of the State Department for short periods, and most of whose contacts with Americans are highly formalized, are especially apt to view America in the light of their preconceived ideas. It has been found that their stereotypes can be successfully combatted by arranging many and varied informal contacts for them with Americans in different settings, reinforced by detailed factual expositions. The best way to demonstrate American patterns of hospitality and family life, for example, is to arrange visits to American homes, and if visitors can participate in some activity, such as letting agricultural experts drive farm machinery on a family farm, so much the better.[11]

The types of personal contact most likely to create favorable impressions and therefore heighten accessibility to each other's views are those the visitors regard as useful. There is a good illustration in a thorough study of a group of young adults from West Germany who were students at American universities for six months to a year. They seemed especially receptive to features of American society that either helped them implement both societies' shared values or provided information they regarded as useful. Thus, they responded favorably to American patterns of give-and-take discussion and to methods of child-rearing, because they saw both as fostering the individualistic orientation they shared, and were particularly interested in American forms of democratic processes and voluntary participation in civic activities, which they believed would make their own society function better.[12]

Visitors want to be treated as individuals rather than as members of a category, and this can be done very effectively by involving them in some ongoing enterprise—that is, by treating them as regular members of the organization whose participation is needed and wanted.[13] Involvement in a common enterprise is an especially useful means of icebreaking, as shown by the gradual thawing of Russian participants in the Olympics: in 1948 they refused to participate and also tried, unsuccessfully, to prevent the participation of satellite countries; in 1952 they participated but segregated themselves from other nations' participants; but since 1956 they have mixed freely with players from other nations.

The need for people of different nationalities to learn to work together is especially acute in international businesses, whose staffs consist of Americans, resident nationals, and people from other countries. An experiment demonstrated convincingly how, with proper planning, mutual understanding can be greatly improved by an intensive experience of cooperation toward the attainment of common objectives. The experiment was done with two companies (one on a Caribbean island and one in Indonesia); the participants represented different levels of management, and the ratio of Americans, residents, and citizens of other countries was the same as in the actual plant; they were divided into teams of seven to ten and worked together for about fifty hours within one week. To preserve the advantage of having different managerial levels represented on the same team while overcoming the obstacles to multi-level communication, each team contained people from several levels but different departments. The assigned task was to learn a particular set of concepts for integrating problems of people and production, and to improve their own working relationships through bringing out and examining differences in attitudes and approaches created by organizational and cultural practices and traditions. Particular stress was laid on the value of candid communication.

At its conclusion, the participants evaluated the program by answering a questionnaire; the evaluation was supplemented by interviews at the close of one program and after several months in the other. The results were the same for both: from 75 to 100 per cent of resident nationals and Americans reported that understanding of each other was increased, and about 90 per cent reported a better understanding of the influence of traditions and past practices on working relationships between Americans and hosts. Almost all believed that the experience would lead them to be more open with each other on the job. And with respect to the method, 95 per cent preferred it to the lectures they had previously been given. One feature thought to have helped the experiment succeed was that the concepts and language to be learned were new to both groups—since neither was in a position to impose its language and concepts on the other, the participants met as true equals.[14]

Visitors' Attitudes and Length of Stay

The considerable amount of research done on the effects of length of stay indicates that as a general rule, the longer the contact, the more differentiated the images visitors and hosts form of each other. But the visitors' image may not change in other respects, as indicated by one study in which the views of a group of African students who had been in the United States less than eighteen months were compared with the views of those who had stayed longer. Both groups liked Americans' informal friendliness and industriousness but disliked their insincerity and materialism—and these perceptions were more widespread in the old-timers than the newcomers.[15]

There seems to be agreement on the general sequence of visitors' reactions during a long stay, although different researchers label them somewhat differently.[16, 17] At first the visitor is a spectator, tending to view the host society through the stereotypes of his own culture and personality; since everything is new and interesting, this phase is usually pleasant. Next he begins to become involved, to react to the different way of life; this is the period of culture shock ("a reaction to a temporarily unsuccessful attempt to adjust to new surroundings and people . . . the person becomes anxious, confused and apathetic" [18]), and from the standpoint of the visitor's personal satisfaction, the lowest ebb. Then he comes to terms with his host country, incorporating some of its ideas and perspectives. Finally, when his departure is imminent he tests and consolidates what he has learned, a process that continues after he returns home.

Aftereffects of International Visits

If cross-cultural contacts are to have any real value, the new attitudes they engender must persist after the visitor returns to his home. An indirect measure of the permanence and degree of the impact of the visit on the visitor would be how much difficulty he had in readjusting to his home country—presumably, the more difficult the readjustment, the more significant the impact of the cross-cultural contact. There are generally no problems after fleeting visits, but after longer visits students, especially those who have not "found themselves" before leaving, have the hardest time,[19] as might be expected—the very characteristics that made them most accessible to the impact of their visit make their return difficult.

The readjustment, actual or anticipated, may be so difficult that the student does not return and thus defeats the whole purpose of the program. This problem is particularly widespread in technical fields: the United States is technically so far advanced that visitors cannot use their American training when they return to their countries, which lack the necessary expensive, highly specialized equipment; and to make matters worse, they are usually assigned to administrative jobs, where the need is greatest. One way to meet the problem might be to send American teachers to schools abroad instead of bringing the students to the United States.

A direct way of measuring a visit's lasting effects is to ask the visitors about it some time after their return home. When the immediate reactions of the German exchange students were compared with those six months after their return, explicit positive comments on democratic values and procedures were highest just before departure, but dropped after six months at home. Such expressions as statements favoring tolerance, civic responsibility, and give-and-take discussion—suggesting that the values had been internalized—increased through their stay, and increased further after their return home.

These findings suggest that well-managed extensive and massive visiting programs—in which stays would be long and visitors would be allowed to perform useful functions, including studying—could powerfully promote world-mindedness. In this connection, two bold and imaginative proposals for interchanges between Americans and Russians deserve mention. One plan—initially conceived as a kind of hostage-exchange to guarantee that neither would launch a nuclear attack, but since cast in more constructive terms—envisages a million people from each country, preferably as prominent as possible but of different ages and walks of life, residing and working in the other.[20] Its sponsors have been able to activate only a small visitors' program, but some day conditions may be suitable for fanning the spark into flame.

The other proposal—which has elicited expressions of interest from American and Russian leaders, although it is still only on paper—would have thousands of American and Russian high school students attend school in the other country for a year.

The youngsters would be particularly suited for exchange programs, since in addition to being especially accessible to new experiences and able to make friends easily, they are by and large too young, inexperienced, and untrained to make good spies, and so would be less likely than adults to arouse suspicion in their hosts.[21]

It is heartening that exchanges on such a massive scale are regarded as feasible.

INTERNATIONAL TECHNICAL AND
ECONOMIC ASSISTANCE

The importance of the proper sort of personal contact in promoting international good will is clearly apparent in the effects of American assistance programs. The movement of industrialized countries toward the economy of affluence will result in a fundamental change in the nature of human relationships because accumulation of wealth by one person or group no longer need be at another's expense. Industrialized nations know how to produce enough goods and food to meet everyone's wants, but they do not know how to implement the knowledge. Most Americans, for example, are shocked by the idea of a guaranteed annual income for everyone, yet this step is certain to come.

Meanwhile, despite its best efforts to share some of its affluence, the United States for the most part has succeeded only in aggravating the problems it is trying to relieve. Since the end of the Second World War, it has been pouring money and food into less fortunate nations, in the hope of building up good will and creating conditions that would reduce international tensions, but except in Europe, unfortunately, these programs have largely miscarried. Since they have not prevented a widening of the gap between rich and poor nations or between rich and poor people in the undeveloped ones, they have aggravated unrest throughout the world and resentment toward the United States.

Psychological Flaws of Aid Programs

Slowly and painfully the United States is learning that many of the factors responsible for this unhappy state of affairs are psychological and that if these programs are to succeed, they must be conducted differently and be accompanied by much more sophisticated and determined efforts to change the recipients' attitudes. To study the psychological problems in any detail would be far beyond the scope of this book, but some are worth mentioning.

Many leaders of undeveloped countries have little sense of national responsibility: as is probably inevitable wherever people live on the edge of starvation most of the time, the leader's first impulse on gaining power seems to be to look out for his own family. Hence, most of America's contributions never reach the intended recipients, but instead enrich the power elite (who invest most of their new wealth abroad for safety's sake); the national economy receives little if any benefit and the relative deprivation of the poor is increased. It is unrealistic to expect the leaders of underdeveloped nations to use American aid to foster political and economic reforms that would reduce their power, however badly these may be needed.

A second problem arises from a lack of adequate planning as to how the aid is to be used. It is difficult to resist the temptation to use aid for prestige items like airlines or for consumer goods, rather than to build needed basic industries—another example of the psychological law that immediate rewards outweigh distant penalties. And sufficient consideration has seldom been given to the disruptive impact on the recipient society of massive industrial programs. For example, they seem to have contributed to India's difficulties by destroying village industries and causing villagers to pour into the already overcrowded cities.

The increased level of health and especially the decline in infant mortality brought about by public health programs has also had an adverse effect. The resulting explosive rise in population eats up any gains in productivity or other direct benefits of aid programs. Through school-lunch and preschool-child food programs Food for Peace, for example, has contributed to the health and nutrition of some forty million children in eighty-five countries, but until population growth is checked, such programs only delay disaster, not prevent it. And the obstacles to population control are mainly psychological: birth control programs have foundered on the population's fatalistic attitude, the fear of not having enough children to care for one in old age, and the view of both husbands and wives that fertility is a sign of sexual prowess.

Aid programs often have adverse effects on the recipient country's attitude toward the donor, for they call attention to his wealth and power. If aid is given as a handout with attempts to control its use, at least as much resentment as gratitude is aroused—no one enjoys being in the position of a beggar. And the sense of relative deprivation among populations of economically deprived nations is increased by their knowledge of others' affluence.

Famine used to be an Act of God, to be accepted with resignation. But starving people in other nations, believing that America could relieve their hunger if it chose, now direct to her the resentment once directed at Fate.

Finally, America's failure to reap the expected benefits from her unprecedented generosity has created in her citizens and leaders a mood of disillusionment and resentment that is imperiling other such activities.

There are a few bright spots, however, in this ominous picture. Family planning finally seems to be gaining ground in some countries like Ceylon and Pakistan, whose governments have begun to appreciate its necessity and are introducing the massive educational programs necessary to make it work; the Japanese birthrate, for example, has actually been substantially reduced. Some good will seems to result from certain modest medical programs, like the hospital ship *Hope,* that offer immediate, direct, and tangible medical care to the suffering and train local practitioners.[22] Actually, most medical programs create good will, even though through their reduction of the death rate their long-term results aggravate the problem.

Ways of Improving Aid Programs—the Peace Corps

These considerations suggest that if foreign assistance programs are to realize their intentions, their recipients must be imbued with the "achievement motive" [23] and must have some sense of nationhood and self-discipline. Perhaps all aid should be accompanied by massive programs of birth control and of education for potential leaders, given either in American schools or by American teachers sent abroad. It would also be important to formulate all such programs as opportunities for Americans to learn as well as teach and to avoid using methods that appear to minimize the recipients' capacity for independent thought. Aid is most likely to promote mutual good will and understanding if it is offered in a context of personal concern and respect for the recipient. This quality exists in programs like Foster Parents Plan and Save the Children Federation, which establish personal contact between giver and receiver, however indirect. The donor's interest in "his" child's welfare also sensitizes him as no amount of reading can to problems in the undeveloped countries: he learns at first hand how the child and his family struggle with adversity and he comes to appreciate their personal worth. Since the aid is given to help the child's personal development by improving his nutrition and enabling him to continue his education, it can be accepted without loss of self-esteem and evokes gratitude rather than resentment.

The Peace Corps, which carries this philosophy further, is perhaps the most hopeful development of all; it has grown from 120 to 10,000 in four years, and is now being emulated by other countries. The principles that have accounted for its success have been devised in conjunction with psychologists and psychiatrists, who also have developed the methods for selecting volunteers. The central principle, as described by one of its senior psychological consultants, is that "The Peace Corps must be seen as a program that is compellingly relevant to the recipients' well being, as a form of assistance that can be accepted without compromise of autonomy or loss of personal dignity." And to this end it operates on "revolutionary" principles: "The volunteer lives simply, with the people. . . . He is assigned to work under the supervision of host nationals within existing administrative structures. . . . There is no money in the program to attract self-seeking interests; all that's there is a person and what he can do. Critical issues in national and international life have been discussed in training; the individual volunteer is trusted to conduct himself intelligently. The volunteer has himself to offer —and that's it." [24]

The Peace Corps' aid projects are defined as collaborative efforts, in which the volunteer learns from as well as teaches the host, and the goal is for the host to take over the job himself. The volunteer works as a peer among peers, not as a superior with inferiors, using the host's language and operating in general on the principle that other people are more receptive to your views if you show that you understand and respect theirs.

Peace Corps volunteers typically go through psychological states analogous to though not quite the same as those experienced by visitors to the United States. First they experience frustration and disappointment at their inability to get things done— the "crisis of engagement," and then they have doubts as to whether what they are doing is really worthwhile—the "crisis of acceptance" (these seem analogous to the culture shock described in visitors to the United States); finally, they come to realize that they have learned at least as much as they have taught.[25] Then comes the familiar problem of readjustment to the home society. Their experience in other lands makes many volunteers more aware of positive and negative aspects of life in the United States and, as a result, often leads them to participate more actively in politics[26] or in various community service programs like Vista or the Domestic Peace Corps.

The Peace Corps is still too minuscule to have a perceptible effect on the course of international events, but as a demonstration of how the mutually beneficial effects of cross-national personal contacts can be successfully increased, it may prove to be a major achievement of our time and a powerful moving force toward world peace.

The next step, and it is around the corner, would be for the

United States to become the recipient of help from other nations' "peace corps" in handling certain types of problems. Americans might learn a good deal from members of Israel's *kibbutzim,* for example, or from directors of cooperatives or those who rehabilitate prisoners in certain Scandinavian countries.

INTERNATIONAL COOPERATION TO ACHIEVE SUPERORDINATE GOALS

There are more efficient ways to reduce international tensions than through the use of mass communications, personal contacts, and aid-giving. If methods were available, the nations themselves could engage in cooperative activities through their representatives. Increased mutual friendliness of their citizens would inevitably follow, for group members' attitudes toward each other depend primarily on the circumstances of the groups' interactions[27]—a generalization, as firm as any about human nature, applicable to all groups, from small artificial ones in psychological laboratories to nations. When strangers are placed in groups that are then brought into conflict, all come to overvalue their fellow group members and their allies and to derogate their opponents, as discussed in Chapter 10. At the national level, as described in Chapter 7, American perceptions of Japanese, Germans, and Russians have been shown to shift drastically, depending on current relations—they are seen as sly when they are enemies and lose this quality when they are allies.

The Robbers' Cave Experiment

The results of an experiment performed some years ago at a boys' camp illustrate that friendship or enmity between members of groups are the products, not the causes, of group interactions. Eleven-year-old, middle-class, American, Protestant, well-adjusted boys, all strangers to each other, were brought to the camp and divided into two groups, which were isolated from each other during the first six days until each had become a cohesive organization with definite leadership structure, local customs, and a name. In the following week the two groups—the Eagles and the Rattlers—were subjected to a series of competitive activities in which one side's victory inevitably meant the other's defeat; this produced a high level of mutual hostility, analogous to that displayed by nations at war. To their own groups the children attributed self-glorifying qualities, but to the other they assigned those traits which justified treating it as an enemy. They improvised and hoarded weapons, raided each other's property, and indulged in other shows of power.

Attempts were then made to restore peace, one spontaneously by a high-ranking member of one group who tried to open negotiations with the "enemy." They took his overtures as attempts to deceive them by pretended expressions of reconciliation, and his departure was accompanied by a hail of "ammunition"—green apples hoarded for use in case of attack. And his own group, far from receiving him as a hero, chastised him for making the attempt. The analogy to the fate of certain international peacemakers is obvious. Nor were there any effects from camp leaders' direct attempts to overcome the mutual stereotypes of the two groups by appeals to fair-mindedness or justice—as would be expected, since the stereotypes were the product, not the cause, of the mutual hostility. Bringing the groups together at meals or movies was equally ineffective, for in such settings the warring factions sat apart from each other, and hurled taunts and spitballs.

But the mutual hostility was finally resolved (measured by one group's members' choosing friends from the other) by a series of experiences in which the groups had to cooperate to attain goals that neither could achieve alone. For example, a very inviting movie could be rented only if the two groups combined their treasuries; more compellingly the camp water supply, secretly interrupted by the counselors, could be restored only by cooperative action; and when the truck carrying food and supplies for an overnight camping trip ran into a ditch and stalled, both groups had to get on the tow rope to pull it out.[28]

Survival as a Superordinate Goal

There are similar "superordinate goals" at the international level that could promote cooperative attitudes among nations and combat hostile ones, and the most obvious, one would think, is survival [29]—a goal surely shared by all nations, and one increasingly jeopardized by the arms race. If threats to survival in the boys' camp were the chief means of drawing the warring factions together, by inference the threat of nuclear annihilation should be useful to draw nations together. Unfortunately, an essential difference between the boys' camp and the international arena is that the boys' joint measures for survival did not weaken them with respect to each other, while nations still regard other nations, not modern weapons, as the main threat to their existence. All want to survive and recognize that disarmament is necessary to achieve this goal, but none is willing to risk reducing its armed power relative to other nations to get the process started—each nation perceives as immediately endangering to itself the steps it must take to achieve ultimate universal security.

Survival as a goal also presents other psychological difficulties. It is not compelling because the danger of modern weapons is not experienced as very real—it is too problematical and too new. Moreover, survival in itself is not especially rewarding; it is merely a prerequisite for the attainment of all other goals. Nevertheless, a more widespread and concerted effort to dramatize the common danger facing all nations would be worthwhile. The inhibitions affecting leaders of major nations in this respect would not apply to the small, militarily weak ones, who could take the initiative. And the UN affords a readily available platform.

New Opportunities for International Cooperation toward Superordinate Goals

Modern scientific and technological advances have created potential international enterprises that would not endanger the security of any nation, and nations working together on them would achieve much greater rewards than any one could obtain alone. Pursuit of these superordinate goals might eventually increase the sense of mutual interdependence and reduce mutual distrust to the point where direct international measures to promote survival might become feasible.

One such undertaking has been running smoothly for some years—the cooperative exploration of the earth's crust and oceans instituted by the International Geophysical Year. And because it is self-enforcing, the treaty demilitarizing the Antarctic, which safeguards this activity, has not caused any trouble; it is to every nation's interest not to violate it because the gains from respecting it outweigh those that might result from an attempt to militarize their zone. The Antarctic venture is a variable-sum game in which the rewards for cooperating far outweigh those for defecting.

Scientists have outlined literally dozens of similar international projects whose payoffs would be enormous.[30] The germ of one already exists in an agreement signed in 1963 by the Soviet Union and the United States to develop a cooperative system of meteorological satellites for a program of long-term weather forecasting. The Soviet satellites have not yet been orbited, but the two nations are exchanging conventional weather information by teletype, and China may also be sending in information, although without public fanfare.

Meteorological satellites connected with computers would make it possible to predict weather two weeks instead of two days in advance—not only would this save billions of dollars annually, but it has even more exciting possibilities. Accumulated data could be used in computer-simulation experiments on weather modification that could not be conducted in reality, thus making it possible to determine the best coordinated program for combatting air pollution over a particular city, for example, or how a proposed dam across the Bering Strait would affect Canada's climate.

Perhaps the most hopeful area for cooperative international research is outer space, including the moon and planets. The payoff in terms of knowledge and therefore potentially in human welfare would undoubtedly be enormous, and the resources necessary for an adequate job are beyond even the richest nation's reach. Since the area is new, no nations have any vested interests and none of those cooperating would start with enough advantage over the others to breed suspicion. In this it would resemble the management experiment described earlier, one of whose advantages was the equal newness of the conceptual scheme to all participants. Space exploration could also substitute for some aspects of war, because it meets the need of many young men to prove their manhood by undergoing dangers and risking their lives. And space heroes already reap at least as much glory as military heroes.

The opening of outer space to exploration is somewhat analogous to the discovery of the New World, an event that probably helped extinguish the religious wars that had devastated Europe by introducing a new type of national hero, the explorer, and more attractive bones of contention. The area of conflict shifted from ideological differences to division of spoils, and the participants' emotional investment gradually followed suit. It was several centuries before Catholics and Protestants could even begin to resolve their religious conflicts, which often intensified the wars over colonies, but actual fighting over religious doctrines died away. It cannot be claimed that Columbus' discovery reduced the number of wars between European nations, but the decline of the ideological component may have reduced their destructiveness for a time.

Competition in outer space may have a similar effect on the intensity of the ideological conflict which is today's main source of danger. Gains in knowledge about outer space do have military implications, of course, and this is the most serious obstacle to international cooperation in this area, but nations so far are willing to forego possible military advantages, as the unanimous United Nations resolution against the orbiting of weapons bears witness. And the potential military implications have not prevented the universally favorable reception given the Russian and American space triumphs; both nations can sincerely congratu-

late each other on new space feats, a response that would be unthinkable to an improved nuclear missile.

In the experiment in the boys' camp all members of the contending groups were involved in the cooperative enterprises to
achieve superordinate goals. It is obviously impossible to involve all citizens of cooperating nations in similar fashion, but
thanks to the human capacity for identification, all members of a
group can participate vicariously in its representatives' activities.
In the experiments cited in Chapter 10 the fact that the debates
were conducted by representatives did not prevent all members
of each group from developing feelings toward the other groups.
Entire student bodies of colleges or large segments of the citizenry of cities become emotionally involved in the fortunes of
their athletic teams, and the hero's receptions accorded astro-
nauts and cosmonauts indicate that the public at large shares the
thrill of their achievements.

These considerations all suggest that if cooperative international ventures are to have the greatest beneficial effect on international attitude, the fact must be dramatized that the participants are their nations' representatives, and not individuals.

Each successful cooperative international project would generate trust and create habits of cooperation that would smooth
the path for the next one. In addition, the international agencies
that would have to be formed to conduct some of these enterprises would set up rules of procedure and precedents which
could gradually become sufficiently extensive and powerful to
withstand international antagonisms as well as to supply part of
the foundations for effective peace-keeping international organizations and world law.

The upshot of these speculations is that the same scientific
activities that threaten to destroy humanity could be powerful
forces for saving it. Modern scientific developments and the new
forms of communication and transportation could be exploited
to break down international misunderstanding and distrust and
to increase mutual appreciation and the sense of community
among nations. The formation of a genuine world state, presumably the end result of these processes, is a necessary condition

for an international system of enduring peace. Whether it would be sufficient, no one knows. States can maintain order within their borders most of the time, yet there are still occasional crime waves, riots, and civil wars.

But there is still the most challenging problem of all—how to create conditions that will permanently keep the human propensity for violence within acceptable bounds.

12 · *Conflict Without Violence*

ONE OF THE few safe generalizations about human existence is that conflict will always be with us. Nor would one wish it otherwise, for conflict adds zest to life; it is the spur to growth and change, and the means by which they occur. Through engaging in conflicts, individuals develop their social and communicative skills, strength of character, self-confidence, and awareness of the scope and limits of their powers. Similarly, social organization and structure grow out of clashes of interest and struggles for dominance between individuals and subgroups within each society.

Humans are continually struggling with each other—parents against children, brother against brother, friend against friend, colleague against colleague. To the extent that an adversary is always frustrating in some sense, all conflict generates some anger and with it the impulse to hurt and destroy; but these are fully compatible with love (the reference here is not to the pathological link between cruelty and sexuality but to the fact that people who can arouse strong affection in each other can also arouse strong anger). In a psychological sense, the two feelings may be sides of the same coin—most murders occur within the family, for example, and there may be some relevance in the suggestion from recent studies of animals that only those species with strong fighting patterns form strong affectional bonds.[1]

Since the basic role of conflict in human existence means that it cannot be eliminated, the task is thus to keep it at a level and guide it into forms in which its constructive aspects outweigh its destructive ones. Affectional ties often prevent conflicts between friends or family members from getting out of hand—that these inhibitions usually (though not always) operate is suggested by the fact that murdering a close friend or relative is regarded as particularly heinous. Institutional safeguards and group expectations control reasonably well the conflicts between members of the same society—there are strong sanctions against injuring or murdering a fellow citizen.

Human conflict can release uncontrolled violence only in conflicts between nations or between groups within a society whose social structure has broken down, that is, where institutions supported by consensus are yet unformed or have become ineffective. Under these circumstances each side regards its own fighters as heroes, not murderers, and the more adversaries they kill, the more they are revered. Although "laws of war" are more often breached than observed, their existence suggests that murdering an enemy is considered legitimate if confined to certain methods of killing and to certain classes of victims.

The growing recognition that war is becoming insufferably dangerous has led to renewed interest in non-lethal forms of conflict, most of which, used so far only within societies, include such forms of pressure without bodily violence as propaganda, subversion, boycotts, strikes, sabotage, and the like. The growing interdependence of societies and the increasing power of public opinion, as well as technological advances, may have increased the applicability of these tactics to international struggles; but since they involve no pyschological innovations, they will not be considered further here.[2]

NON-VIOLENT ACTION

A category of non-lethal conflict that is as old as history but seems to be taking genuinely new forms abjures violence in principle—non-violent action. Not only is this type of conflict compatible with human survival, but its aims are constructive rather than destructive: it is seen by its advocates and practitioners as a means of hastening social and political reforms.

Methods of non-violent action are being re-explored by religious pacifists as well as historians, political scientists, military strategists, students of conflict, psychologists, and others, each from his own viewpoint and using his own conceptual scheme,[3] with the result that the subject of non-violence is currently particularly untidy, conceptually and descriptively. I am not so rash as to attempt a systematic description or evaluation of its present status, but I will indicate both a few of its concepts based on religious principles that appear to have considerable psychological relevance, and the questions they raise. Then, primarily to show that it is possible to think about the question, I shall briefly explore the possibility of non-violent action in international relations.

Before proceeding with this reckless undertaking, I should like to correct a common misapprehension whose basis is primarily linguistic: the confusion of "non-violence" with "passivity." English has no term for "refusal to use violence as a positive act"; all terms imply some kind of renunciation, not affirmation, and words like non-violence, passive resistance, pacifism, civil disobedience, non-cooperation, and so on, conjure up images of people standing by with saintly or pained expressions while armed men massacre their wives and sisters (one cynic has defined non-violence as "defense by scowling"). Despite the Hindu religion's supposed emphasis on non-violence, Hindi contained no word adequate to express what Gandhi had in mind, so he coined one: "*satygraha,*" usually translated "soul force." It is important to remember that the type of behavior to be described is a very active effort to defeat, by means other than violence, a possessor of superior destructive power, and that it requires at least as much courage, discipline, and initiative as violent combat.

The central psychological question raised by programmatic non-violence is: In the absence of personal ties or institutional restraints, is it possible for an antagonist in a desperate struggle to act in ways that could bring victory while simultaneously inhibiting his adversary from resorting to violence? The question may seem patently absurd, but it has become worth asking because of the results of the quantum jump in weaponry. To aid in approaching it with an open mind, it may be well to recall that when conditions change drastically, the familiar, "realistic" ways of behaving are almost certain not to work. Common sense is usually the best guide in the solution of traditional problems because it contains the experience of time, and habitual approaches always seem more realistic than new ones because they have worked in the past. But unprecedented problems require unprecedented solutions, and the correct one is likely to appear bizarre or ridiculous simply because it is so unfamiliar (the atomic physicist Leo Szilard once described how he and Enrico Fermi burst out laughing when they hit upon the solution to a problem in constructing atomic reactors, because it seemed so absurd).

Principles of Non-Violence

Every conflict is basically a clash of wills in which each combatant's goal is to make the other acknowledge that he is the master; this acknowledgment may range from the loser's simply admitting that he was wrong to his putting his life in the victor's hands. The most effective way of imposing one's will has always been to make the opponent suffer until he gives in or to kill him if he persists in his obstinacy.

One antagonist's stronger determination can outweigh the other's possession of considerable superiority in weaponry and tactical skill, hence one powerful way to demonstrate strength of will is to show a willingness and capacity to suffer for one's beliefs. This may be more effective than fighting back under some circumstances, because instead of stimulating the adversary to further violence, it inhibits and demoralizes him. This insight is probably as old as mankind—religions have preached the power of suffering to redeem oneself and one's opponent alike, and history is dotted with examples of individuals and groups who have prevailed by non-violent means—but until very recently these examples were not taken seriously and were only splendid topics for sermons, forgotten at the church door by both congregation and preacher.

Then a genius, Mohandas Gandhi, brought non-violence from the pulpit into the arena by systematically developing ways of waging combat without bloodshed and showing their extraordinary effectiveness in some circumstances. And Martin Luther King, Jr., and others have recently shown that with modifications, Gandhi's methods could be transplanted to another society with some success.

Gandhi's central appeal was to his opponent's conscience—he attempted to "raise the deliberate suffering of a man of outraged conscience to the status of a moral sanction that would compel respect and secure results" [4]—which required that a sharp distinction be maintained between the antagonist and his deeds. His target was not the persons in certain positions who did reprehensible things, but the social structure that forced them to, and he credited his opponent with having a conscience and acting righteously according to his own standards: "Man and his deed are two distinct things. Whereas a good deed should call forth approbation and a wicked deed disapprobation, the doer of the deed, whether good or wicked, always deserves respect or pity as the case may be." [5]

Just as he refused to dehumanize his opponent, he also acted to make it difficult for the opponent to dehumanize him. And his insistence, to this end, that forms of resistance be constructive had the added value of maintaining morale. An authority on Gandhi summarizes his position as follows: "In a group struggle you can keep . . . the ability to work effectively for the realization of the goal stronger than the destructive violent tendencies and the tendencies to passiveness and despondency only by . . . giving all phases of your struggle, as far as possible, a constructive character." [6] Thus, to oppose the salt tax, he organized a march to the sea to make salt. Analogously, King named his organization of the Montgomery, Alabama, bus boycott the Montgomery Improvement Association, implying that an end to bus segregation would be good for all the citizens of Montgomery.

Through his candor, courage, sense of responsibility, personal dignity, and adherence to the highest ethical principles, the non-violent fighter continually reminds himself and his adversary that they are both moral human beings—he tries to win by morally embarrassing his adversary. It is easy to dismiss moral and religious motives as ineffective, but as the history of martyrdom suggests, they can be powerful determinants of human behavior.

The type of non-violent behavior Gandhi advocated may also mobilize the inhibitions to violence rooted in man's biological ancestry, as described in Chapter 3. Like all other behavior, violent behavior is not self-sustaining—its increase or decrease depends partly on how the victim responds, and it can sometimes be inhibited by a calm, friendly attitude that implies the victim's concern for the attacker's welfare as well as his own.

As the following anecdote suggests, violence in humans, as in animals, is probably inhibited by certain rituals that convey this attitude: A missionary's wife in China, whose husband was away, learned that the inhabitants of their village were planning to massacre her and the children because they blamed a drought on the anger of the gods at the presence of foreigners. When the armed mob broke into the house, she walked calmly up to the tall, surly leader and offered him a cup of tea. Nonplussed, he accepted, and the others uncertainly followed his example— after which they could do nothing but leave peacefully. Fortunately for the sake of the story, the drought was broken by a rainstorm the following day.[7] This example may be exceptional, for if an attempt to meet violence with non-violence fails, there may be no survivor to tell the story. Yet if a person can find the courage to meet aggression with calm friendliness, it may have a powerfully inhibiting effect.

Certain types of behavior may be more inhibitory than rituals of courtesy. The posture of prayer or supplication often seems to have this effect, provided the attacker comes from the same culture so that he recognizes it, as does a simple willingness to endure suffering without retaliation. There are many anecdotes about British soldiers who were unable to continue clubbing non-resisting Indians, for example, and some white policemen in the South (U.S.) have reacted similarly to civil rights demonstrators. Similarly, some Russian soldiers were executed because they refused to fire on unarmed East Germans during the non-violent revolt in 1953.

Non-violent action is a group affair, for while very few individuals would have the moral courage to persist in renouncing violence in the face of threatened death, members of cohesive groups can sometimes manage it.* The morale of groups in violent combat rises initially and continues high in both until one begins to be defeated. We know from the experiences of Gandhi and King that sometimes when a group using force is met with non-violence, its morale declines and that of the non-violent group increases. German troops were so demoralized by the spontaneous and loosely organized campaigns of non-violent resistance in Denmark and Norway that they had to be frequently rotated. And at a more trivial level, the only psychological casualty during a non-violent campaign to desegregate a Baltimore motion picture theatre was a white police captain who attacked a white reporter.

Questions Concerning Non-Violence

Successful contemporary non-violent campaigns have been led by those whose strong religious faith proclaimed the ultimate supremacy of love and the redemptive power of suffering. They have been conducted by groups who felt they had no hope of winning with violence against opponents whom they correctly believed to be accessible to certain types of non-violent pressures, which involved extensive face-to-face and mass-media contact with their adversaries. To the extent that they are essential, each of these features would severely limit the range of applicability of non-violent action.

* The successful renunciation of violence by the staff of a psychiatric admission ward illustrates the power of a group's standards for its members (see Chapter 8, p. 146n), although the dominant group took the initiative in that case. The crucial problem is whether a similar initiative by the underdog could also succeed.

Gandhi held that every successful non-violent campaign successively aroused five responses in its opponents: indifference, ridicule, abuse, repression, and finally, respect; if it did not survive the fourth stage, it did not amount to anything. His deep religious faith gave him the steadfastness of purpose that, with some lapses, held his followers to non-violence through the stage of repression; and a similar faith has sustained leaders of the non-violent civil rights movement in the United States. Two questions arise in this connection: Must non-violent campaigns be based on this particular faith? And must all the participants share the leaders' faith?

The experience of the Danish and Norwegian resistance movements shows that patriotism can supply the necessary fortitude. All fighters, violent or non-violent, subscribe to the phrase in the American national anthem, "Conquer we must, for our cause it is just," and perhaps any powerful ideal can equally well sustain violent and non-violent fighters in the face of death. It is also perfectly clear that participants in non-violent action need not share their leaders' particular philosophy as long as they have faith in them. Gandhi had only a few hundred totally committed disciples, but much of the time he was able to inspire millions of Indians to adhere to his methods. There is no reason to think that they were personally less prone to violence than any comparable group of citizens—in fact, some of his most effective followers were Pathans, members of a warrior tribe, whose military virtues of courage and group discipline made them especially effective non-violent fighters. Similarly, American Negroes, who have waged successful non-violent campaigns, have a high rate of violent crime.

While not all participants in a non-violent campaign need to share the leaders' philosophy, it is questionable whether such tactics can succeed in the total absence of a sustaining ideology, because the temptation to abandon them as soon as they appear not to be working is very strong. The present growing resort to violence in the American civil rights struggle strongly suggests that non-violence cannot be maintained in the absence of allegiance to a leader who is sustained by an ideology.

A related question, one requiring further exploration, is whether those types of non-lethal combat that violate moral principles, such as deceit and sabotage, can be used successfully without weakening or destroying what Gandhi felt to be the core of non-violence—appeal to the adversary's conscience. The two modes of combat theoretically should not be miscible but actually they have been—the Norwegian and Danish resistance movements, for example, included all available violent as well as non-violent tactics.

Non-violent action probably cannot succeed as a set of tactical maneuvers unsupported by ideals, and it will probably also fail if based on ideology without discipline. Non-violent fighting demands of its adherents fully as much group discipline as violent fighting, a point often overlooked by some radical pacifists whose principles cause them to reject submission to any authority that has not secured their willing consent. Thus, they consider themselves bound only by decisions arrived at by consensus, refuse to accept leadership themselves, obstruct others' leadership, and are extremely reluctant to delegate authority. A group whose members hold this philosophy may be able to function if it is highly cohesive, but "participatory democracy" cannot work without a true sense of community. Those who adhere to this viewpoint may be indirectly expressing rebelliousness and hatred of all authority, for such people often use insistence on consensus as an excuse to express opposition but do not take responsibility for clarifying positive alternatives.

That refusal by a group's members to submit to discipline can result in paralysis and disaster when it is faced with the necessity of thwarting an invader by non-violent means was vividly demonstrated by a sociodramatic experiment in which a Quaker camp in Canada was called upon to defeat an armed occupation by representatives of a right-wing Canadian government. Despite ample warning, the defenders never succeeded in getting organized, formulating a consistent plan of resistance, or establishing adequate means of communication with the invaders, but instead frittered away their time in debates to attempt to achieve consensus. After thirty-one hours of rising tensions on both sides, an emotional defiance of orders by one of the defenders, not clearly sanctioned by the group, precipitated a massacre by the invaders that brought the experiment to an inglorious close.[8]

Gandhi never fell into the trap of underestimating the importance of discipline—perhaps the essence of his genius was his infusion of hard-boiled, ingenious, highly disciplined non-violent tactics with the religious idealism necessary to sustain them. As he once remarked, those who accused him of being a saint trying to be a politician were wrong: he was really a politician trying to be a saint.

It is widely held that non-violent methods can succeed only against a group committed to orderly processes of law and some concern for the individual, like the Americans and British. The Jews' fate under Nazism is often offered as support for this view, but it is not very convincing, for some predicaments are hopeless —no method of fighting can succeed—and after World War II was well under way, this was true of the plight of the Jews. It is often forgotten that the extermination camps were set up only after Germany was at war (whether even the Nazis could have perpetrated such atrocities in peacetime is questionable) and at that point the Jews had three choices, none of which could have saved their lives: violent resistance, non-violent resistance, and fatalistic acquiescence. The best they could do was die in the way most compatible with their own self-respect and most likely to win sympathy for them abroad; most did not resist but simply acquiesced apathetically in their own destruction.[9] There are many moving anecdotes of Jews who, having received a notice to report to the police station, would go to their non-Jewish friends and say farewell, without expressing any thought of attempting to escape. No one knows what might have happened had the Jews resorted to non-violent action before the Nazi regime had consolidated itself and when it still wished to create a favorable impression abroad. Suppose, for example, in organized fashion they had refused to wear the stigmatizing armbands and forced the police to drag them off to prison; this might have made it more difficult for Germans to ignore what was going on, and it might have mobilized earlier, more effective opposition in other nations.

It is too simple to attribute the success of non-violent campaigns in India and the United States to the humanitarianism of the British and the Americans, although this undoubtedly helped. But neither the British nor the Americans shrink from brutality under certain circumstances—the history of American treatment of the Indians or British treatment of the "lesser breeds without the law" does not inspire confidence in their compassion, any more than does their more recent use of extreme violence in combatting the Mau Mau rebellion in Kenya. Nor were the Nazis themselves impervious to non-violent resistance: they could not break the Norwegian teachers' strike.[10]

Non-violent tactics against a group like the Nazis would have to be very different, of course, from those that worked against the British. It has been said that the non-violent movement in India would have failed had the English taken Hitler's advice to shoot Gandhi and his lieutenants; such measures might well have succeeded against his tactics, especially if they had received no publicity, but they probably could have been counteracted by dispersal of leadership, clandestine communications, and other "underground" tactics. Dictatorships actually might be more vulnerable to suitably organized non-violent campaigns than to violent ones, because except, perhaps, for a brief halcyon period, they are riven by internal tensions and mutual suspicions, and maintaining them requires constant personal contact between the dictator's henchmen and members of the population. In such a situation violent opposition keeps the dictatorship cohesive by supplying an object on which it can displace internal hatreds and frustrations without guilt. Conversely, non-violent tactics would tend to intensify internal tensions by giving them no appropriate outlet and by mobilizing latent guilt feelings.

Mention of the nineteenth-century American treatment of the Indians and the British of the "natives" does raise the question of whether non-violent campaigns could succeed against a group with whom there is no possible common basis for understanding. Successful non-violent campaigns have been waged thus far only against groups with whom there existed some potential meeting ground, however circumscribed. Leaders of the non-violent campaigns in India subscribed to religious principles that the British respected; trained in England, they knew how to disconcert the English by appealing to their sense of fair play. Negroes and whites in the United States have been brought up in the same culture and indoctrinated with the same dreams; the Negro's most effective appeal is to the "American dream" of equal opportunity for all.

Some of the effectiveness of the non-violent anti-Nazi campaigns of the Danes and Norwegians may have stemmed from the German regard for them as Nordics; they could thus demoralize the Nazis by treating them with contempt. But in this respect the Jews in Germany represent an equivocal case, for while the Nazis excluded them from the human race, the Jews shared many cultural characteristics with the Germans that they might have been able to exploit. The most severe test of non-violent action would be the attempted use by, for example, the blacks in South Africa against the Afrikaners, who refer to them as "things" and do not include them in census figures, for it is hard to conceive of any type of appeal that in the face of such an attitude would have an inhibitory or demoralizing effect.

Groups have adhered to non-violent methods only when the power balance was so unequal that there was no hope of winning with violent ones. But will they remain non-violent when they believe that violence might bring victory? Some American-Negro factions possibly advocate resort to violent tactics because they have come to realize that although their access to violent means is far below that of the whites, it can still create considerable havoc. It remains to be seen, however, whether Black Power's destructive features will set back or advance its aims, since what it gains by intimidation it may lose by removing the whites' inhibitions against counter-violence, and its violent activities can suffice to disrupt American society but not construct the kind its advocates want. Its leaders may succeed, like Samson, only in pulling the temple down about their ears.

Since mobilization of public opinion has become a very powerful weapon in non-violent campaigns, much of the effectiveness of non-violence depends on continued face-to-face or mass-media contact between the contending groups. Would clandestine communication channels be sufficient to replace the mass media if access to them were denied? Resistance movements (most of which, of course, were violent) did remarkably well during the last war with relatively primitive equipment, so censorship might be even more easily circumvented in the future.

Perhaps the most disquieting consideration with respect to non-violence is that it has succeeded only within a context of violence; the threat of violence has always lurked in the wings. The British knew that too harsh suppression of Gandhi and his followers would stimulate violent revolutionary movements, and they were fighting for their national existence against the Germans and Japanese. The Danes and Norwegians might have failed had the Nazis not been defeated in war. The federal courts in the United States can mobilize overwhelming power in defense of Negro rights, as Mississippi learned, and Martin Luther King has wondered in print whether the Montgomery bus boycott would have succeeded without the Supreme Court decision.

Moreover, leaders of non-violent movements constantly remind their opponents that if their demands are not met, they may not be able to keep their followers in check. Their tactics sometimes appear to be aimed at provoking the local white population to violence in order to mobilize public opinion against them and force federal intervention. In short, non-violent campaigns always include an element of brinkmanship, and it is hard to imagine that they could succeed without it. To what extent it is a serious limitation or implies that violence really cannot be eliminated from conflict remains an open question.

Achievements of Non-Violence

By now the reader may well be inclined to dismiss non-violence as without promise and irrelevant to the problem of war. But let us remember that the campaigns of Gandhi and King have chalked up two remarkable achievements: they have demonstrated that non-violent methods could work against an opponent who possesses and is prepared to use superior destructive power; perhaps equally significant in the long run, they have succeeded in breaking the psychological link between masculinity and violence, thus circumventing one of the major psychological supports for war.

Since no form of waging conflict always wins, the most that can be asked of non-violent techniques is that where they fail—and they will certainly fail sometimes—violent methods would have failed more completely and left a greater legacy of mutual hate. Perhaps the most encouraging feature of non-violent campaigns is their unforseen success—who would have dared predict that a little man clad in a loincloth would drive the British out of India by non-violent methods, or that Norwegian teachers could reduce the Nazis to impotence by simply not cooperating, or that Mrs. Parks' refusal to give up her bus seat to a white man could have such far-reaching effects?

The economist and peace researcher Kenneth Boulding has promulgated Boulding's First Law: What exists, is possible. Non-violent action exists and has succeeded under some circumstances, and this alone destroys the contention that non-violent methods of conflict are hopelessly at variance with human nature.

Non-violent action should be viewed not as a single technique but as a new class of fighting, in which strategy and tactics will differ from one campaign to the next. King modified Gandhi's methods for maintaining the morale and discipline of non-violent fighters to fit conditions in the United States: fasting, Gandhi's most powerful technique for this purpose, would have been relatively useless in the United States, so instead King used frequent prayer meetings with hymn singing, which would have helped Gandhi's followers very little.

The second great achievement of Gandhi and King is that in two different societies and with people whose traditions are very different, they have reversed the relationship between masculinity and violence, and shown that this may be based more on cultural expectations than on the usually assumed biology of maleness. They succeeded in establishing group standards in which willingness to die rather than resort to violence was the highest expression of manly courage. In Gandhi's words: "Heroic as it undoubtedly is for a handful of people to offer armed resistance . . . it is far more heroic to stand up against overwhelming numbers without any arms at all." [11]

Evidence supporting this point has been obtained by studies of participants in the sit-in movements. An interesting report of a six-year follow-up of a group of Negro children who at ages five to fifteen participated in the first lunch-counter sit-in in an Oklahoma city stresses their persisting feeling of latent power, based in part on a strong conscious sense of being able to control their own aggressive feelings in the service of ideals.[12] Similarly, extensive interviews with adolescents and young adults who participated in sit-ins and Freedom Rides have revealed that by refusing to resort to violence, the participants gain a heightened feeling of manliness and a sense of moral superiority over their opponents, who in effect, act out their own aggressive impulses for them.[13] The increased self-respect of participants in civil rights demonstrations may account for the drop in crime rates among Negroes in the locale of the demonstration.[14]

NON-VIOLENCE IN INTERNATIONAL CONFLICT

The major question remains: Do non-violent methods of fighting have any place in the conduct of international relations? Much international conflict has taken such non-violent forms as economic and psychological pressures, but these have never seemed sufficient when the chips were down. To rely exclusively on non-violent methods of conflict in international struggles would mean substituting something new and untried for a pattern of behavior as old as humanity and deeply ingrained by success, under which circumstances it is impossible to prove that non-violent methods would be superior to violent ones or even that they would work at all.

All I can hope to do is show that the question deserves to be taken seriously, and to this end, let me indulge in a brief flight of fancy, taking off from the unrealistic assumption that the United States has decided to renounce violence as a tool of foreign policy, a decision that would have to be based on two premises. First, it cannot achieve its aims—the protection of its citizenry and the promotion of our way of life—by violent means. The industrialized nations can exert enormous violence, but control over limitless destructive power is, paradoxically, equivalent to control of none, for in neither case can violence bring victory. All nations, even the most powerful, will soon be in the position of Gandhi's Indians and King's Negroes, if they are not so already. Second, the United States leadership would have to be convinced that communism could be effectively combatted by non-violent methods.

The core of the American way of life is the supreme importance it attaches to individual freedom, and America's main quarrel with communist states is over their restrictions of it. America has indicated a willingness to live with a variety of socioeconomic systems as long as they share this value. I believe that the American philosophy will eventually prevail, and will do so earlier in a world without war, for all human beings aspire to freedom. The common denominator of all psychiatric illnesses is their imposition of limits on the patient's freedom; his longing to be free of the tyranny of his symptoms is a very strong motive for accepting the work and suffering often entailed by psychotherapy. At the level of societies, men have always strived for freedom, but they have sometimes been made willing by poverty, ignorance, and fear to accept tyranny as the price of food and safety. As Gandhi said: "For the starving men and women, liberty and God are merely letters put together without the slightest meaning; the deliverer of these unfortunate people would be the one who brought them a crust of bread." A rising level of education and prosperity in a world at peace is regularly accompanied by a growth of freedom. Evidence of the growth of individual freedom in Russia is overwhelming, and only those completely blinded by the stereotype of the enemy can fail to see this. American commitment to the renunciation of force, far from being a surrender to communism, might be the most effective way to fight its tyrannical aspects and foster a growth within communist societies of the values Americans believe in. For if the United States does have a superior way of life, it will prevail in a disarmed world; if it does not, nuclear war will not save it. Commitment to non-violent forms of power would immediately remove disarmament from the context of weakness or surrender. Disarming would become part of an overall plan for strengthening America's world position, thereby greatly facilitating negotiations. And negotiations would still be necessary. Commitment to renunciation of violence would not necessarily require abrupt unilateral disarmament any more than belief in the decisive power of superior violence requires the immediate launching of a nuclear attack. Drastic disarmament by the United States, without considerable advance preparation, might actually plunge the world into chaos by creating panic among nations reliant on our armed strength.

Since ultimate values, however, guide day-to-day behavior, a commitment to non-violent methods of conflict would lead to a change of attitude at the conference table. The United States today selects at each choice point the alternative most likely to preserve its military preponderance; instead, it would choose the one most likely to foster the development of a world of enduring peace. The choice involves risks, but all alternatives are risky, and the dangers involved with promoting disarmament would at worst be no greater than those involved with the continual accumulation of weapons. The United States would seek agreements that included inspection and control methods, as Russia and other nations would permit, but its disarmament would not be made contingent on having precisely the controls it desired. As the United States disarmed in accordance with a prearranged schedule, with some assurances that other nations were also disarming, it would be taking certain other very important steps— disarmament as a means of carrying out a program of nonviolence could not occur in a vacuum.

Consequences for Internal Social Organization

Commitment to a policy of non-violence in international affairs would undoubtedly require profound and widespread changes in American society's internal organization, but I shall mention only three directly related to military activities. Internally, it would have to abolish armies, war colleges, and general staffs, or at least drastically change their functions. This would necessitate large domestic educational and propaganda campaigns, and failure to provide them would be evidence of bad faith and so would jeopardize progress. The United States would also have to make the economic readjustments necessary for absorbing the resources now spent on munitions. Since arms contribute nothing to the national wealth—nations would not be poorer if they shoveled arms into the sea as fast as they made them—the biggest obstacles to conversion to a peacetime economy would be psychological, and these would be formidable, involving policies of taxation and government spending that violate long-established traditions, and the relocation and retraining of workers and the like, but they are not insurmountable.

Finally, America would have to train citizens in methods of civilian defense,[15] and to do this effectively, she would have to rely on the military. Their function would still be to protect the nation but by different means: their mission would be to train the civilian population throughly in the philosophy, strategy, and tactics of non-violence and to organize and lead them in case of an attempted occupation by foreign powers. These measures would include the creation of a tightly disciplined, well-trained leadership group, with provision for its concealment and diffusion, the creation of a clandestine communications network, and other tasks that could keep the military establishment as busy as preparation for war does today.

Consequences for Conduct of Foreign Affairs

Internationally, the United States would devote resources now squandered on arms to hasten the industrial and political development of the nations whose embittered, impoverished populations are the only soil in which communism flourishes. America's commitment to non-violence would thus require concomitant massive efforts to promote the sense of world community, build international organizations for the preservation of peace, and close the gap between rich and poor nations through programs including not only massive economic aid but full-scale attacks on illiteracy and the population explosion.

The arms race now absorbs almost two-thirds of America's scientists and technicians and half the money spent on research and development, and a comparable proportion of the brains and money necessary for the advancement of science and technology is probably tied up in other countries—this is exclusive of the huge percentages of national budgets being spent on arms production. These intellectual and financial resources devoted to promoting human welfare would cause a great forward surge in living standards, health, and food production.

Using international mass-communication channels, the United States would try to mobilize world public opinion in favor of such peaceful activities and against any nation that attempted to return to a war system, a type of deterrent that will grow stronger as the interdependence of nations increases. These efforts might well include support of a Court of International Delinquency, as described in Chapter 11.

Unfavorable Contingencies—Internal Revolution and External Invasion

This program's most favorable outcome would be that each successive disarmament step would become progressively easier as its advantages to all countries became increasingly obvious, culminating in an increasingly prosperous world containing strong inhibitions against resort to violence and increasingly effective institutional means for peaceful resolution of disputes.

The process could go awry in two ways at any point, however, and there would have to be preparations to meet these contingencies. First, if a doctrine of non-violence ever showed signs of winning the adherence of a majority of the American people, those who still believed that force is necessarily an instrument of policy would almost certainly attempt to seize power. In this situation most of the values of the ruling group and the opposition would be the same, and it might be possible, as it was in India, to inhibit the ruling group's violence by appealing to its ideals. The outcome would depend on whether the non-violence proponents were fully convinced of its superiority, had been sufficiently trained in its methods, and could be steadfast in their purpose. An internal dictatorship could not maintain itself against a persistent mass refusal to cooperate (in this connection, it will be recalled that no law is enforceable over the long pull without the acquiescence of at least 90 per cent of the population).

The second contingency in a world moving toward or having achieved disarmament would be one country's attempt to use a secreted stockpile of weapons against the United States. But if matters had run smoothly to this point, the attempt would be less easy than first appears, for with inspection increasing step-by-step with disarmament, the accumulation of such a cache would be more and more difficult.

Assuming that a nation had succeeded in concealing some weapons, however, it would face strong inhibitions, beyond those the United States could muster, against attempting to use them. Even with complete control of the mass-communications media, a dictator cannot make policy changes as drastic as this without considerable advance preparation of the population, and it would thus be very hard to preserve the element of surprise. (Hitler conducted history's most intensive internal campaign to glorify war, yet even he needed several years to rouse the Germans' martial fervor sufficiently to enable him to start World War II.) Other nations would have time to rearm, and everyone's enemy would be the nation which made the nuclear threat. Since nations would not have forgotten how to make weapons, and bacteriological and chemical ones are very cheap and easy to produce, the nation contemplating blackmail would have a virtually impossible job of policing on its hands. A nation's return to reliance on armed force in a world at peace would also jeopardize the progressive advance in living standards, under which circumstances the aggressor nation's leaders would also have to face the prospect of considerable demoralization and resistance among their own citizens.

Nevertheless, the United States would have to consider how to meet three further contingencies: a massive attack with nuclear or other weapons, an effort at occupation, and an attempt to weaken its international influence by threatening its allies and the uncommited nations.

The danger of nuclear attack seems very small, because the main incentive—fear of a pre-emptive attack by the United States—would be gone. It is pointless to destroy another country unless it is perceived as a threat to one's own existence, and the United States would no longer be one. The risk exists, of course, but in view of the infinitely greater risks involved in the arms race, it seems worth taking.

An occupation by an enemy possessing superior arms seems to be what American political leaders fear most—as one expressed it: "In the face of Communist ideology any nation that lays down its arms can expect immediate occupation." [16] Sometimes the fear of occupation takes the form of a nightmare of hungry, armed Asians and Africans swarming over us, a fear I find hard to take seriously. Most people do not leave home that easily, and if life were getting steadily better at home and they were no longer hungry, the major incentive for such a mass migration halfway around the world would be gone. The chief safeguard against such a possibility would be the raising of the impoverished nations' living standards which would progress rapidly once the preposterous burden of armaments was lifted.

Occupation would be more likely to be attempted by a rival like Russia, and in a disarmed world there would be powerful deterrents to such an act. But they might fail, and then the United States would be faced with the necessity of defeating the occupation by non-violent means.[17] This might appear hopeless in the light of the many historical examples of the crushing of resistance by occupation armies, but in all these a winning nation at the peak of its morale occupied a demoralized and defeated nation whose citizens were untrained in the techniques of non-violence; and even under these conditions an occupation army's morale soon sags.

Modern weapons and methods of transportation and communication have increased the ability of small groups to subdue and control hostile populations, but they do not protect the rulers against psychological pressures. The ultimate question would really be whether the invader's group standards are sufficiently strong to sustain a program of oppression and slaughter long enough to break the resistance of an undefeated population, trained in methods of resistance calculated to inhibit aggressiveness, weaken morale, and convert the opponent. Dictatorships and armies of occupation, as already indicated, may be particularly susceptible to such types of pressure.

The remaining contingency would be the rearmed nation's use of a covert threat of military force to combat American influence in other countries. But the new deterrent would be that such tactics, like other attempts to revert to the use of force, would shatter international order. And in an affluent, disarmed world, the present incentives to dominate other nations would be greatly weakened—large nations would no longer need to control small ones to maintain military alliances or to protect their markets and sources of raw materials. Nations would still influence each other, but the weaker ones would favor those among the stronger that offered them the greatest help or presented the best models. The United States could equal or excel other large nations in both respects, and it also has a particular advantage over communist nations because its pluralist philosophy leads it to welcome diversity in political and socioeconomic matters; hence, nations who looked to it would feel less pressure to conform to alien standards than would those that turned toward the communist nations. America's case would be strengthened by the resentment sure to be aroused by blackmailing tactics; she might lose ground in some areas, as she does now by relying on force, but considering the much larger potential gains accruing from a policy that includes renunciation of force, the risk would appear well worth taking.

NON-VIOLENCE: SUMMARY

In its modern manifestations non-violent action is a method of waging group combat that derives from both religio-philosophical and psychological sources. From the former comes the conviction that it is possible to appeal successfully to an enemy's conscience, because as a fellow human he cannot help being affected by the demonstration of willingness to suffer for one's convictions without bitterness or retaliation. The non-violent fighter refuses to dehumanize his opponent and acts to make it very hard for his opponent to dehumanize him. From a psychological standpoint, non-violence can be seen as a determined attempt to prove to the enemy that he cannot gain his ends by violence while simultaneously behaving so that his use of violence is inhibited. This includes not showing fear and not counter-attacking physically or verbally, but rather treating him with respect and trying, even in the midst of the struggle, to understand his viewpoint and enlist his aid in finding a solution that will satisfy the interests of both.

The assumption on both counts is that the non-violent fighter's moral stance and his violence-inhibiting behavior will eventually cause his adversary's violence to grind to a halt. In actual practice, non-violent fighting has seldom been confined to such high-minded arms and actions, raising some awkward questions: Would deceit and sabotage destroy the moral basis for non-violence on which its effectiveness may rest? Could a non-violent "underground" movement, requiring secrecy rather than full publicity, succeed? The answers to such questions are yet to be determined, but non-violence has at least become a legitimate field for scientific study, and in this may lie the greatest hope for its further development.

The applicability of non-violent action is more easily seen in domestic rather than foreign quarrels, and perhaps its use in the latter would reduce to discouraging a planned occupation or defeating an attempt. This would meet only part of the problem, but if leaders could be convinced that an enemy occupation could be defeated by non-violent means, the most feared possible consequence of another nation's gaining military superiority would be removed, freeing national leaders' imaginations and energies to take other steps toward a world of enduring peace.

In one sense non-violence is very ancient; in another it is a mere infant, less than fifty years old. Now that Gandhi and others have shown its new potentials, there is no reason to think that non-violent fighting will not undergo the same type of development as war did over the centuries, with geniuses periodically devising new revolutionary means. One is reminded of Faraday's retort to a visitor's scornful question on seeing the first electric motor—a wire swaying in a magnetic field: "What earthly use is that?" Faraday answered: "What earthly use is a newborn baby?"

COMMITMENT TO PEACE ACTIVITIES— FINDINGS OF A QUESTIONNAIRE

If modern nations are to give up reliance on force as the final resort in settling international disputes, a change in attitudes of the magnitude of a mass religious conversion or such a major revolution as the overthrow of czarism would be necessary. A nation like the United States that glorifies its violent frontier heritage and has never been defeated in war would be particularly unlikely to undergo such a conversion, and the little that is known about conditions fostering conversion of individuals or groups is not encouraging.

Religious conversions are typically experienced after a prolonged period of despair—to use a phrase well known to alcoholics, before the conversion a person has "hit bottom." And if at that moment a person or group holds out a new view of life that promises surcease from suffering, and renewed hope and acceptance by a new group, the sufferer may experience a strong emotional release, followed by adherence to the new view.

Probably only a major nuclear catastrophe could shock modern nations into abandoning war as an instrument of national policy, but until that happens, all other methods that might promote this result, however inadequate they seem to be, must be brought to bear.

Some alcoholics manage to see bottom before they hit it— which at least opens the possibility that nations could do the same. In this connection there may be some relevance in the findings of a questionnaire study of people who became active in working for peace as the result of a "crucial episode." In the absence of a control group, and considering that the sample was self-selected, the findings can be no more than suggestive.[18,19] Most respondents were already concerned but felt helpless about nuclear weapons before the crucial episode; then something happened which made the dangers of these weapons psychologically real to them and at the same time suggested a course of action. The events of 1961—the building of the Berlin Wall, Russia's resumption of atmospheric nuclear tests, and the flurry over home fallout shelters—were the most common triggers, and they had greater effect on respondents with children.

Practically every respondent reported a moderately or very strong emotional response during the crucial episode, usually some combination of anger and fear, directed at the danger as well as at leaders on whom they were relying for protection or to fight for disarmament, and who they felt were letting them down. Moreover, the intensity of their emotion seemed related to the degree of attitude change.

Coupled with this surge of feeling was the new sense of responsibility the respondents felt for doing something instead of relying on others, leading them to take some initiative—this might be simply reading up on the subject, talking with someone already active in the peace movement, participating in demonstrations, or writing a letter to the editor. After a burst of rather intense activity their efforts leveled off, but they remained more active than they had been, and they were sustained by a conviction of the rightness of their acts, an increased sense of self-worth, and a reduction of unpleasant emotions like anxiety. Support from family and from the new friends made when their activity patterns changed also helped, as did new sources of information and opinion of which they had become aware.

By and large, the people who responded to the questionnaire were characterized by a high degree of initiative, a lively concern for human welfare, and independence of thought, qualities which in combination may have increased their awareness of the dangers of nuclear weapons, made them less willing to accept official policies uncritically, and more inclined to take some action once their energies were mobilized.

A marked change of attitude was reported by a much larger proportion of respondents under rather than over twenty-five. Women proved to be more accessible to such personal influence as listening to a speaker, talking with a friend, or participating in a demonstration, while men were more moved by such impersonal influences as a news event, article, or book.

Though tentative and fragmentary, these findings may have some value for organizations trying to win converts to programs for promoting peace, including reliance on non-violent means of combat. The most reachable people appear to be those who are concerned but do not know what to do, which suggests that continuing efforts to educate the public about the nature of the danger, even though there are no immediate results, are worth pursuing as means of preparing the ground. The best time to get people involved would seem to be after some news event has made these dangers vivid; those most likely to be affected are parents, which would agree with the general observation that concern over the welfare of one's offspring ranks as high as or higher than concern about oneself.

The findings suggest that public actions like demonstrations have some value in mobilizing those who are on the fence, while strengthening the morale of those already committed by heightening their sense of solidarity with others of like mind.

EDUCATION FOR PEACE

For the long pull, main reliance must be placed on the education and training of the upcoming generations—the first of the post-atomic age. To enable them to create a world without war, education and child-rearing will have to inhibit recourse to violence to settle conflicts.

Reducing the Individual's Propensity to Violence

The most widespread method of child-rearing is based on corporal punishment, which does nothing to inhibit violence and may encourage it. The relationship between the propensity to violence of a nation's individual citizens and that nation's readiness to go to war is, of course, highly complex; it is possible, although hard to imagine, that there is no relation at all.

It seems safe to conclude on the basis of present evidence that the strongest internal controls are developed by children whose parents have shaped their behavior by affection, praise, and reason rather than by physical punishment and deprivation of privileges. Corporal punishment seems to increase aggressive behavior by frustrating the child and by supplying him with an aggressive model to imitate. It is not known, however, whether children brought up by affectionate parents who do not use corporal punishment are, as adults, less easily aroused to fight an enemy or make worse soldiers than those brought up by the rod. Similarly, educational methods like that of the *kibbutz* stress group responsibility, and while they may inhibit violence within the group, their graduates are excellent soldiers. There is no reason to think, however, that child-rearing methods that reduce violence among group members necessarily increase the propensity for violence directed at other groups. Since the fostering of violence has no positive value, nothing would be lost by efforts to instill a different attitude toward it.

The greatest progress to this end, at least in the United States, could probably be made by drastic reforms in mass-media offerings. American children and youth are currently taught in many ways that violence is fun and, by implication, that indulgence in it is a sign of manliness—movies, the comics, and television provide a steady diet of violence, often mixed with sex, while hundreds of thousands view the U.S. Army's public demonstrations of garrotting, stabbing, and other methods of killing.

Obviously, it would be desirable if the opposite attitude toward violence were presented instead. The mass media should stop glorifying the violent man and present him as the villain, not the hero and his punishment should be prompt. One type of hero appears occasionally who deserves much more emphasis— the heroic cowboy or sheriff who throws away his gun and faces the villain down by sheer will power: while such scenes usually culminate in a splendid fist-fight, basically they glorify the man who can inhibit someone with superior destructive power from using it.

Military heroes should be downgraded and heroes of peace played up. Some, like King and Gandhi, are famous for the way they conducted conflict: and leaders like Wilson and Roosevelt who, although they led the nation into war, worked mightily to create a world at peace could be included in this category. Given the resources and talents available to the mass-entertainment media, it would certainly be possible to dramatize the lives of the many peacetime heroes, often persons of extraordinary courage, whose efforts in many fields have enriched human life —Michelangelo, Pasteur, Florence Nightingale, Thomas Edison are random examples.

If suggestions along these lines are to have any hope of realization, a drastic change of attitude would be required of the purveyors of mass entertainment. They would have to realize that as controllers of powerful educational media, they have considerable responsibility for shaping the attitudes of Americans, especially young ones, so that their choice of programs should not be motivated solely by profit.[20] Unfortunately, the purveying of crime and violence pays well, and this is a formidable roadblock to reform. A huge expansion of educational television might be the most hopeful approach.

Although certain child-rearing methods and the types of information emphasized or avoided by the mass media may reduce the propensity to indulge in violence, they cannot eliminate it entirely, for humans will always find frustrations that incite them to destructive behavior. Furthermore, since many males seem to feel that they prove their masculinity by risking their lives, and a preferred way to do this is through fighting, a world without war must also include ways to divert or control the impulses to violence that find their outlet in war. It is in this realm that the greatest imagination is needed, and the best hope may lie in the development of methods of non-violent conflict, since these require individual heroism and also attempt to attain directly the group objectives served by war. Other possibilities offered by the modern world are a vast expansion of international sports, activities like the Peace Corps, and undersea and outer-space exploration. All offer new opportunities for spectacular acts of individual and group heroism and healthy competition, and they afford ample opportunities to express aggression in the service of constructive goals.

Reducing Recourse to International Violence

In addition to reducing the attractiveness of violence and finding alternatives for its expression, the maintenance of international peace requires the creation of effective peace-making machinery. This is primarily a political and legal problem, but education can hasten progress toward this goal. By promoting understanding and appreciation among people of different cultures and nations, it can hinder the formation of the enemy image and promote the sense of world community on which acceptance of a world government must be based. Communication satellites have created magnificent new opportunities for television to break down cultural barriers that have not begun to be exploited. The teaching of history and current affairs, now too often devoted to glorifying one's own nation and derogating certain others, could also become a powerful force for promoting international understanding.

Schools and colleges must also develop new courses on the futility of modern war and the need for creating effective international peace-keeping organizations.

Peace education should be introduced into school curricula in the earliest grades. Presentation of antiwar material by teachers has been shown to change students' attitudes, at least as measured by responses to a questionnaire, and repeated presentations are much more effective than single ones: two or three lectures against militarism changed students' attitudes not two or three times as much as one lecture, but five to ten times as much.[21] Over several months, those exposed were found to slide back toward their initial viewpoints, but not all the way.

Peace education is showing a healthy shift from exhortation to supplying information. It is directed increasingly toward analyzing the obstacles to the development of international order (seen as a problem of systems change) rather than merely emphasizing the evils and dangers of war and the desirability of peace. It is also beginning to engage the help of artists and writers, recognizing that to change attitudes, mobilization of feelings is necessary. A small private group, the World Law Fund, has had remarkable success in gaining college and high school teachers' acceptance of materials with these orientations, a most encouraging development.[22] Such programs cannot have maximal effects until they are incorporated into the educational curricula of all nations, but their growing reception in the United States gives grounds for hope that their spread may be rapid.

In comparison with the deepseated and pervasive psychosocial forces supporting war, the suggestions summarized here are admittedly trivial. If they have any value, it is in pointing out certain directions of thought and activity that could strengthen individual and group psychological supports for a world without war. The road to this goal is long and hard, perhaps impassable, but even the longest journey begins with the first step.

Epilogue:
The Problem
in Perspective

THIS EXPLORATION into psychological aspects of war and peace has led into so many byways and covered such a variety of terrain that it may have been difficult to maintain perspective. A few general remarks may therefore help to bring the total picture back into focus.

Wars have always been attributed to certain features of their eras' dominant sociopolitical organization. Conflicting religious creeds, dynastic ambitions, munitions manufacturers, the struggle for markets—all have had the accusing finger pointed at them, but the simple fact is that organized societies have always found something to fight about. Societies may change, but wars go on. Economic, ideological, dynastic, political, and other sources of international conflict can all apparently mobilize war fever, for they could not cause men to slaughter each other if this were not so.

The conclusion is inescapable that aspects of human nature are necessary, although not sufficient, causes for war, but it is hard to discern what these aspects are because they manifest themselves only through sociopolitical institutions, and these change from one era to the next. Perhaps behind all the appearances are two related human impulses—to power and to violence.

Humans, or at least men, seem impelled to aggrandize themselves and their groups by trying to bend the environment, both human and non-human, to their will. They have performed prodigies of endurance and ingenuity in progressively subduing the non-human environment and in attempting to subdue each other. These activities take the form of struggles for dominance and wealth within societies, and for territorial or ideological expansion between them. In both cases individuals and groups aggrandize themselves until checked by external forces—group codes, expectations, and institutions within groups, and the power of rivalry between groups.

The second human psychological feature underlying war is the latent potential for violence which can be activated by such causes as imitation and obedience, but the most pervasive cause is probably frustration, especially frustration of expectations. The most ubiquitous source of frustration is other human beings who promote interests that clash with one's own.

Neither the drive for power nor the potential for violence can be excised from the human psyche, especially since they are the obverse and reverse of a coin. The drive for power keeps humans perpetually dissatisfied by creating a permanent gap between performance and expectations: since their reach always exceeds their grasp, they will eventually feel frustrated no matter how well off they are; and since as likely as not the source of the frustration will be another human being or group of human beings whose drive for self-aggrandizement has led them into a collision course, no degree of affluence or self-fulfillment will in itself assure that humans will live peacefully together.

Fortunately, self-aggrandizement and the potential for violence are counterbalanced by forces at least equally strong that are perhaps best summed up by the phrase "moral sense," as expressed in the teachings of all the major religions. It includes the desire to love and be loved, concern with others' welfare, joy in cooperative enterprises, and the general satisfactions of communal living. Humans generally would rather love than hate and feel more fulfilled by acts of affiliation than hostility. The positive features of human behavior are elicited most readily by those whom they perceive as belonging to the same group.

Survival today depends on reducing, controlling, channeling, and redirecting the drive for power and the impulse to violence and fostering the countervailing drives toward fellowship and community. These can be done because of the extraordinary flexibility of humans, arising from their unique power to symbolize, which permits an almost endless variety of expressions of any particular impulse.

But the crucial question is whether the necessary changes in human institutions, especially in the international sphere, can be created rapidly enough. Affiliative forces have thus far been sufficiently strong to keep aggressive forces from destroying humanity, and humans have been able to change their behavior rapidly enough, though not without considerable stress and strain, to keep up with the changes they have created in their environment.

To meet today's drastic and still rapidly changing conditions requires changes in human behavior more rapid and widespread than ever before, and the obstacles to achieving these changes seem formidable, if not insurmountable. This book has focused mainly on the constraints limiting human adaptability, especially in the realm of international relations. Fortunately, many customary patterns of human interaction are still valid or require only slight modification—the basic virtues of honesty, trustworthiness, and consideration for others are as good guides for conduct today as they ever were. Institutionally, much could be accomplished by more effort to remove recognized blocks to making existing arrangements work more effectively. There is a great deal of accumulated experience from relations between smaller and larger political units, about the techniques for resolving disputes between conflicting interest groups, and about a wide variety of political and legal institutions useful for the resolution of international conflict.

There is no ignoring, however, that one fundamental change in the international system is required for survival: the concept of unlimited national sovereignty and, its corollary, reliance on destructive capacity as the final resort in the settlement of international disputes must be replaced by an orderly rather than anarchic international system and by the development of faith in new non-destructive forms of power.

The magnitude of the task is unprecedented, but so are the new means available for mastering it and the positive and negative incentives for doing so. The new means lie in the advances in mass communication and transportation and the technological gains in many fields that are knitting the world ever more closely together, as well as in budding international organizations like the United Nations and its subsidiaries. Together, these forces are making nations more interdependent and bringing this interdependence into awareness.

The new negative incentive is the growing realization that continuance of the war system will lead to the destruction of civilization and possibly the human species. War has been tolerable until now because wars have always left behind enough survivors, and enough social and political structure in the victorious society, for civilization to be able to survive and continue to advance. But since the invention of genocidal weapons, this has no longer been true.

The new positive incentive is the growing realization by peoples of all nations that for the first time in human history, they have the knowledge and the techniques to reduce or eliminate famine, disease, poverty, and ignorance. Moreover, these goals could be reached within a generation if the vast material and human resources tied up in preparing for waging war could be applied to them—in a few decades we could create a world of plenty that could not have figured in our ancestors' wildest dreams. With ample leisure the arts and sciences would flourish as never before, and the enrichment of experience and knowledge would proceed at a fabulous pace.

In the last analysis, the main source of hope that mankind will avert the looming disaster is the recognition that while man's survival has always been problematical, the human species has always been able to muster the resources and ingenuity to enable it to come through by the skin of its teeth. Although it is a subject for ironic reflection, it is also hopeful that the main threats now come from man himself instead of nature, because it implies that he can use his new mastery of his environment to enhance his welfare instead of hasten his destruction.

Today it looks as if mankind is doomed like Moses to perish in sight of the Promised Land, yet it could be reached if humans would stop trying to achieve their ends by killing each other. If enough people grasp this simple truth in time, humans could rapidly move forward into a world in which, for the first time, all would have the opportunity to realize their full potentialities.

Like many individuals, nations will probably not be able to make the drastic changes in habitual attitudes and behavior necessary for survival in a nuclear world until they come to the brink of disaster. At that moment, though probably not before, enough national leaders may see bottom before they hit it and abandon resort to war as the ultimate recourse for resolving international disputes. The chance that such a massive change of heart will occur in time is very small. If it does happen, perhaps the spadework of all those who have been analyzing the sources of war and working out non-violent methods of settling international disputes will have helped tip the balance in favor of survival.

References

I

1. V. W. Sidel and R. M. Goldwyn, "Chemical and Biologic Weapons—A Primer," *New England Journal of Medicine,* 274 (1966), 21–27, 50–51.
2. B. Johnson, *Baltimore Sun,* February 5, 1960, p. 1.
3. Sidel and Goldwyn.
4. Statement of the Federation of American Scientists, New York City, November 23, 1958.
5. T. Stonier, *Nuclear Disaster* (Cleveland: World, Meridian Books, 1963).
6. H. Zinsser, *Rats, Lice and History* (Boston: Little, Brown, 1935), p. 153.
7. H. Kahn, *On Thermonuclear War* (Princeton: Princeton University Press, 1960), p. 92.
8. L. C. Van Atta, "Arms Control: Human Control," *American Psychologist,* 18 (1963), 39.
9. E. P. Wigner *et al.,* "Project Harbor Controversy," *Scientist and Citizen,* 7 (August 1965), 1–5; 8 (February–March, 1966), 26–31.
10. R. S. McNamara, Testimony before House Armed Services Committee (February, 1963), quoted by Sen. George McGovern, *Congressional Record* (August 2, 1963).
11. J. B. Wiesner and H. F. York, "National Security and the Nuclear-Test Ban," *Scientific American,* 211 (October, 1964), 35.
12. *Proceedings of Pugwash Conference of International Scientists on Biological and Chemical Warfare,* Pugwash, Nova Scotia, August 24–30, 1959, 5-6.

2

1. L. S. Cottrell and E. Eberhart, *American Opinion on World Affairs in the Atomic Age* (Princeton: Princeton University Press, 1948).
2. *U. S. News & World Report*, December 21, 1959, p. 53 (speaker unidentified).
3. M. Howard, "Telling the Patient," *The Spectator*, 203 (July 3, 1959), p. 9.
4. I. L. Janis and R. F. Terwilliger, "An Experimental Study of Psychological Resistances to Fear Arousing Communications," *J. Abn. and Soc. Psychology*, 65 (1962), 402–410.
5. A. Modgliani, "The Public and the Cold War," *War/Peace Report* (September, 1963), 7–9.
6. *The Wall Street Journal*, March 25, 1959, pp. 1, 16.
7. Sen. George A. Aiken, *Baltimore Evening Sun*, May 30, 1960.
8. K. Tynan, *The New Yorker*, April 4, 1959, pp. 114–115.
9. W. N. Plymat, "The Power Problem is Solvable: A Formula to Think Ourselves Out of Our War Psychosis," *Peace and Power* (Washington, D. C.: The Division of Peace and World Order of the Board of Christian Social Concerns of the Methodist Church, 1960), p. 88.
10. M. Pilisuk and T. Hayden, "Is There A Military Industrial Complex Which Prevents Peace?: Consensus and Countervailing Power in Pluralistic Systems," *J. Social Issues*, 21 (July, 1965), 67–117.
11. D. Eggan, "The General Problem of Hopi Adjustment," *Amer. Anthropologist*, 45 (1943), 372–373.
12. A. Kardiner *et al.*, *The Psychological Frontiers of Society* (New York: Columbia University Press, 1945), p. 49.

3

1. K. Lorenz, *On Aggression* (New York: Harcourt Brace and World, 1966).
2. I. Eibl-Eibesfeldt, "Aggressive Behavior and Ritualized Fighting in Animals," in J. H. Masserman, ed., *Violence and War, with Clinical Studies* (New York: Grune and Stratton, 1963), pp. 8–17.
3. E. von Holst and U. von St. Paul, "Electrically Controlled Behavior," *Scientific American*, 206 (1962), 50–59.
4. W. P. Chapman, H. R. Schroeder, G. Geyer, M. A. B. Brazier, C. Fager, J. L. Poppen, H. C. Solomon, and P. I. Yakovlev,

"Physiological Evidence Concerning Importance of the Amygdaloid Nuclear Region in the Integration of Circulatory Function and Emotion in Man," *Science*, 120 (December, 1954), 950.

5. D. W. Liddell, "Observations on Epileptic Automatism in a Mental Hospital Population," *J. Mental Science*, 99 (1953), 741.
6. H. Brill, "Postencephalitic Psychiatric Conditions," in S. Arieti, ed., *American Handbook of Psychiatry* (New York: Basic Books, 1959), II, pp. 1163–1174.
7. J. Recktenwald, "Woran hat Adolf Hitler Gelitten? Eine Neuropsychiatrische Deutung," *Psychologie und Person*, Bd. 3 (Munich: E. Reinhardt, 1963).
8. J. P. Scott, *Aggression* (Chicago: Chicago University Press, 1958), p. 71.
9. *Ibid.*
10. *Ibid.*, pp. 18–21.
11. W. A. Scott, "Psychological and Social Correlates of International Images," in H. C. Kelman, ed., *International Behavior* (New York: Holt, Rinehart and Winston, 1965), pp. 70–103.
12. S. Putney and R. Middleton, "Some Factors Associated with Student Acceptance or Rejection of War," *Amer. Sociological Rev.*, 27 (October, 1962), 655–667.
13. M. J. Rosenberg, "Images in Relation to the Policy Process: American Public Opinion on Cold-War Issues," in Kelman, pp. 278–334.
14. S. Oskamp and A. Hartry, "A Factor-Analytic Study of Attitudes toward U.S. and Russian Actions in World Affairs," paper read at the American Psychological Association meeting, Chicago, September, 1965.
15. L. Berkowitz, *Aggression: A Social-Psychological Analysis* (New York: McGraw-Hill, 1962), 269–71.
16. J. P. Scott, pp. 62, 64.

4

1. *Time*, April 15, 1966, p. 27.
2. H. Brandon, "An Untold Story of the Cuban Crisis," *Saturday Review*, March 9, 1963, p. 57.
3. Col. A. J. Glass, "Observations upon the Epidemiology of Mental Illness in Troops during Wartime," in *Symposium on Preventive and Social Psychiatry* (Washington, D.C.: Walter Reed Army Institute of Research, U.S. Government Printing Office, 1957), pp. 185–198.

4. *Baltimore Evening Sun,* October 4, 1960.
5. C. L. Sulzberger, "The Case of the Unknown Colonel," *The New York Times,* February 15, 1958.
6. *Air Force Manual 160–55,* "Guidance for Implementing Human Reliability Program," February 28, 1962; also Air Force Regulations 35–9.
7. T. C. Schelling, *The Strategy of Conflict* (New York: Oxford University Press, 1963), pp. 257–266.
8. P. H. Liederman and J. H. Mendelson, "Some Psychiatric Considerations in Planning for Defense Shelters," in S. Aranow, F. R. Ervin, and V. W. Sidel, eds., *The Fallen Sky: Medical Consequences of Thermo-Nuclear War* (New York: Hill and Wang, 1963), pp. 42–54.
9. M. Torre, "How Does Physical and Mental Illness Influence Negotiations between Diplomats?", *Int. J. Social Psychiatry,* 10 (Summer, 1964), 170–176.
10. R. L. Noland, "Presidental Disability and the Proposed Constitutional Amendment," *Amer. Psychologist,* 21 (March, 1966), 230–235.
11. I. Gregory, *Psychiatry, Biological and Social* (New York: W. B. Saunders Co., 1961), pp. 459, 469.
12. A. A. Rogow, *James Forrestal: A Study of Personality, Politics and Policy* (New York: Macmillan, 1963).
13. ———, "Disability in High Office," *Medical Opinion and Review,* 1 (April, 1966), 16–19.
14. Lord Moran, *Churchill* (Boston: Houghton Mifflin, 1966), p. 245.
15. *Ibid.,* p. 193.
16. *Santa Barbara News-Press,* June 30, 1966, p. B–1.
17. N. Kleitman, *Sleep and Wakefulness* (Chicago: University of Chicago Press, 1963) rev. ed., p. 229.
18. S. Pally, "Cognitive Rigidity as a Function of Threat," *J. Personality,* 23 (1954), 347–355.
19. E. L. Cowen, "The Influence of Varying Degrees of Psychological Stress on Problem-solving Rigidity," *J. Abn. and Soc. Psychology,* 47 (1952), 512–519.
20. J. W. Moffitt and R. Stagner, "Perceptual Rigidity, Closure and Anxiety," *J. Abn. and Soc. Psychology,* 52 (1956), 354–357.
21. O. Klineberg, *The Human Dimension in International Relations* (New York: Holt, Rinehart, and Winston, 1964), pp. 65–67.
22. Rogow, "Disability in High Office."

5

1. J. E. Hokanson, M. Burgess, and M. F. Cohen, "Effects of Displaced Aggression on Systolic Blood Pressure," *J. Abn. and Soc. Psychology,* 67 (1963), 214–218.
2. R. E. Ulrich, R. R. Hutchinson, H. H. Azrin, "Pain-Elicited Aggression," *The Psychological Record,* 15 (January, 1965), 111–126.
3. A. Bandura and R. H. Walters, *Adolescent Aggression* (New York: Ronald Press, 1959).
4. E. Aronson, "Threat and Obedience," *Trans-action,* 3 (1966), 25–27.
5. *Ibid.,* 27.
6. U. Bronfenbrenner, "Soviet Methods of Character Education: Some Implications for Research," *Amer. Psychologist,* 17 (1962), 550–564.
7. M. E. Spiro, *Children of the Kibbutz* (New York: Shocken Books, 1965).
8. A. Freud, *The Ego and the Mechanisms of Defense* (New York: International Universities Press, 1946), p. 121.
9. J. P. Scott, pp. 20–22 (Ch. 3, note 8 *supra*).
10. A. Bandura, D. Ross, and S. A. Ross, "Transmission of Aggression through Imitation of Aggressive Models," *J. Abn. and Soc. Psychology,* 63 (November, 1961), 575–582.
11. ———, "Imitation of Film-Mediated Aggressive Models," *J. Abn. and Soc. Psychology,* 66 (1963), 3–11.
12. ———, "Vicarious Reinforcement and Imitative Learning," *J. Abn. and Soc. Psychology,* 67 (1963), 601–607.
13. E. E. Maccoby, "Effects of the Mass Media," in M. L. and L. W. Hoffman, eds., *Review of Child Development Research* (New York: Russell Sage Foundation, 1964), I, p. 345.
14. W. Schramm, J. Lyle, and E. B. Parker, *Television in the Lives of Our Children* (Stanford: Stanford University Press, 1961).
15. H. T. Himmelweit, A. N. Oppenheim, and P. Vince, *Television and the Child* (London and Ontario: Oxford University Press, 1958).
16. F. Wertham, *Seduction of the Innocent* (New York: Rinehart, 1954), pp. 147–171, 353–384.
17. H. E. Krugman, "The Impact of Television Advertising: Learning without Involvement," *Public Opinion Quarterly,* 29 (1965), 349–356.
18. D. Pearson, "Army Exhibit Good for Youth?" *The Santa Barbara News-Press,* August 27, 1966.
19. J. Dollard, L. Doob, N. Miller, O. Mowrer, and H. Sears,

Frustration and Aggression (New Haven: Yale University Press, 1939).

20. L. Solomon, "The Influence of Some Types of Power Relationships and Motivational Treatments upon the Development of Interpersonal Trust" (New York: Research Center for Human Relations, New York University, January, 1957), cited in J. W. Thibaut and H. H. Kelley, *The Social Psychology of Groups* (New York: Wiley, 1959), p. 229.

21. D. O. Hebb and W. R. Thompson, "The Social Significance of Animal Studies," in G. Lindzey, ed., *Handbook of Social Psychology* (Reading, Mass.: Addison Wesley, 1954), I, p. 550.

22. Berkowitz, p. 69 (Ch. 3, note 15 *supra*).

23. *Ibid.*, p. 70.

24. J. W. Thibaut and H. Riecken, "Authoritarianism, Status, and Communication of Aggression," *Human Relations*, 8 (1955), 95–120.

25. L. A. Coser, "Violence and the Social Structure," in J. H. Masserman, ed., *Violence and War with Clinical Studies* (New York: Grune and Stratton, 1963), pp. 30–42.

26. P. Sukman, "South America's Shattered Showcase," *Fortune*, November, 1965, p. 202.

27. Hebb and Thompson, p. 551.

28. A. Miller, "The Bored and the Violent," *Harpers*, November, 1962, p. 51.

29. L. Berkowitz, "The Effects of Observing Violence," *Scientific American*, 210 (1964), 35–41.

30. ———, "The Concept of Aggressive Drive: Some Additional Considerations," in L. Berkowitz, ed., *Advances in Experimental Social Psychology* (New York: Academic Press, 1965), 2, pp. 314–318.

31. L. Weeler and A. R. Caggiula, "The Contagion of Aggression," *J. Exp. and Soc. Psychology*, 2 (1966), 1–10.

32. S. Milgram, "Behavioral Study of Obedience," *J. Abn. and Soc. Psychology*, 67 (1963), 371–378.

33. S. Milgram, "Some Conditions of Obedience and Disobedience to Authority," *Human Relations*, 18 (1965), 57–76.

34. S. L. A. Marshall, *Men Against Fire* (New York: William Morrow, 1947), pp. 50–57.

35. W. H. Cary, Jr., *Madmen at Work, The Polaris Story* (Philadelphia: The American Friends Service Committee, undated).

36. M. Gluckman, *Custom and Conflict in Africa* (New York: Free Press, 1955), p. 4.

37. R. A. LeVine, "Socialization, Social Structure, and Intersocietal Images," in Kelman, ed., pp. 53–62 (Ch. 3, note 11 *supra*).

38. H. L. Neiburg, "Uses of Violence," *J. Conflict Resolution,* 7 (1963), 43–54.
39. E. E. Maccoby, J. P. Johnson, and R. M. Church, "Community Integration and the Social Control of Juvenile Delinquency," *J. Social Issues,* 14 (1958), 38–51.
40. H. D. Fabing, "On Going Berserk: A Neurochemical Inquiry," *Amer. J. Psychiatry,* 133 (1956), 409–415.
41. R. Linton, *Culture and Mental Disorders* (Springfield, Mass.: Charles C. Thomas, 1956), p. 116.
42. C. W. Kennedy, quoted in E. C. Jessup, *War or Sport* (Roslyn, New York, 1940), p. 25.
43. Lorenz, pp. 280–282 (Ch. 3, note I *supra*).
44. K. W. Deutsch, "Power and Communication in International Society," in A. de Rueck and J. Knight, eds., *Conflict in Society* (Boston: Little Brown, 1966), p. 305.
45. W. H. Goodenough, "Arms Control and Behavioral Science," *Science,* 144 (May 15, 1964), 821–824.

6

1. M. Sherif and C. W. Sherif, *In Common Predicament: Social Psychology of Intergroup Conflict and Cooperation* (Boston: Houghton Mifflin, 1966), pp. 12–14.
2. D. Katz, "Nationalism and Strategies of International Conflict Resolution," in Kelman, pp. 354–390 (Ch. 3, note II *supra*).
3. D. G. Pruitt and R. C. Snyder, *Theory and Research on the Causes of War* (unpub. ms., 1965), B 2, 3.
4. P. T. Hopmann, "International Conflict and Cohesion in the Communist System," cited in R. C. North, J. F. Triska, R. A. Brody, and O. R. Holsti, *Stanford Studies in International Conflict and Integration, Progress Report* (March, 1966).
5. B. M. Bass and G. Dunteman, "Biases in the Evaluation of One's Own Group, Its Allies and Opponents, *J. Conflict Resolution,* 7 (1963), 16–20.
6. E. B. McNeil, "The Nature of Aggression," in E. B. McNeil, ed., *The Nature of Human Conflict* (Englewood Cliffs, N.J.: Prentice-Hall, 1965), p. 37.
7. R. Tanter, "Dimensions of Conflict Behavior Within and Between Nations, 1958–60," *J. Conflict Resolution,* 10 (1966), 41–64.
8. M. Haas, "Some Social Correlates of International Political Behavior," cited in North, Triska, and Brody, *Stanford Studies* (July, 1963).
9. M. N. Walsh, "A Contribution to the Problem of Recurrent

Mass Homicide," *J. Hillside Hosp.*, 15 (April, 1966), 84–93.

10. K. E. Boulding, "National Images and International Systems," *J. Conflict Resolution*, 3 (1959), 120–131.

11. J. C. Stoessinger, *The Might of Nations* (New York: Random House, 1965), rev. ed., pp. 393–409.

12. J. W. Fulbright, *The Arrogance of Power* (New York: Random House, 1966), p. 5.

13. CBS News, "Results of a Nationwide Survey Concerning Vietnam War" (December 14, 1965).

14. C. Geertz, "The Impact of the Concept of Culture on the Concept of Man," *Bull. Atomic Scientists*, 22 (April, 1966), 2–8.

15. Many psychologists have discussed this process. Good descriptions relevant to international conflict are to be found in H. Cantril and L. Free, "Hopes and Fears for Self and Country," *Amer. Behav. Scientist*, 2 (1962), 6; and R. Stagner, "The Psychology of Human Conflict," in McNeil; pp. 45–63.

16. J. W. Bagby, "A Cross-Cultural Study of Perceptual Predominance in Binocular Rivalry," *J. Abn. and Soc. Psychology*, 54 1957), 331–334.

17. A. L. Edwards, "Political Frames of Reference as a Factor Influencing Recognition," *J. Abn. and Soc. Psychology*, 36 (1941), 35–40.

18. J. K. Galbraith, "The Age of the Wordfact," *Atlantic Monthly*, September, 1960, p. 87.

19. M. Rokeach and L. Mezei, "Race and Shared Belief as Factors in Social Choice," *Science*, 151 (1966), 167–172.

20. L. Festinger, S. Schachter, K. Bach, *Social Pressures in Informal Groups: A Study of a Housing Community* (New York: Harper, 1950), pp. 72–100.

21. B. Wedge, "Toward International Understanding: The Contributions of Comparative National Psychology," Edward L. Bernays Lecture, Edward R. Murrow Center of the Fletcher School of Law and Diplomacy, Tufts University, March 14, 1966.

22. M. Rokeach, *The Open and Closed Mind* (New York: Basic Books, 1960), 401.

23. H. H. Hyman and P. B. Sheatsley, "Some Reasons Why Information Campaigns Fail," *Public Opinion Quarterly*, 11 (1947), 412–423.

24. K. Deutsch and R. L. Merritt, "Effects of Events on National and International Images," in Kelman, p. 183.

25. Klineberg, p. 95 (Ch. 4, note 21 *supra*).

26. Geertz, 8.

27. R. F. Murphy, "Intergroup Hostility and Social Cohesion," *Amĕr. Anthropologist*, 59 (1957), 1028.

28. C. E. Osgood, "Cognitive Dynamics in the Conduct of Human Affairs," *Public Opinion Quarterly,* 24 (Summer, 1960), 365.
29. T. Caplow and R. J. McGee, *The Academic Marketplace* (New York: Basic Books, 1958), p. 105.
30. J. T. Gullahorn and J. E. Gullahorn, "An Extension of the U-Curve Hypothesis," *J. Soc. Issues,* 19 (1963), 36.
31. B. M. Wedge, "The Russian Mass Mind," *Yale Sci. Mag.,* 34 (February, 1960), 2–8.
32. U. Bronfenbrenner, "Allowing for Soviet Perceptions," in R. Fisher, ed., *International Conflict and Behavioral Science* (New York: Basic Books, 1964), p. 171.
33. R. Hingley, "Will Communism Survive Vranyo?", *Current,* 26 (June, 1962), 42.
34. Boulding, 123.
35. B. Chisholm, *Prescription for Survival* (New York: Columbia University Press, 1957).
36. L. J. Halle, *The Society of Man* (London: Chatto and Windus, 1965), p. 103.
37. H. Begbie, *Twice-Born Men: A Study in Regeneration* (New York: Fleming H. Revell, 1909).
38. J. D. Frank, *Persuasion and Healing* (Baltimore: Johns Hopkins Press, 1961), pp. 81–94.
39. M. Argyle, *Religious Behavior* (London: Routledge and Kegan Paul, 1958), p. 57.
40. L. Festinger, *A Theory of Cognitive Dissonance* (New York: Harper & Row, 1957).
41. H. Wheeler, "The Role of Myth Systems in American-Soviet Relations," *J. Conflict Resolution,* 4 (1960), 182.
42. R. K. White, "The Cold War and the Modal Philosophy," *J. Conflict Resolution,* 2 (1958), 50.
43. Boulding, 131.

7

1. J. D. Singer, "Threat-Perception and the Armament-Tension Dilemma," *J. Conflict Resolution,* 2 (March, 1958), 96.
2. M. Sabshin, D. A. Hamburg, R. R. Grenker, H. Persky, H. Basowitz, S. J. Korchin, and J. A. Chevalier, "Significance of Pre-experimental Studies in the Psychosomatic Laboratory," *A.M.A. Archives Neurol. and Psychiat.,* 78 (August, 1957), 207–219.
3. G. D. Berriman, "Fear Itself: An Anthropologist's View," *Bull. Atomic Scientists* (November, 1964), 9.
4. U. Bronfenbrenner, "The Mirror Image in Soviet-American

Relations: A Social Psychologist's Report," *J. Social Issues,* 17 (1961), 46.

5. R. C. Angell, V. S. Dunham, and J. D. Singer, "Social Values and Foreign Policy Attitudes of Soviet and American Elites," *J. Conflict Resolution,* 8 (1964), 329–491.

6. H. H. Kelley, in Discussion, Third Session: "The Structural Properties of the Actor, in K. Archibald, ed., *Strategic Interaction and Conflict* (Berkeley, Calif.: Institute of International Studies, University of California, 1966), p. 182.

7. K. Krauskopf, "Report on Russia: Geochemistry and Politics," *Science,* 134 (August 26, 1961), 542.

8. R. K. White, "Misperception and the Vietnam War," *J. Soc. Issues,* 22 (July, 1966), 18.

9. F. W. Barnes, Letter to *Washington Sunday Star,* January 21, 1962.

10. M. Rokeach, *The Open and Closed Mind* (Ch. 6, note 22 *supra*).

11. I. L. Janis and M. B. Smith, "Effects of Education and Persuasion on National and International Images," in Kelman, p. 209 (Ch. 3, note 11 *supra*).

12. Rokeach, *The Open and Closed Mind,* p. 416.

13. M. J. Rosenberg, "Images in Relation to the Policy Process, American Public Opinion on Cold-War Issues," in Kelman, 324–328.

14. H. P. Smith and E. W. Rosen, "Some Psychological Correlates of World-Mindedness and Authoritarianism," *J. Personality,* 26 (1958), 170–183, cited by Janis and Smith in Kelman, p. 209.

15. Putney and Middleton, 655–667 (Ch. 3, note 12 *supra*).

16. B. Christiansen, *Attitudes Toward Foreign Affairs as a Function of Personality* (Oslo: University of Oslo Press, 1959), cited by Janis and Smith in Kelman, p. 210.

17. M. G. Hermann, "Some Personal Characteristics Related to Foreign Aid Voting of Congressmen" (Masters thesis, Northwestern University, 1963, mimeographed); cited by J. A. Robinson and R. C. Snyder, "Decision-Making in International Politics," in Kelman, p. 445.

18. J. W. Thibaut and J. Coules, "The Role of Communication in the Reduction of Inter-Personal Hostility," *J. Abn. and Soc. Psychology,* 47 (1952), 770–777.

19. *The Baltimore Sun,* November 8, 1959, p. 1.

20. *The New York Times,* November 1, 1959, p. 20.

21. *Ibid.,* April 19, 1966, p. 1.

22. P. Ram and G. Murphy, "Recent Investigations of Hindu-

Muslim Relations in India," *Human Organization*, 11 (Summer, 1952), 13–16.
23. G. W. Allport, *The Nature of Prejudice* (Cambridge, Mass.: Addison-Wesley, 1954), p. 3.
24. U. Bronfenbrenner, "Why Do the Russians Plant Trees Along the Road?", *Saturday Review* (January 5, 1963), p. 96.
25. S. Oskamp, "Attitudes Toward U.S. and Russian Actions: A Double Standard," *Psychological Reports*, 16 (1965), 43–46.
26. O. R. Holsti, "The Belief System and National Image: A Case Study," *J. Conflict Resolution*, 6 (1962), 244–252.
27. R. Bauer, "Problems of Perception and the Relations between the United States and the Soviet Union," *J. Conflict Resolution*, 5 (September, 1961), 223–229.
28. E. Fromm, *May Man Prevail?* (Garden City, N. Y.: Doubleday, 1961), p. 19.
29. G. Icheiser "Misunderstandings in Human Relations," *Amer. J. Sociology*, 55 (part 2) (1940), 1–70, cited in M. Deutsch, "A Psychological Approach to International Conflict," in G. Sperazzo, ed., *Psychology and International Relations* (Washington, D.C.: Georgetown University Press, 1965).
30. H. Wheeler, "The Role of Myth Systems in American-Soviet Relations," *J. Conflict Resolution*, 4 (1960), 182.
31. M. Rokeach, "The Organization and Modification of Beliefs," *Cent. Rev.*, 7 (Fall, 1963), p. 386.
32. M. Haire, "Role-perceptions in Labor-Management Relations: An Experimental Approach," *Indust. Labor Rel. Rev.*, 8 (1955), 204–212.
33. The Gallup Poll, " 'Image' of Red Powers," *The Santa Barbara News-Press* (June 26, 1966).

8

1. *The Baltimore Sun*, November 11, 1960.
2. W. W. Rostow, "The Test: Are We the Tougher?", *The New York Times Magazine* (June 7, 1964), pp. 112, 113.
3. G. Kateb, "Kennedy as Statesman," *Commentary* (June, 1966), p. 59.
4. H. Kahn, "The Arms Race and Some of its Hazards," in D. G. Brennan, ed., *Arms Control, Disarmament and National Security* (New York: George Braziller, 1961), pp. 89–121.
5. J. D. Singer, "Stable Deterrence and its Limits," *Western Political Quarterly* (September, 1962), 460–464.
6. B. Bettelheim, "Remarks on the Psychological Appeal of Totali-

tarianism," *Amer. J. Economics and Sociology,* 12 (1952), 89–96.

7. R. K. Merton, *Social Theory and Social Structure* (Glencoe, Ill.: Free Press, 1957), pp. 421–436.

8. H. A. Wilmer, "Toward a Definition of the Therapeutic Community," *Amer. J. Psychiatry,* 114 (1958), 824–834.

9. For excellent popular presentations see H. Kahn, *Thinking about the Unthinkable* (New York: Avon, 1962); and T. C. Schelling, *The Strategy of Conflict* (Ch. 4, note 7 *supra*), and *Arms and Influence* (New Haven: Yale University Press, 1966).

10. Schelling, *The Strategy of Conflict,* p. 89.

11. ———, "Uncertainty, Brinkmanship, and the Game of 'Chicken,' " in K. Archibald, ed., *Strategic Interaction and Conflict* (Berkeley: University of California Institute of International Studies, 1966), pp. 74–89.

12. E. P. Wigner, "Reply to S/C's Criticism of the Project Harbor Summary," *Scientist and Citizen,* 7 (August, 1965), p. 5.

13. Wiesner and York, 33 (Ch. 1, note 11 *supra*).

14. S. Escalona, *Children and the Threat of Nuclear War* (New York: Child Study Association Publication, 1962).

15. A. Freud and D. T. Burlingame, *War and Children* (New York: Medical War Books, 1943).

16. Committee on Social Issues, Group for the Advancement of Psychiatry, *Psychiatric Aspects of the Prevention of Nuclear War* (New York: Group for the Advancement of Psychiatry, September, 1964), 280.

17. M. Mead, "Science, Freedom and Survival," *Amer. Association for the Advancement of Science Bull.,* 7 (1962), cited in P. H. Leiderman and J. H. Mendelson, "Some Psychiatric Considerations in Planning for Defense Shelters," in Arnow, Ervin, and Sidel, p. 44 (Ch. 4, note 8 *supra*).

18. L. Aumack, "Action Research Regarding Civil Defense Preparedness and Attitudes of V.A. Hospital Employees," (August 14, 1964), mimeographed, p. 14. (Abstract published in *Newsletter for Psychology,* VAC, Kecoughtan Station, Hampton, Va., 6 [1964], 12–13).

19. M. J. Lerner, "The Effect of Preparatory Action on Beliefs Concerning Nuclear War," *J. Social Psychology,* 65 (1965), 225–231.

20. F. K. Berrien, C. Schulman, and M. Amarel, "The Fall-out Shelter Owners: A Study of Attitude Formation," *Public Opinion Quarterly,* 27 (Summer, 1963), pp. 206–216.

21. Modgliani, 7–9 (Ch. 2, note 5 *supra*).

22. P. Solomon *et al.,* eds., *Sensory Deprivation* (Cambridge, Mass.: Harvard University Press, 1961).

23. S. E. Cleveland, I. Boyd, D. Sheer, and E. E. Reitman, "Effects of Fallout Shelter Confinement on Family Adjustment," *Arch. Gen. Psychiatry*, 8 (1963), 43.

24. J. A. Vernon, *Project Hideway: A Pilot Feasibility Project of Fallout Shelters for Families* (Washington, D.C.: U.S. Government Printing Office, December, 1959), cited in Leiderman and Mendelson, p. 49.

25. J. W. Altman *et al.*, *Psychological and Social Adjustment in a Simulated Shelter, A Research Report* (Washington, D.C.: U.S. Government Printing Office, 1960), cited in *ibid.*, p. 50.

26. W. L. Langer, "The Next Assignment," *The Amer. Hist. Rev.*, 63 (January, 1958), 283.

27. N. J. Demerath, "Some General Propositions: Interpretive Summary," *Human Organization*, 16 (Summer, 1957), 28.

28. R. A. Dentler and P. Cutright, *Hostage America* (Boston: Beacon Press, 1963), pp. 74–76.

29. M. Hachiya, *Hiroshima Diary: The Journal of a Japanese Physician, August 6–September 30, 1945*, W. Wells, ed., (Chapel Hill, North Carolina: University of North Carolina Press, 1955).

30. R. J. Lifton, "Psychological Effects of the Atomic Bomb in Hiroshima—The Theme of Death," *Daedalus*, 92 (1963), 462–497.

31. ———, "On Death and Death Symbolism: The Hiroshima Disaster," *Psychiatry*, 27 (1964), 191–210.

32. S. Stouffer *et al.*, *Studies in Social Psychology in World War II*, Vol. II, *The American Soldier: Combat and its Aftermath* (Princeton, N.J.: Princeton University Press, 1947), p. 84.

33. L. E. Abt and L. Bellak, eds., *Projective Psychology* (New York: Alfred A. Knopf, 1950), pp. 53–54.

34. M. Sherif and O. J. Harvey, "A Study in Ego Functioning: Elimination of Stable Anchorages in Individual and Group Situations," *Sociometry*, 15 (August–November, 1952), 302.

35. Frank, pp. 42 ff. (Ch. 6, note 38 *supra*).

36. Schelling, *Arms and Influence*, pp. 74 ff.

37. E. J. Lieberman, "Threat and Assurance in the Conduct of Conflict," in R. Fisher, ed., *International Conflict and Behavioral Science: The Craigville Papers* (New York: Basic Books, 1964), pp. 110–122.

38. T. W. Milburn, "The Concept of Deterrence: Some Logical and Psychological Considerations," *J. Social Issues*, 17 (1961), 3–11.

9

1. B. M. Rutherford, "Psychopathology, Decision-making, and Political Involvement," *J. Conflict Resolution*, 10 (December, 1966), 387–407.
2. Lord Moran (Ch. 4, note 14 *supra*).
3. N. Kogan and M. A. Wallach, *Risk Taking: A Study in Cognition and Personality* (New York: Holt, Rinehart and Winston, 1964), p. 86.
4. L. Grinspoon, "Interpersonal Constraints and the Decision-Maker," in Fisher, pp. 238–247 (Ch. 8, note 37 *supra*).
5. D. Cartwright and A. Zander, *Group Dynamics: Research and Theory*, 2nd Ed. (Evanston, Ill.: Row, Peterson, 1960).
6. M. A. Wallach, N. Kogan, and D. J. Bem, "Group Influence on Individual Risk-Taking," *J. Abn. and Soc. Psychology*, 65 (1962), 75–86.
7. ———, "The Roles of Information Discussion and Consensus in Group Risk Taking," *J. Exper. and Soc. Psychology*, 1 (1965), 1–19.
8. *Ibid.*, 18.
9. Unless otherwise indicated, the findings concerning the 1914 crisis are taken from O. R. Holsti, "Perceptions of Time, Perceptions of Alternatives, and Patterns of Communication as Factors in Crisis Decision-Making," *Peace Research Society: Papers, III*, Chicago Conference (1965).
10. R. S. McNamara, Address Before American Society of Newspaper Editors, Queen Elizabeth Hotel, Montreal (May 18, 1966), news release, p. 8.
11. Cf. M. McLuhan, *Understanding Media: The Extensions of Man* (New York: McGraw-Hill, 1964).
12. CBS News, "Results of Nationwide Survey Concerning Vietnam War," (December 14, 1965), Question 14.
13. M. Mead, *And Keep Your Powder Dry* (New York: William Morrow, 1942), pp. 156–157.
14. M. J. Rosenberg, "Images in Relation to the Policy Process: American Public Opinion on Cold-War Issues," in Kelman, pp. 278–334 (Ch. 3, note 11 *supra*).
15. L. Festinger, H. Riecken, and S. Schachter, *When Prophecy Fails* (Minneapolis: University of Minnesota Press, 1956), pp. 208–212.
16. Schelling, *Arms and Influence*. p. 97 (Ch. 8, note 9 *supra*).
17. O. R. Holsti, and R. C. North, "Comparative Data from Content Analysis: Perceptions of Hostility and Economic Variables in the 1914 Crisis," in R. L. Merritt and S. Rokkan, eds., *Com-

paring Nations, The Use of Quantitative Data in Cross-National
Research (New Haven, Conn.: Yale University Press, 1966),
pp. 169–190.

18. R. C. North, R. A. Brody, and O. R. Holsti, "Some Empirical
Data on the Conflict Spiral," *Peace Research Society Papers,*
III, Chicago Conference, (1963, 1964), 12–13.

19. ———, "Violencia y Hostilidad: El Camino Hacia la Guerra
Mundial," *Revista De Estudios Politicos,* Nums. 141–142
(1965), 33–54.

20. E. Taylor, *The Fall of the Dynasties* (Garden City: Doubleday, 1963), pp. 220 ff.

21. O. R. Holsti, "The Value of International Tension Measurements," *J. of Conflict Resolution,* 7 (September, 1963), 612.

22. O. R. Holsti and R. C. North, "The History of Human Conflict," in McNeil, p. 167 (Ch. 6, note 6 *supra*).

23. Holsti, "The Value of International Tension Measurements,"
611.

24. Holsti and North, "History of Human Conflict," p. 169.

25. J. P. Coogan, "The Psychopolitical Path to War," *Smith, Kline
& French Psychiatric Reporter* (May–June, 1965), 13–17.

26. Stanford Studies in International Conflict and Integration, "Crisis and Crises, III. Helping Decision-Makers Decide," *Stanford
Today* (Spring, 1963), pages unnumbered.

27. I. Ziferstein, "Psychological Habituation to War: A Sociopsy-
chological Case Study," *Amer. J. Orthopsychiatry,* 37 (1967),
457–468.

28. *Psychiatric Aspects of the Prevention of Nuclear War,* 245–
256 (Ch. 8, note 16 *supra*).

29. R. V. Malinowsky, *The New York Times,* May 2, 1966, p. 1.

30. B. Tuchman, *The Guns of August* (New York: Macmillan,
1962) (quotes taken from paperback edition [New York: Dell,
1964], pp. 353–354).

31. Berkowitz, p. 194 (Ch. 3, note 15 *supra*).

32. A. Horne, "Verdun—The Reason Why," *The New York Times
Magazine,* February 20, 1966, p. 42.

33. S. S. Tomkins and C. E. Izard, eds., *Affect, Cognition and Per-
sonality* (New York: Springer, 1965), cited in M. Deutsch,
"Vietnam and the Start of World War III: Some Psychological
Parallels," Presidential Address to the N. Y. State Psychological
Association (May 7, 1966), mimeograph p. 14.

34. Tuchman, p. 60.

35. *Ibid.,* p. 211.

36. *Ibid.,* p. 217.

37. *Ibid.,* 293.

38. Schelling, *Arms and Influence,* pp. 131–141.

10

1. See, for example, E. Jackson, *Meeting of Minds* (New York: McGraw-Hill, 1952); F. C. Ikle, *How Nations Negotiate* (New York: Harper & Row, 1964); N. R. F. Maier, *Principles of Human Relations, Applications to Management* (New York: Wiley, 1952).
2. L. J. Halle, "The Struggle Called 'Coexistence,' " *The New York Times Magazine* (November 15, 1959), p. 110.
3. S. de Madariaga, "Disarmament? The Problem Lies Deeper," *The New York Times Magazine* (October 11, 1959), p. 74.
4. J. F. Kennedy, quoted in *Science*, 137, (August 24, 1962), p. 591.
5. H. G. and H. B. Kurtz, *War Safety Control Report* (Chappaqua, New York: War Control Planners, Inc., 1963).
6. E. B. McNeil, "Personal Hostility and International Aggression," *J. Conflict Resolution*, 5 (1961), 279–296.
7. J. D. Singer, "Media Analysis in Inspection for Disarmament," *J. Arms Control* (July, 1963), 248–260.
8. L. C. Bohn, "Non-Physical Inspection Techniques," in Brennan, pp. 347–364 (Ch. 8, note 4 *supra*).
9. E. B. McNeil, "Psychological Inspection," *J. Arms Control*, 1 (1963), 124–138.
10. S. Melman, "Inspection by the People," in Q. Wright, W. M. Evan, and M. Deutsch, eds., *Preventing World War III: Some Proposals* (New York: Simon and Schuster, 1962), pp. 40–51.
11. W. M. Evan, "An International Public Opinion Poll of Disarmament and 'Inspection by the people': A Study in Supernationalism," in S. Melman, ed., *Inspection for Disarmament* (New York: Columbia University Press, 1958), pp. 231 ff.
12. L. Szilard, " 'Minimal Deterrent' vs. Saturation Parity," *Bull. of the Atomic Scientists*, 20 (1964), 10.
13. R. W. Gerard, "Truth Detection," in Wright, pp. 52–61.
14. C. E. Osgood, *An Alternative to War or Surrender* (Urbana, Ill.: University of Illinois Press, Illini Book, 1962).
15. A. Etzioni, "The Kennedy Experiment," *Western Political Quarterly*, 20 (June, 1967), 361–381.
16. H. Nicholson, *The Congress of Vienna* (New York: Harcourt Brace, 1946), p. 19.
17. F. Bacon, *The Essays, or Counsels Civil and Moral* (London: Oxford University Press, 1921), p. 146.
18. M. Torre, "How Does Physical and Mental Illness Influence Negotiations between Diplomats?," *International J. Social Psychiatry*, 10 (Summer, 1964), 170–176.

19. Klineberg, p. 163 (Ch. 4, note 21 *supra*).
20. B. M. Wedge and C. Muromcew, "Psychological Factors in Soviet Disarmament Negotiation," *J. Conflict Resolution*, 9 (March, 1965), 18–36.
21. E. S. Glenn, "Across the Cultural Barrier," *The Key Reporter*, 31 (Autumn, 1965), 3.
22. H. H. Kelley, "A Classroom Study of the Dilemmas in Interpersonal Negotiations," in Archibald, pp. 63 ff. (Ch. 7, note 6 *supra*).
23. R. Fisher, "Fractionating Conflict," in Fisher, pp. 91–110 (Ch. 6, note 32 *supra*).
24. Schelling, *The Strategy of Conflict*, pp. 45 ff. (Ch. 4, note 7 *supra*).
25. B. M. Wedge, "A Note on Soviet-American Negotiation," in M. Miller, ed., *Proceedings of the Emergency Conference on Hostility, Aggression and War* (Washington, D.C.: American Association for Social Psychiatry, 1961).
26. G. Best, "Diplomacy in the United Nations," (doctoral dissertation, Northwestern University, 1960), cited by C. F. Alger, "Personal Contact in International Exchanges," in Kelman. pp. 527–531 (Ch. 3, note 11 *supra*).
27. D. Rusk, "Parliamentary Diplomacy—Debate vs. Negotiation," *World Affairs Interpreter*, 26 (1955), 127.
28. C. F. Alger, "Decision-Making Theory and Human Conflict," in McNeil, pp. 274–294 (Ch. 6, note 6 *supra*).
29. *Ibid.*, p. 289.
30. Rusk, 126.
31. H. Guetzkow, C. Alger, R. Brody, R. Noel, and R. Snyder, *Simulation in International Relations: Developments for Research and Teaching* (Englewood Cliffs, N.J.: Prentice Hall, 1963).
32. L. N. Solomon, "Simulation Research in International Decision-Making," in Sperazzo, pp. 37–52 (Ch. 7, note 29 *supra*).
33. Kelley.
34. K. R. Hammond, "New Directions in Research on Conflict Resolution," *J. Social Issues*, 21 (July, 1965), 44–66.
35. R. R. Blake and J. S. Mouton, "Loyalty of Representatives to Ingroup Positions during Intergroup Competition," *Sociometry*, 24 (1961), 177–183.
36. ———, "Competition, Communication and Conformity," in I. A. Berg and B. M. Bass, eds., *Conformity and Deviation* (New York: Harper & Row, 1961), pp. 199–229.
37. ———, "Loyalty of Representatives to Ingroup Positions during Intergroup Competition," *Sociometry*, 24 (1961), 177–183.

38. R. R. Blake, "Psychology and the Crisis of Statesmanship," *Amer. Psychologist*, 14 (1959), 90–93.
39. R. R. Blake and J. S. Mouton, "Comprehension of Own and of Outgroup Positions under Intergroup Competition," *J. Conflict Resolution*, 5 (1961), 304–310.
40. ———, "Comprehension of Points of Communality in Competing Solutions," *Sociometry*, 25 (1962), 56–63.
41. ———, "Competition, Communication and Conformity."
42. ———, "The Intergroup Dynamics of Win-Lose Conflict and Problem-Solving Collaboration in Union-Management Relations," in M. Sherif, ed., *Intergroup Relations and Leadership* (New York: Wiley, 1962), p. 102.
43. ———, "Overevaluation of Own Group's Product in Intergroup Competition," *J. Abn. and Soc. Psychology*, 64 (1962), 237–238.
44. Bass and Dunteman, 16–20 (Ch. 6, note 5 *supra*).
45. Blake and Mouton, "The Intergroup Dynamics of Win-Lose Conflict and Problem-Solving Collaboration in Union-Management Relations," p. 105.
46. A. Rapoport, *Fights, Games and Debates* (Ann Arbor: University of Michigan Press, 1960), pp. 71 ff.
47. ———, "Research for Peace," *The Listener* (March 31, 1966), p. 455.
48. J. L. Loomis, "Communication, the Development of Trust and Cooperative Behavior," *Human Relations*, 12 (1959), 305–315.
49. M. Deutsch, "Bargaining, Threat, and Communication: Some Experimental Studies," in Archibald, pp. 19–41 (Ch. 7, note 6 *supra*).
50. H. H. Kelley, "Experimental Studies of Threats in Interpersonal Negotiations," *J. Conflict Resolution*, 9 (March, 1965), 79–105.
51. R. J. Meeker, G. H. Shure, and W. H. Moore, Jr., "Real-Time Computer Studies of Bargaining Behavior: The Effects of Threat upon Bargaining," *American Federation of Information Processing Societies Conference Proceedings*, 25 (1964), 115–123.
52. G. H. Shure, R. J. Meeker, and E. A. Hansford, "The Effectiveness of Pacifist Strategies in Bargaining Games," *J. Conflict Resolution*, 9 (March, 1965), 106–117.
53. A. Stevenson, Godwin Lecture, Harvard University, 1955.
54. J. Cohen, "Reflections on the Resolution of Conflict in International Affairs," *Proceedings of the International Congress on Applied Psychology*, 1 (Copenhagen: Munksgaard, 1962), 59.
55. S. Hayakawa, "On Communication with the Soviet Union, Part I," *Etc.: A Review of General Semantics*, 17 (1960), 396–400.
56. Blake.

57. L. Coch and J. R. P. French, Jr., "Overcoming Resistance to Change," *Human Relations*, 1 (1948), 512–532.
58. R. R. Blake, H. A. Shepard, and J. R. Mouton, *Managing Intergroup Conflict in Industry* (Houston, Texas: Gulf Publishing Co., 1964), pp. 97 ff.

11

1. G. Bateson, "The Patterns of an Armaments Race, Part II: An Analysis of Nationalism," *Bull. Atomic Scientists*, 7, 8 (1946), 26–28.
2. E. Thorneycroft, *Personal Responsibility and the Law of Nations* (The Hague: Martinus Nishoff, 1961).
3. N. Cousins, "Talking to the Russians: Part 3," *Saturday Review* (September 15, 1962), p. 14.
4. R. K. White, " 'Socialism' and 'Capitalism,' An International Misunderstanding," *Foreign Affairs* (January, 1966), pp. 216–228.
5. House Committee on Foreign Affairs, International Organizations and Movements Subcommittee, *Modern Communications and Foreign Policy*. Report No. 5 on Winning the Cold War: The U.S. Ideological Offensive (Washington, D.C.: U.S. Government Printing Office, 1967).
6. Berkowitz, p. 193 (Ch. 3, note 15 *supra*).
7. I. De S. Pool, "Effects of Cross-National Contact on National and International Images," in Kelman, p. 123 (Ch. 3, note 11 *supra*).
8. D. T. Allen and W. P. Matthews, eds., *A Handbook of Procedure for Children's International Summer Villages* (Oslo: Children's International Summer Villages, 1961).
9. Pool, pp. 124–128.
10. *Ibid.*, p. 121.
11. B. Wedge, *Visitors to the United States and How They See Us* (New York: Van Nostrand, 1965), pp. 123–139.
12. J. Watson and R. Lippitt, "Cross-cultural Experience as a Source of Attitude Change," *J. Conflict Resolution*, 2 (1958), 61–66.
13. H. C. Kelman, "Changing Attitudes through International Activities," *Journal of Social Issues*, 18 (1962), 68–87.
14. R. R. Blake and J. S. Mouton, "International Managerial Grids, Getting Better Teamwork through Improving Intercultural Relations," *Training Directors Journal* (May, 1965).
15. J. Veroff, "African Students in the United States," *J. Social Issues*, 19 (1963), 48–60.

16. Watson and Lippitt.
17. S. Lundstet, "An Introduction to Some Evolving Problems in Cross-Cultural Research," *J. Social Issues*, 19 (1963), 1–9.
18. *Ibid.*, 3.
19. Gullahorn and Gullahorn, 36 (Ch. 6, note 30 *supra*).
20. S. D. James, "Exchange Plan Gains in Acceptance," *War/Peace Report*, (October, 1964), 15.
21. J. H. Masserman, "Or Shall We All Commit Suicide?", in J. H. Masserman, ed., *Current Psychiatric Therapies* (New York: Grune and Stratton, 1962), II, pp. 273–281.
22. R. B. Stark, "Medicine as a Force for Peace," *Journal of the American Medical Association*, 195 (January 3, 1966), 108–110.
23. D. C. McClelland, *The Achieving Society* (New York: Van Nostrand, 1961).
24. N. Hobbs, "A Psychologist in the Peace Corps," *Amer. Psychologist*, 18 (1963), 53.
25. J. T. English and J. G. Colmen, "Psychological Adjustment Patterns of Peace Corps Volunteers," *Psychiatric Opinion*, 3 (December, 1966), 29–35.
26. M. I. Stein, *Volunteers for Peace* (New York: Wiley, 1966), pp. 230–235.
27. Sherif and Sherif, *In Common Predicament* (Ch. 6, note 1 *supra*).
28. M. Sherif, O. J. Harvey, E. J. White, W. R. Hood, and C. W. Sherif, *Intergroup Conflict and Cooperation: The Robbers Cave Experiment* (Norman, Oklahoma: University of Oklahoma University Book Exchange, 1961).
29. M. Sherif, "Creative Alternatives to a Deadly Showdown," *Trans-Action*, 1 (January, 1964), 3–8.
30. "Official Statement of COSWA VII," *Bull. Atomic Scientists*, 18 (January, 1962), 25–30.

12

1. Lorenz, pp. 165–219 (Ch. 3, note 1 *supra*).
2. A. I. Waskow, "Nonlethal Equivalents of War," in Fisher, pp. 123–144 (Ch. 8, note 37 *supra*).
3. A good annotated bibliography of 277 references, primarily historical and religious, is A. Carter, D. Hoggett, and A. Roberts, *Non-Violent Action, Theory and Practice, A Selected Bibliography* (London: Housmans, 1966).
4. R. N. Iyer, "On Gandhi," in H. A. Freeman, R. Rustin, R. Lichtman, *et al.*, *Civil Disobedience* (New York: Fund for the Republic, 1966), p. 20.

5. M. K. Gandhi, *An Autobiography: The Story of My Experiments with Truth* (Boston: Beacon Press, 1957), p. 276.
6. A. Naess, "A Systematization of Gandhian Ethics of Conflict Resolution," *J. Conflict Resolution*, 2 (1958), 144.
7. P. Buck, cited in A. R. Fry, ed., *Victories Without Fear* (London: Edgar G. Dunstan, 1950), pp. 69–71.
8. T. Olson and G. Christiansen, *Thirty-one Hours* (New London: Grindstone Press, 1965).
9. H. Arendt, *Eichmann in Jerusalem: A Report on the Banality of Evil* (New York: Viking, 1963).
10. G. Sharp, "Tyranny Could Not Quell Them!" (London: Fish & Cook), republished from *Peace News* (undated pamphlet).
11. Quoted by Iyer (in Freeman *et al.*), p. 25.
12. C. M. Pierce and L. J. West, "Six Years of Sit-Ins: Psychodynamic Causes and Effects," *Int. J. Social Psychiatry*, 12 (1966), 29–34.
13. F. Solomon and J. R. Fishman, "The Psychosocial Meaning of Nonviolence in Student Civil Rights Activities," *Psychiatry*, 27 (1964), 91–99.
14. F. Solomon, W. L. Walker, G. O'Connor, and J. R. Fishman, "Civil Rights Activity and Reduction in Crime Among Negroes," *Archives of General Psychiatry*, 12 (March, 1965), 227–236.
15. G. Sharp, " 'The Political Equivalent of War'—Civilian Defense," *International Conciliation* (November, 1965).
16. Congressman Holifield, reported in *The Baltimore Sun* (February 28, 1962).
17. S. King-Hall, *Defence in the Nuclear Age* (London: Camelot Press, 1958), pp. 133–127.
18. J. D. Frank and E. H. Nash, "Commitment to Peace Work: A Preliminary Study of Determinants and Sustainers of Behavior Change," *Amer. J. Orthopsychiatry*, 35 (January, 1965), 106–119.
19. J. D. Frank and J. Schoenfeld, "Commitment to Peace Work: II. A Closer Look at Determinants," *Amer. J. Orthopsychiatry*, 37 (1967), 112–119.
20. H. S. Ashmore, "Cause, Effect, and Cure," in *W. H. Ferry and Harry S. Ashmore on Mass Communication* (New York: Fund for the Republic, 1966), pp. 28–38.
21. H. J. Eysenck, "War and Aggressiveness: A Survey of Social Attitude Studies," in T. H. Pear, ed., *Psychological Factors of Peace and War* (London: Hutchinson, 1950), pp. 66–68.
22. R. A. Falk, "The Revolution in Peace Education," *Saturday Review* (May 21, 1966), p. 59.

Index

ABOUT THE AUTHOR

Dr. Jerome D. Frank has been a practicing psychiatrist with the Henry Phipps Psychiatric Clinic in Baltimore and is Professor Emeritus of Psychiatry at the Johns Hopkins University School of Medicine. In addition to *Sanity and Survival in the Nuclear Age*, Dr. Frank has published, with Florence Powdermaker, *Group Psychotherapy: Studies in Methodology of Research and Therapy, Persuasion and Healing: A Comparative Study of Psychotherapy,* and *Psychotherapy and the Human Predicament: A Psychosocial Approach* (edited by Park Elliott Dietz), as well as numerous articles that have appeared in psychiatric and psychological journals, and in popular publications. He has received numerous honors and awards in the United States and abroad.

Dr. Frank was born in New York City, and graduated from Harvard University with honors. He holds an M.D. from Harvard Medical School, as well as a Ph.D. in psychology from Harvard. Dr. Frank served in the United States Army during World War II. He and his wife live in Baltimore.

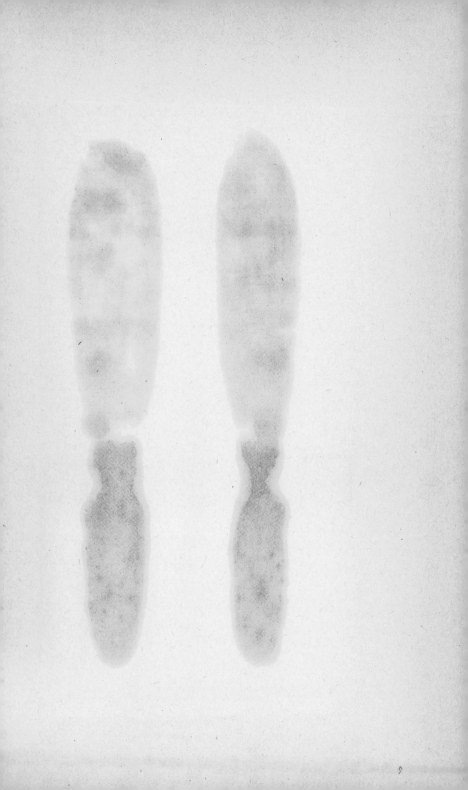

DATE DUE

MAR 2 3 1996	
MAR 30 2010	

GAYLORD   PRINTED IN U.S.A.